LAW AND SOCIETY IN A POPULIST AGE

Balancing individual rights and the common good

Amitai Etzioni

BRISTOL
UNIVERSITY
PRESS

First published in Great Britain in 2019 by

Bristol University Press
1-9 Old Park Hill
Bristol BS2 8BB
UK
t: +44 (0)117 954 5940
www.bristoluniversitypress.co.uk

North American office:
c/o The University of Chicago Press
1427 East 60th Street
Chicago, IL 60637, USA
t: +1 773 702 7700
f: +1 773-702-9756
e:sales@press.uchicago.edu
www.press.uchicago.edu

© Bristol University Press 2019

British Library Cataloguing in Publication Data
A catalogue record for this book is available from the British Library.

Library of Congress Cataloging-in-Publication Data
A catalog record for this book has been requested.

ISBN 978-1-5292-0026-3 paperback
ISBN 978-1-5292-0025-6 hardback
ISBN 978-1-5292-0028-7 ePub
ISBN 978-1-5292-0029-4 Mobi
ISBN 978-1-5292-0027-0 ePdf

The right of Amitai Etzioni to be identified as author of this work has been asserted
by him in accordance with the 1988 Copyright, Designs and Patents Act.

Cover design by blu inc, Bristol
Front cover image: www.alamy.com

Other books by Amitai Etzioni

The New Normal:
Finding a Balance Between Individual
Rights and the Common Good (2015)

Privacy in a Cyber Age: Policy and
Practice (2015)

Law in a New Key (2010)

My Brother's Keeper: A Memoir and a
Message (2003)

The Active Society: A Theory of
Societal and Political Processes (1968)

Contents

Acknowledgments

These chapters appeared in earlier form as noted below. All chapters have been updated and modified, some extensively.

Chapter 1

Segments from Amitai Etzioni, "We Must Not Be Enemies," The American Scholar (Winter 2017); and from Amitai Etzioni, "Communitarian Antidotes to Populism," *Society* 54, no. 2 (2017): 95-99 (© Springer Science+Business Media New York 2017). With permission of Springer.

Chapter 2

Amitai Etzioni, "Reining in Private Agents," *Minnesota Law Review Headnotes* 101 (2016): 279-331.

Chapter 3

Amitai Etzioni, "Corporate Capture" in *Encyclopedia of White-Collar and Corporate Crime*, 2nd edn, ed. Lawrence M. Salinger (Los Angeles: SAGE, 2013).

Chapter 4

Amitai Etzioni, "Moral Dialogs," *The Social Science Journal* 55, no. 1 (2018): 6-18.

Chapter 5

Amitai Etzioni, "The Standing of the Public Interest," *Barry Law Review* 20, no. 2 (2015): 193-219.

Chapter 6
Amitai Etzioni, 'A Liberal Communitarian Approach to Security Limitations on the Freedom of the Press', 22 *Wm. & Mary Bill Rts. J.* 1141 (2014).

Chapter 7
Amitai Etzioni, "Liberal Communitarian Approach to Privacy and Security," *Homeland and National Security Law Review* 1, no. 1 (2014): 55-79.

Chapter 8
Amitai Etzioni, "How Liberty Is Lost," *Society* 40, no. 5 (2003): 44-51 (© Springer 2003). With permission of Springer.

Chapter 9
Amitai Etzioni, "Defining Down Sovereignty: The Rights and Responsibilities of Nations," *Ethics and International Affairs* 30, no. 1 (2016): 5-20, reproduced with permission.

Chapter 10
Amitai Etzioni, "Nationalism: The Communitarian Block," *Brown Journal of World Affairs* 18, no. 1 (2011): 229-247.

Chapter 11
Originally published in the *Vanderbilt Journal of Entertainment & Technology Law*, Volume 19, Issue 1, Fall 2016, under the title "Keeping AI Legal."

Chapter 12
Amitai Etzioni, "A Cyber Age Privacy Doctrine: A Liberal Communitarian Approach," *I/S: A Journal of Law and Policy for the Information Society* 10, no. 2 (2014): 641-669.

List of abbreviations

ACLU	American Civil Liberties Union
AI	artificial intelligence
CRA	consumer reporting agency
CWC	Commission on Wartime Contracting
DOJ	Department of Justice
DPD	Data Protection Directive
ECPA	Electronic Communications Privacy Act
EU	European Union
FBI	Federal Bureau of Investigation
FCRA	Fair Credit Reporting Act
FISA	Foreign Intelligence Surveillance Act
GAO	Government Accountability Office
HIPAA	1996 Health Insurance Portability and Accountability Act
ICC	International Criminal Court
NSA	National Security Agency
PAC	political action committee
PMC	private military contractor
SMU	shared moral understanding
TSA	Transportation Security Administration

Introduction

This book can be read in three different ways: First, as a response to rising populism. Much attention has been paid, for good reason, to the rise of rightwing populism in many countries, especially in democratic ones. However, if by populism one means a direct political bond between a charismatic leader and the masses, a bond that occurs outside established institutional channels, leftwing populism should also be taken into account. To use the US as an example, Bernie Sanders was not a member of the Democratic Party when he ran for nomination as its presidential candidate, and he was about as critical of the Democratic Party as Trump was of the Republican Party. Both were opposed by the establishment of the two parties. (Macron won the French presidential election, against all candidates of established parties, and created his own party in the process.) Viewed this way, one notes that although rightwing populism is not embraced by the majority of the public in most of the nations in which it is rising, if one adds those on the left who are deeply troubled by the existing political regime, one finds that a large majority of the citizens are alienated and distrust major institutions of their countries. For instance, Gallup polling shows that in 2017, roughly two-thirds of Americans have reported feeling "dissatisfied with the way things are going in the United States."[1] According to a 2016 poll, "The overall average of Americans expressing 'a great deal' or 'quite a lot' of confidence in 14 [U.S.] institutions [was] below 33%."[2]

As I see it, these majorities have strong reasons to be disaffected. To dismiss their concerns as merely reflecting ignorance, prejudice, or credulity is both empirically wrong and unhelpful in dealing with the crisis they pose to the legal order of liberal democracy. I fully recognize that the populist response to loss of jobs and benefits, increased economic insecurity, and accelerating social and cultural changes is deeply troubling and must be corrected. However, to proceed one should recognize that their disaffection is driven by valid concerns. This book tries to outline a response that does not dismiss these concerns but rejects the ways populists react to them. It looks for paths toward the reintegration of these masses into a society based on the rule of law (even if some of the laws involved may have to be recast in the process).

A second way to read this book is to see it as seeking to address a fundamental issue that used to be defined, before we become sensitized to prejudice built into our languages, as 'to put man on top again.' Modernity is characterized by technological and economic developments that stress the existing legal, ethical, and political institutions; these institutions lose their ability to ensure that these new sources of means will be dedicated to pro-social rather than anti-social purposes. Like the Golem, or the Sorcerer's Apprentice, society has lost control of these developments and is buffeted by them. The book examines a whole slew of such developments and asks how the institutional lag may be closed and society—drawing on its lawmaking, policy-setting institutions—will be able to guide the forces that have been unleashed rather than captured by them.

Finally, the book may be read as an attempt to outline an agenda for research and deliberations by those interested in the relationship between law and society. I join those who view law as a subsystem of a dynamic societal system. The phrase 'law in society,'[3] seems to be a sound one.

The law-based, political institutions in many democratic societies are challenged by populist movements, parties, and leaders. In other nations, the state is failing. These historical changes invite greater attention to the role society plays in forming and challenging laws—and to the role of the law in coping with these challenges. Hence, there is reason to expect that legal scholarship and policy makers, as well as citizens interested in public affairs, will be even more interested in studies of the relations between law and society than they have been in the recent past. In recent years, other schools—especially law and economics—were particularly influential, while law and society programs were less so. This book assumes that these schools as well as 'traditionalists' will continue to be influential, but that there will be (or at least should be) more attention paid to law-in-society considerations.

Those unfamiliar with law in society as a discipline may benefit from the characterization of the field by some of its leading scholars. According to Lawrence Friedman "The law and society movement is the scholarly enterprise that explains or describes legal phenomena in social terms."[4] This might include a focus on "ways in which law is socially and historically constructed, how law both reflects and impacts culture, and how inequalities are reinforced through differential access to, and competence with, legal procedures and institutions."[5] "'Law and society movement' is a rather awkward term," Friedman wrote in 1986. "But there is no other obvious collective label to describe the efforts of sociologists of law, anthropologists of law, political scientists who study judicial behavior, historians who explore the role of nineteenth-century lawyers, psychologists who ask why juries behave as they do, and so on."[6] As an interdisciplinary field, law and society borrows methods and theories from various disciplines.[7]

Furthermore, according to Robert Ellickson, scholars of law and society "do not agree on, and often don't show much interest in developing basic theoretical building blocks."[8] Although Ellickson views the eclectic nature of the movement as a hindrance to its scholars,[9] Patricia Ewick and Austin Sarat hold that eclecticism has resulted in a rich body of scholarship that promotes a sophisticated understanding of the topic at hand. Acknowledging that, "from the perspective of any particular scholar, law and society work may seem incoherent and amorphous," they believe that approaching the scholarship from a wider angle demonstrates the field's maturity.[10]

The following chapters examine, in one major arena after another, specific sources of alienation and offer some preliminary deliberations on how the challenges they pose may be addressed. The most general treatment of this subject in found in the first chapter. These more specific sources include the privatization of force (Chapter Two); the capture of public domain by concentrations of private power (Chapter Three); and ways in which obsolescent legitimacy can be replaced by newly formed legitimacy (Chapter Four). These chapters are assembled in Part One. Read together, these chapters show that in order for the public at large to be served rather than having large segments of the population feel left out and antagonized, we need a major reallocation of power as well as a new source of legitimacy. Both of these developments require the kind of major societal change historically brought about only by social movements.

In Part Two the book turns to the tensions between those who seek ever more governmental powers to bolster national security and defense as well as environmental protection and climate control, and those who hold that such concentrations of power undermine their rights. It first explores the very concept of the common good, which is contested by libertarians (Chapter Five) and introduces a liberal communitarian conception of a balance between individual rights and social responsibilities (Chapter Six). The following chapter examines this conception in a particular and important case, the tension between privacy and security (Chapter Seven). Many hold that liberty is lost as one right after another is curtailed. Chapter Eight points out that often liberty is lost when the common good is neglected.

Part Three is concerned with the relations between the national communities and the attempts to build more encompassing, so-called supranational (or regional) communities. The most advanced of these is the European Union (EU). The fact that Britain chose to leave the EU is often cited as a key example of the rise and victory of populism. One can also see it as an example of multilateral overreach; of concentrating power in Brussels and violating national sovereignty—before most people transferred their loyalty to the nascent European community (Chapter Nine).

In response to genocides, a near worldwide consensus evolved that when a national government does not discharge its responsibilities to protect its people, does not protect them from atrocities, other nations have a right to intervene. (This concept is known as the Responsibility to Protect, or RtoP). However, after this moral and legal concept was abused when it was invoked to justify coercive regime changes, RtoP lost much of its standing. Nevertheless, its popular support can be regained (Chapter Ten). Ignoring genocides and raging civil wars is a moral outrage that alienates people who are otherwise good citizens of liberal democracies.

Part Four concerns itself with responses to major technological development. Automation, often benefiting from breakthroughs in artificial intelligence, is eliminating many jobs, and is especially challenging people with lower education levels and those who previously held traditional manufacturing jobs such as coal miners and steel workers. Soon many other professions will be affected. Some fear the development of autonomous weapons (another case of loss of control). Still others are alarmed that robots will outsmart us and dominate us, the ultimate Golem. Chapter Eleven outlines the way for humans to stay in charge. The rise of the internet—itself a technological development—and other technologies that exploit it has led many to conclude that privacy is dying. Indeed, it faces many challenges; however, privacy can be much better protected if one takes into account the distinct qualities of cyberspace (Chapter Twelve).

Part One
Power and Legitimacy

ONE

A response to populism

Liberalism provides an incomplete moral language to address the populism that is rising in many democratic polities. Communitarian conceptions must be included in order to provide a more comprehensive moral language. This addition, however, raises issues because liberal and communitarian conceptions are in conflict with one another to some extent. In the following discussion I suggest ways that this conflict can be limited, and I outline a liberal communitarian approach as an effective response to populism.

One should note from the outset that this approach holds that societies cannot be designed to follow one overarching principle, because of differences in the needs, interests, and values of their various members. That is, no value can be maximized.

The discussion is centered on two recent variants of philosophical positions that have a long and rich history: *globalism*, a subcategory of contemporary classical liberalism—and *nationalism*, a particular form of communitarianism. Thus, globalism draws on liberal elements, but other forms of liberalism do not necessarily share the globalists' positions, as is true for contemporary classical liberalism and so-called welfare liberalism. Nationalism is a form of communitarianism because it views the nation as the major community (whether real or imagined). Other communitarians do not necessarily share this view—for instance, those who see their main community as their confessional or ethnic one.

Populism: definition and causes

The hallmarks of populism include a demagogue who appeals to the masses in highly emotive terms, attacking the institutions of civil society, offering ready-made solutions for society's complex challenges, and promising to deliver those solutions. Cas Mudde characterizes populism as a "thin ideology," one that provides an ideological framework, according to which good people are being abused by a corrupt elite.[1] (He contrasts it with pluralism, which accepts the legitimacy of many different groups and sets of values.) Similarly, Jan-Werner Müller argues that populists are antipluralist, that populism is a form of identity politics, and is always critical of elites.[2] The rise of populism in many democratic polities in the 2010s is often attributed to a nationalistic reaction to the ascent of globalization, whose champions hold many of the same positions as contemporary liberals. They favor open societies—open to the flow of goods, people, and ideas. They are universalists who view all people as endowed with the same *human* rights, and as rational deliberative people, able to make their own reasoned decisions.

Globalization, scholars hold, is opposed by current waves of populism that are propelled by nationalists. These are individuals and groups that are parochial (or particularistic), who view their commitments to their local and national communities as trumping global considerations. They are depicted as opposed to the spread of rights ('deplorable')[3] and to immigration (especially of people whose culture and ethnicity differs from the national one); as people who adhere to the traditional values of their communities and hence oppose liberalism; and as protectionists (limiting access to the markets of their nation).[4] For globalists, "national boundaries are increasingly obsolete and perhaps even immoral … progressive pundits and journalists increasingly speak a dialect of ethical cosmopolitanism or globalism—the idea that it is unjust to discriminate in favor of one's fellow nationals against citizens of foreign countries," according to Michael Lind. George Monbiot adds that

> When confronted with a conflict between the interests of your country and those of another, patriotism, by definition, demands that you should choose those

of your own. Internationalism, by contrast, means choosing the option which delivers most good or least harm to people, regardless of where they live. It tells us that someone living in Kinshasa is of no less worth than someone living in Kensington, and that a policy which favours the interests of 100 British people at the expense of 101 Congolese is one we should not pursue.[5]

Drawing on these definitions, a considerable number of observers view globalists as enlightened, progressive, and on the right side of history, and nationalists as seeking to preserve a traditional, anachronistic, and unjust social order. Pankaj Mishra sees in Trump's America—and in Europe, India, and Russia—whole countries that "seethe with demagogic assertions of ethnic, religious, and national identity." These movements threaten "the great eighteenth-century venture of a universal civilization harmonized by rational self-interest, commerce, luxury, arts, and science."[6] Nationalists reject the wisdom of the great thinkers of the Enlightenment, Mishra writes, and instead follow the authoritarian philosophy of Jean-Jacques Rousseau.

Another line of analysis sees the rise of populism as being caused in part by globalization, because it undermines both local and national communities. Put differently, globalization helped to engender the forces that oppose it. The argument runs as follows: as people moved from villages to the cities, they lost many of the social bonds that provided them with emotional security. Ferdinand Tönnies refers to the change as a movement from a communal society (*Gemeinschaft*) to an associational one (*Gesellschaft*).[7] Those social bonds, however, had protected them from the Siren calls of would-be demagogues because individuals who were well anchored in communities relied on each other and on their communal leaders (heads of families, religious figures, and other authority figures) to resist outsiders' appeals. Once the society of communities turned into a mass society—a society composed of individuals who had lost much of their social moorings[8]—they became susceptible to demagogues. This was particularly said to be the case when their economic conditions deteriorated. The conditions in pre-Nazi Germany are often cited. These included massive unemployment, hyperinflation, and loss of dignity (emanating from humiliation following Germany's defeat in World War I and the punishing terms imposed on it by the nations that won the war). Racial nationalism is said to have provided Germany with a new sense of community, meaning, and dignity. "As the political and social fragmentation of the Weimar period imparted a sense of apocalyptic collapse for many Germans, the Nazi millennial worldview in turn conferred a sense of oneness via its racial concept of a unified Volk (race or people), a community of shared blood," writes David Redles.[9]

When this analysis is applied to contemporary populism, it suggests, in the terms already introduced, that what we are witnessing is a nationalist reaction to the rise of globalization. Large segments of the population are reported to have experienced job loss (partly because freer trade led to jobs moving to developing countries), most of those who are employed have gained little or no increases in real income, all involved have experienced growing income insecurity and inequality, as well as a loss of dignity (associated with the loss of traditional jobs such as coal mining). The same people are also found to be reacting to growing diversity due to immigration, and to cultural changes which are the result of extensions of individual rights (e.g. legalization of gay marriages). The affected people view the rise of diversity both as undermining their social standing and as a loss of shared core values and habits.[10] And they feel that they are snubbed by globalist elites. Steven Kull adds that, "Trump effectively mirrored back to voters what they have been saying for years, that they feel like they are being ignored in a system dominated by special interests."[11]

Americans' openness to "authoritarian alternatives" is on the rise; "Among all age cohorts, the share of citizens who believe that it would be better to have a 'strong leader' who does not have to 'bother with parliament and elections'" increased from 24 percent in 1995 to 32 percent in 2011.[12] Furthermore, "The share of U.S. citizens who think that it would be a 'good' or 'very good' thing for the 'army to rule'" has risen from one in sixteen in 1995 to one in six in 2016.[13] Indeed, most mature democracies, including Germany, the United Kingdom, and Sweden, exhibit a similar trend.[14] Globalists do not ignore the communitarian causes that drive populism; however, they tend to view them as the pathological reactions of people seeking to hold on to the past and to traditional social structures that were discriminatory and authoritarian, and are historically indefensible in view of the unstoppable rise of globalization. They tend to see nationalists as misinformed, misled, or captured by the emotive appeals of demagogues. Moreover, globalists often view the weakening of particularistic bonds—including the weakening of commitments to local or national communities—as liberating. They draw on writings such as those by Peter Singer, who argues that one should treat all children as one treats one's own;[15] and on the work of Martha Nussbaum, whose *For Love of Country* argues we should view ourselves as citizens of the world.[16] History is seen as a march from particularism to universalism, from close local and national communities toward a global one.

Globalists, like many liberals, have no room for communities in their moral and philosophical vocabulary. They see people as free-standing individuals, endowed with rights by the mere fact that they are human and not because they are members of this or that community or nation. They hold that people are free (or ought to be free) to move across borders. Above all, each person ought to be free to choose their own definition of the good and not be hindered because their habits, tastes, or values differ from those of others. Diversity and pluralism trump the restrictive demands for conformity of various communities and their core values.

The essentiality of communities

The globalists miss what Aristotle has observed—that human beings are social animals. Individuals need bonding with others in order to flourish. A considerable number of studies show that when people are cut off from their social moorings, when they are isolated—in prison cells, in high rise buildings (especially the elderly), or in psychological experiments—they show many signs of diminished cognitive and emotive capacity. Scores of other studies show that they thrive when they are involved in lasting meaningful relations with others.[17] That is, communal bonds—which are *prima facie* particularistic, because all communities, including families, local communities, and nations, exclude most people—are an essential part of that which constitutes an individual.

The absence of sufficient communal bonds is a major reason why people feel detached, alienated, and powerless and either withdraw or act out in anti-social ways, including joining gangs and militias (to find community) or abusing drugs and alcohol, or each other.

Identity too is profoundly tied to communities, and thus to particularistic bonds. As Joseph de Maistre put it, "There is no such thing as *man* in the world. In the course of my life, I have seen Frenchmen, Italians, Russians etc.; I know, too, thanks to Montesquieu, that one can be a Persian. But as for *man*, I declare that I have never met him in my life; if he exists, he is unknown to me."[18] Michael Sandel puts it well when he writes that we cannot understand ourselves but "as the particular persons we are—as members of this family or community or nation or people, as bearers of this history, as sons and daughters of that revolution, as citizens of this republic."[19]

Strong involvement of people in their particularistic communities, rather than in some kind of universal social grouping, is highlighted by the fact that millions of people are willing to die for their nation but very few for the United Nations (or even the European Union (EU)). Globalists might argue that the fact that identity is tied to nations is one reason for wars and the world's great difficulties in coping with global problems. However, these are not feelings that most people have; on the contrary, most find such globalist ideas strange, if not alien. It follows that seeking to deprive people of their national sources of identity and bonding fosters nationalism and populism (at least, as long as they neither develop nor are provided with other sources of identity and bonding that they find compelling). A colleague noted at this point: "If they didn't have 'national sources of identity' but they had jobs and dignity, is it really that there'd still be populism? That strikes me as unlikely." In response, one notes that most of those who voted for Trump (and for other populist leaders in other societies) had jobs and the dignity they confer. They seem to have felt nevertheless that globalists' demands (real and imagined) assaulted their identity and community.[20]

Furthermore, one cannot ignore that communities form the individuals that are the mainstay of liberalism. Infants are born with human potential; however, they will not even learn to walk upright or to communicate with words unless they are "socialized," studies show. Parents, families, local communities (as captured in the phrase, "it takes a village") forge individuals, not global systems. And when these communities falter, so does the education of the people within them. To put it differently, the rational, free agents that liberalism sees are the product of communities (some as small as families, others as large as nations, with the smaller ones nestled within the more encompassing ones). One cannot grow one without the incubation provided by the other. (David B. Wong adds that to learn to be duty-bound and to act in a universalistic way, one first must have relationships of trust with others, i.e., particularistic relations.[21])

When children become adults, they still need communities to foster a social order that is pluralistic, tolerant, and civil, i.e. a liberal order. Communities provide the informal social controls that uphold norms by chiding violations and praising compliance. The more effective they are, the less need there is for the state to employ coercive means to maintain social order.[22] In short, the liberal polity assumes a communitarian society—the kind of society that nationalists champion.

True, communities can be overpowering and oppressive. Historically, most communities were indeed too thick and many are still found in parts of the world as different as Singapore and Saudi Arabia. And national communities are prone to conflict with each other because there is only a limited sense of obligation toward the other. However, communities in democratic societies tend to be much "thinner," because people can leave communities that they find too "thick"[23] and often are members of more than one community (e.g. work and residence) and hence are less psychologically dependent on any one community.

A sounder globalist philosophy will seek modes of social design that foster thin communities rather than promote individualism to the extent that it entails attacking communities, especially nations, as troublesome relics of the past. This can be accomplished by combining globalist (universalistic, liberal) principles with nationalist (particularistic communitarian) ones. In other words, if one places at one end of the normative spectrum globalist liberalism and at the other end authoritarian communitarianism, the middle ground of the spectrum is liberal communitarianism. It provides the antidote both to populism (by undergirding communities) and to authoritarianism (by incorporating liberal principles). The challenge is to find ways to develop a normative framework that will incorporate the values of globalization with those of nationalism, and to find ways to limit their contradictions, while recognizing that a measure of conflict and tension between these two core elements of liberal communitarianism is inevitable. This approach is outlined next.

Yuval Levin dedicated a book to the subject which he calls communitarian liberalism.[24] M. Daly writes: "Most liberals and a good many communitarians would like the liberal ideals of equality and freedom to be integrated with community commitments in all aspects of American society and families, educational institutions, businesses, health care institutions, religions, and political institutions. Such integration would realize the communitarian ideal of a democratic community."[25]

This philosophy has been summarized in popular terms by David Brooks: "I suspect the coming political movements will be identified on two axes: open and closed and individual and social ... Donald Trump is probably going to make the G.O.P. the party of individual/closed ... The Democrats are probably going to be the party of social/closed ... I've been thinking we need a third party that is social/open."[26] Such a party, according to Brooks, would "support the free trade and skilled immigration that fuel growth. But it would also flood the zone for those challenged in the high-skill global economy—offering programs to rebuild community, foster economic security and boost mobility."[27]

An important counterargument to the line of argument laid out so far is that the mass society thesis is mistaken, that communities have far from disappeared. Residential communities abound and there are a large number of non-residential communities, such as the gay community and various ethnic and racial ones. In response, I note that some segments of the population have lost communal bonds. Freer trade and automation force people to relocate to where the new jobs are, leaving their communal bonds and institutions behind. As often, if they develop new communal bonds, a shift in the labor markets requires them to relocate again. For instance, people moved from West Virginia to Montana when coal declined and gas production increased, only to be forced to move again when prices for energy collapsed but the auto industry revived.

Granted, an important correction to the mass society is called for. Many populists (arguably the major segment) are in traditional communities that are antagonistic to globalization. Much has been written about the reasons why these communities are antagonistic. Causes are said to include fragmentation of the news, gerrymandering, self-segregation, and political polarization.

For the purpose at hand, it matters little whether people feel that they are losing their communities or that the values of their communities are under attack. Either way, they react antagonistically. One may argue that many traditional values ought to be attacked. However, as I see it, a head-on confrontation is not the most effective way to change values, and the social costs of such confrontations are high. Progressive observers often argue that when we deal with drug addicts or felons, we should approach them in a therapeutic way, seeking to rehabilitate them and reintegrate them into society. There seems to be no reason why nationalists should be treated more severely.

No less important is the sense that both those who have lost their local communities and those who are members of antagonistic ones hold that their national community is under attack by globalists' conceptions of supranationalism. These include respect for the UN, the International Criminal Court, and more general international law, which are all perceived as an assault on sovereignty.

A globalist suggested to the author that people can satisfy their communitarian needs in families or some other small communities—and should avoid investing themselves in the nation. However, one notes that because of geographic mobility people are losing many of their bonds with their extended families; that the nuclear family is declining (as fewer people marry, or stay married, or they marry later and have fewer children); and that other communities are hollowed out, leaving the nation as a major focus of bonding and identity. True, many of the problems national governments find difficult to cope with are regional or global in nature (including wars, terrorism, climate change), and would be much easier to manage if people treated humanity as one imagined community, the way they now treat their nation. However, to claim speciously that such a global community is currently in place feeds populism rather than helps to curb it.

Elements of liberal communitarianism

If one seeks to curb populism, violence, prejudice, and xenophobia, then one must nurture communities, rather than override them. The discussion next turns to examine ways that the conflict between globalists and nationalists can be reduced. The examination covers major areas of contention: the clash between the advocates of free and fair trade; the debate about limiting the free movement of people (immigration); the objections to communities that are insular and excluding; free speech that is sensitive to community values; and the minting of new rights and community adjustments. The section closes with a discussion of the ways that the two conflicting principles can be accommodated, using the relationship of privacy (as a human right) and national security as a case study.

Limiting free trade?

When globalists champion free trade, they stress that it enriches all those involved, making for less costly consumer products as each nation focuses on what it is best equipped to produce, a condition referred to in popular terms as win–win. Actually, the ethical situation that free trade entails is illustrated by a familiar challenge raised in reference to utilitarianism, i.e. when one asks how many Christians one may throw in the arena to contend with the lions if a very large number of Romans are going to enjoy the spectacle. The point is that sacrificing even a small number of lives cannot be justified even if it enhances the happiness of a much larger number. The Christians of free trade are the hundreds of thousands of workers in coal, steel, and other sectors, who lost their jobs as a result. Economists respond that most jobs were lost due to automation and other technological developments, and not to trade. True, but nonetheless, since 2000 at least five million manufacturing jobs in the U.S. were lost to trade.[28] Free traders do not deny this loss but respond that it can be handled through Trade Adjustment Assistance (TAA), which uses public funds to retrain the displaced workers for new jobs.

This response fails on two counts. First of all, TAA has so far been unable to help most of these displaced people. It is hard to make steel workers into computer programmers. And many of the new jobs available are low paying, with few or no benefits, especially when compared to the jobs lost. And flipping hamburgers at McDonald's or selling T-shirts at Target is not the sort of meaningful work that coal miners, steel workers, and others previously took pride in.

Furthermore, free trade champions ignore the effects of free trade on people's essential communitarian needs. They often fail to take into account that people lose their communal bonds when they move—that they leave behind friends they can call on when they are sick or grieving. Their children miss their friends and everyone in the family is ripped away from the centers of their social lives: school, church, social club, union hall, or American Legion post. And when these people finally bring their families along and form new communities, changes in free trade often force them to move again. Thus, after a boom in Montana, prices of oil and gas fall, and so many of the workers who moved there now need to relocate again. In this way, free trade churns societies, exacting high social costs by undermining communities.

These high social costs do not mean that nations should stop trading with one another; rather, they mean that those who are concerned about the social effects of new trade treaties are not know-nothings, white trash, or rednecks, but people with valid concerns. These might be addressed by much greater investments in TAA. It could provide those who cannot be retrained—often the older workers—with early retirement or jobs in an infrastructure corps. At best, ramped-up TAA programs should not require workers to relocate, because relocations increase costs and undermine communities.

Finally, one notes that all countries impose some limitations on trade in the name of national security, consumer protections, protecting famers, and quite a few other concerns. Hence, to add some limits, especially if they are time-limited, to allow groups hard-hit by job loss to have time to adjust is not a sign that dark populism won, but that measures often taken in the past by "free" trade partners have been extended.

Limiting immigration?

Globalists favor the free movement of people across national borders. They strongly support the Schengen Agreement, which removes border controls among many European nations. They strongly supported Angela Merkel, the German chancellor, when she opened the doors to more than a million refugees. And they view Trump's call for building a wall on the Mexican border and restriction on immigration from Muslim countries as typical right-wing, xenophobic, reactionary, nationalist policies.[29]

Several social scientists, however, point to a tension between open-ended immigration, especially of people from different cultures, and sustaining communities. Communities benefit from a measure of stability, continuity, and a core of shared values. Social psychologist Jonathan Haidt views mass immigration as the trigger that set off populism in many nations. He concludes that it is possible to have moderate levels of immigration from "morally different ethnic groups"—so long as they are seen to be assimilating into the host culture—but high levels of immigration from countries with different moral values, without successful assimilation, will trigger a backlash.[30] Haidt suggests that immigration policies ought to take into account three factors: the percentage of foreign-born residents at any given time; the degree of moral difference between the incoming group and the members of the host society; and the degree to which assimilation is being achieved. Globalists do not approve of this approach. They embrace a libertarian perspective toward immigration, and the "core principle of libertarianism," as Jacob Hornberger writes, "is that freedom entails the right to live your life anyway you want, so long as your conduct is peaceful." Thus, "There is only one libertarian position on immigration, and that position is open immigration or open borders."[31] One may suggest that the idea of open borders is just a theoretical position; that nobody truly believes in unlimited immigration. However, this position describes exactly what took place in the EU when several nations joined the Schengen Agreement, which allows free movement of people across national borders. The resentment that followed is a major reason for Brexit. (A reviewer of a previous draft noted here, "But the major immigrant group to the UK is *Polish*. They're not 'morally different'. So this wouldn't have met the

Haidt criterion!" As I see it, whom people consider sociologically different is in the eye of the beholder. Indeed, often people seek to avoid and even exclude from their communities people who are rather similar to themselves, such as Sunni and Shia of the same nationality, or Japanese and Koreans.) (For more discussion of Brexit, see Chapter Six.)

Brookings' William Galston cites public opinion polls that show that Americans have become more concerned about the United States becoming a majority non-white country. In 2016, 21 percent of Americans said that such a majority would "bother" them, up 7 percentage points from 2013. Furthermore, "fifty percent of all Americans acknowledged being bothered when they came into contact with immigrants who spoke little or no English."[32] Galston reminds his readers that in an earlier era, when the United States implemented immigration restrictions and caps, immigration fell significantly and "'ethnics' from central and southern Europe were gradually assimilated into white America, a process that many scholars believe contributed to the relatively placid and consensual politics of the postwar decades."[33]

Some nationalists hence call for at least a "pause" on immigration, especially from Muslim nations. Globalists continue to favor immigration and a short pathway to citizenship for millions of undocumented immigrants. A liberal communitarian will focus on accelerated integration of immigrants, first by properly defining what such integration entails (which, we shall see, makes accelerated integration more achievable) and by taking specific measures to advance it.

To proceed, a liberal communitarian approach benefits from drawing on a strategy that might be referred to as "diversity within unity," which can help to lower social tensions in countries that accept large numbers of immigrants while tolerating particularistic diversity—by not seeking full assimilation into the culture of the new homeland. The United States has in effect followed such a strategy, with considerable success, compared to the more assimilationist European countries, as well as to Japan and South Korea.

Assimilation, in its strongest form, requires that immigrants abandon their distinct cultures, values, habits, and connections to their country of origin in order to integrate fully into the culture of their new country. France stands out as an archetype of this approach. For many years, it was regarded as discriminatory to even recognize the country of origin or religion of a French citizen. In this spirit, France passed a law in 2004 banning all religious symbols from public schools. The law is so far-reaching, and has been interpreted so broadly, that several schools have demanded that female Muslim students not wear long dresses.[34] Towns and cities have banned "burkinis," bathing attire that follows Muslim prescripts for covering women in public.[35] Schools in several French towns have decided to stop serving pork-free meals.[36] This anti-communitarian approach is provoking tension because immigrants are required to give up values and behaviors that are central to their identity. Furthermore, such excessive homogenization is not necessary to obtain a sound state of community. The high level of alienation in immigrant and minority communities in France— and the corresponding alienation of the majority—reveal that this approach is not working and is indeed counterproductive.

In contrast, diversity within unity is a combination of partial assimilation and community building along with a high level of tolerance for differences in others, for pluralism and respect for individual rights. It presumes that all members of a given society will respect and adhere to certain core values and institutions that form the basic shared framework of the society. (This is the unity component.) At the same time, every group in society, including the majority, is free to maintain its distinct subculture—those policies, habits, and institutions that do not conflict with the shared core. (This is the diversity component.) Respect for the whole and respect for all are the essence of this approach; when these two come into conflict, then respect for the national community (which itself may change over time) is to take precedence.

Among the core values are adherence to the law, acceptance of democracy as the way to resolve differences and create public policy, and belief in civility in dealing with others. Religion, a core value for many European societies, need not be a unity value. However, a measure of patriotism should be expected, especially when loyalty to the new, host nation clashes with commitments to the nation of origin. (Thus, if the United States were to go to war with another country, our immigrants from that country would be required to support our effort.) Under diversity within unity, all immigrants are expected to learn the national language but are welcome to keep their own and speak it with their children as a secondary language. They are free to follow their own rituals but also expected to partake in the national ones, such as pledging alliance to the flag.

In recent years, much attention has been paid to the level of immigration, which many of Trump's supporters view as far too high and some social scientists hold is overwhelming American communities and their core values. The level of immigration that communities can tolerate, however, is affected by the pace and scope of integration. In other words, higher levels of immigration will have less anti-communitarian effects when integration is more effective.

To illustrate: in the United States, there is a great shortage of classes to teach English to adult immigrants. Obviously, a strong command of the language is an essential element of acculturation. Moreover, the language classes also serve as opportunities to introduce immigrants to American values and lifestyles, as well as to form personal contacts between immigrants and established residents who teach these classes. One could call for a new massive federal program to provide English and civics classes to immigrants. However, this is a mission particularly suited to volunteers. To teach English and to share values does not require a degree from a teaching college. Volunteers are more likely to be members of local communities than civil servants.

In short, the stress that large-scale and diversifying immigration poses for local and national communities, which is one cause that drives populism, can be mitigated if one follows the liberal communitarian approach. It seeks diversity within unity rather than assimilation and favors accelerated integration. It follows, though, that to the extent that this approach cannot be implemented, immigration will need to be capped if populism is to be reined in.

Limiting communities

Many millions of Americans live in a gated community of one form or another, many of which are called homeowner associations.[37] These are criticized by globalists as violating universal rights.[38] Furthermore, the "spatial segregation [resulting from gated communities] has been criticized as troubling and a continuation of many of the historically discriminatory social policies of the past such as racial and socio-economic segregation, redlining and discrimination."[39] But gated communities are places that provide their members with varying levels of community, mostly far from thick ones. Liberal communitarianism calls for a two-layered approach to these communities. They should not be allowed to violate basic rights, discriminate, ban books, suppress speech, infringe upon the freedom of religious expression, and so on. If they do, after proper warning, these communities should be compelled by fines or denial of public funds, and if these measures do not suffice, forced to comply. However, in all other matters, these communities should be welcome to form their own policies, to fashion particular rules that only their members will be required to follow. These may include rules concerning the appearance of their communities (homes, lawns), certain types of behavior by their members (loud music after midnight), places they may park their cars, and scores of other matters, expressing the particular preferences of the members of these communities.

In short, particularism can be well tolerated as long as it occurs within the limits of rights enumerated in the Constitution and its Bill of Rights as interpreted by the courts, augmented with considerations based on a globalist framework, that of universal human rights.

Critics argue that even if communities do not violate rights they nevertheless are insular, isolating, and thus undermining of the societal fabric. To conclude that to avoid such effects one should take measures to curb the development of communities, one ignores the critical role that thick relations play in human life and that they are essential to avoid mass societies and their ill consequences, including populism. A communitarian response is to note the need to form bridging social bodies that are composed of communities rather than individuals,[40] and to nestle local communities within more encompassing communities—but not to agitate against the basic building block of solid communities (albeit ones that observe rights).

New rights, more empathy

Until recently, media reports and narratives about transgender people treated them mainly as outliers, typically discussed as people with individual struggles and peculiar needs. Questions were raised about the age at which transgender surgery should be considered ethical, and what factors led individuals to seek to change their assigned gender, and other such personal considerations.

As of 2012, transgender people have been increasingly referred to as a group and as one that has distinct rights. Public leaders and elected officials started to associate gay and lesbian rights with those of transgendered people, increasingly using the term LGBTQ. For instance, during the 2016 elections Hillary Clinton's campaign stated she had "plans to protect the rights of women, workers, minorities, and the LGBTQ community."[41]

In 2013, California passed a law allowing transgender students to use bathrooms aligned with their identity rather than their gender at birth. In 2015, the Charlotte City Council voted to expand the city's nondiscrimination ordinance to allow people to use bathrooms that correspond with their gender identity. In March 2016, however, House Bill 2 (HB2), also known as the Public Facilities Privacy and Security Act, was passed by the General Assembly in North Carolina to pre-empt the Charlotte bill. HB2 requires people to use public restrooms (the law does not apply to private universities or businesses) in accordance with the sex listed on their birth certificate.

In response, the U.S. Department of Justice asserted that HB2 is a violation of federal civil rights law, including under Title VII, which protects against workplace discrimination on the basis of race, color, religion, sex, or national origin, and Title IX, which protects against sex-based discrimination in education. In May 2016, it notified North Carolina of HB2's violation of the Civil Rights Act. In response, North Carolina filed a lawsuit against the Department of Justice (DOJ), and a few hours later, the DOJ filed a lawsuit against North Carolina. The Obama administration announced that it was considering withholding federal aid to North Carolina for schools, highways, and housing.[42]

In February of 2017, the Trump administration retracted the federal guidelines issued by the Obama administration, which stated that students had the right to use the restroom that corresponds to their gender identity. Oral arguments before the Supreme Court for the case of Gavin Grimm, a transgender high school student from Virginia prevented from using the boys restroom at school, had been scheduled for March 2017. However, after the Obama-era guidelines were removed, the Supreme Court decided to remand the case to the Fourth Circuit.

From a globalist, human rights viewpoint the minting of a new right, through an extended interpretation of Titles VII and IX, is but one more step in a long, progressive development of rights. Indeed, much of American history can be told as an expansion of rights, beyond those understood as enumerated in the Bill of Rights in its original form. These include extending the right to vote and to run for office to people without property; extending it to women; ending slavery and providing African Americans both a de jure and a de facto right to vote; forming the right to privacy; extending rights to people with disabilities, and to gay people to be married.

From a liberal communitarian viewpoint these developments went a long way to correct an imbalance, to correct a social world in which values that prescribed obligations were strongly etched but protections of the individual were weak. However, communitarians raised the question whether extending these developments serves both the individual and the community well, and if there are other ways to respond to newly recognized needs and articulated grievances. Communitarians point to three considerations: the effect of the inflation of rights, the merit of communal treatments, and the need for adaptation and empathy. These points are next illustrated.

In the early 1990s communitarians pointed out that there was a strong tendency toward minting new rights.[43] In Santa Monica, California, men were found dealing drugs in public women's rooms on the beaches and in parks. To combat the abuse, the city council passed an ordinance that prohibited men and women from using the opposite sex's facilities unless they were in urgent need (which was defined as a line of three or more in front of them). A local activist, Gloria Allred saw in the ordinance a violation of a woman's right to urinate in any public facility, at any time. Referring to a similar ordinance in Houston, Texas, she stated: "Little did I know that such a nightmare might soon be reenacted in this fair city."

Ms. Allred warned: "This is the first step down a long dark road of restricting women's rights in the name of public safety."[44]

Death-row inmates at San Quentin have sued to protect their reproductive rights to provide artificial insemination. An attorney in the case reports that "these inmates believe that they are being subjected to cruel and unusual punishment because not only are they being sentenced to die, but future generations of their family are being executed also ..."[45]

Lisa Dangler, a mother in Yorktown, New York, sued the local school district for not admitting her son into the high school's honor society. She argued that his rejection reduced his chances of being accepted by a select college and medical school. She further claimed that he was being punished because the Danglers were outspoken critics of the school—and hence his rejection was actually a violation of the family's right of free speech. A jury rejected her suit. The presiding judge stated that if the jury had ruled in Ms. Dangler's favor, he would have overturned the verdict. He added: "By attempting to elevate mere personal desires into constitutional rights and claiming denial of their civil rights whenever their desires are not realized, these persons are demeaning the essential rights and procedures that protect us all."[46]

The American Bankers Association took out a full-page ad in the *Washington Post* (when Congress was considering putting a cap on the interest banks may charge credit-card holders) that bore the headline, "Will Congress deny millions of Americans the right to keep their credit cards?"[47]

These examples illustrate that one can trivialize rights by claiming that whatever one seeks is due to one because it is a constitutionally protected right, and hence should be enforced by courts and, if need be, by the full force of the federal government. Like with other currencies, such an inflation of rights undermines the value. In a *New York Times* editorial entitled "Tempest in a Toilet," Frank Bruni asks rhetorically, "What species of sentry or manner of inquisition would assess the external and internal anatomy of the bathroom-bound? Shall we divert government spending to this? We skimp on money to repair America's infrastructure, but let's find funds to patrol America's lavatories."[48] He notes that male sexual predators going into women's restrooms (the concern of many who advocate for bathroom bills) would already be breaking other laws against lewdness, harassment, and molestation. Bruni writes "I understand the anxiety that many Americans feel. I get their confusion. I'm not immune to it myself ... Let's navigate these waters calmly. Let's flush away the nonsense."[49]

David Benkoff writes:

> The Bathroom Battle can be easily resolved if respectful people focus on practicalities rather ideology. Options include communal showers with individual stalls, alternative private bathrooms for gender nonconforming children, and special hours for changing and showering. The idea that such accommodations will draw negative attention to transgender kids is frankly silly. Do we really think kids don't already know which of their peers is transitioning?[50]

I am not arguing that the transgender people's quest for using the facilities they prefer is a trivial one, but ask whether it should be treated as a constitutionally protected right or if there is some other way to address it.

Communitarians point to the value of drawing on communal treatments of new issues rather than rushing to involve the courts. Communitarians see an advantage in alternative dispute resolutions (and integrative justice) such as arbitration and mediation over using courts, especially for "lighter" offenses. Good divorce lawyers urge couples to work out their differences about custody of children and distribution of assets on their own, rather than using lawyers and courts. These recommendations are based on the realizations that the advocacy model characteristic of American courts tends to increase antagonism between the parties and make amiable, civil community-building outcomes much less likely. In this model there are only two sides, and each side presents its interpretation of the facts in the way that most strongly supports its position. The advocacy model assumes that the clash of two strong one-sided views will lead to a just conclusion, reasonable judgments, and sound public policies. This is rarely the case.

In the case at hand, various accommodations were proposed to deal with the special bathroom and locker needs of transgender people. For instance, in 2015 Illinois's largest school district offered a separate room to a transgender student as a place where she could change. This proposal was rejected by the U.S. Department of Education.[51] Harper Jean Tobin, policy director at the National Center for Transgender Equality, noted in response to the proposal, "It's a very different thing to say 'Here's the facility. Here's how everyone else can use the facility, except you. We've determined there's something wrong with you that you cannot use the facility in the same way that everyone else can.'"[52] This is similar to what the Gloucester County Public Schools opted for in the case of Gavin Grimm: offering him use of a unisex restroom in the nurse's office. The American Civil Liberties Union (ACLU) argues that such a policy is unacceptable because it singles out transgender students and subjects them to different treatment.[53]

Once an issue is framed in legal terms, it is difficult to see how it might have benefited from less coercive treatments, at least as a first and second cut. The following new concern, shared by some members of the LGBTQ community, may serve as a way to explore the point at hand because it deals with an issue that has not been turned into a question of rights so far.

The issue is a quest for a gender-neutral language; for example, the use of Mx. as a gender-neutral honorific. Mx. is favored as an option for transgender individuals or anyone who does not want a gender-specific identification of themselves.[54] "I think Mx. should be adopted as the standard form of address for everyone, because the real promise of the transgender movement was not the freedom to figure out ways to become more fully male or fully female, but rather freedom from gender entirely. Loosening the gender grip on language is a step in that direction," writes Wake Forest University Professor Shannon Gilreath.[55] In 2014, the Vancouver school board introduced a policy which recognizes gender-neutral pronouns (xe, xem, and xyr for third person singular, plural, and possessive, respectively) for students who do not identify as male or female.[56] A web designer who uses zie and hir (to replace he/she and his/her) notes that people "seem to want to prioritize rigid linguistic rules over people's well-being and self-identification. It's funny because language is ever-evolving along with people, and I find it counter-productive to be so inflexible because of 'linguistic challenges.'"[57]

One may favor or oppose such moves, but they are much less of a concern as long as it is left to public dialogue to agree which honorific one ought to use. Such dialogues led in the past to the shift from referring to women by their husbands' names (e.g., Mrs. John Doe), to referring to them by their own name—and to wide acceptance of the honorific Ms. Such developments would be much more contentious if the law required a change in honorific and leveled penalties against those who used the "wrong" one. This does not mean that coercive means have to be avoided in general, but that society is better served if it relies on them more sparingly and takes into account that feelings on both sides are going to be ruffled.

Nationalists are losing the culture wars, as abortion remains legal, divorce has been normalized, and gay marriages have been approved by the highest court in the land. At the same time, immigrants bring ways of life that conflict with those of nationalists. And their economic conditions prevent nationalists from maintaining the standard of living they were used to. The Charlotte ordinance seems to be, for many of them, the straw that broke the camel's back, although one may well argue that they felt that it had already been broken, repeatedly, before.[58] As Arlie Russel Hochschild points out,

> For the Tea Party around the country, the shifting moral qualifications for the American Dream had turned them into strangers in their own land, afraid, resentful, displaced, and dismissed by the very people who were, they felt, cutting in line ... Liberals were asking them to feel compassion for the downtrodden in the back of the line, the "slaves" of society. They didn't want to; they felt downtrodden themselves.[59]

To list these deprivations experienced by nationalists, their sense that their ways of life are being assaulted, is of course not to justify their prejudices. However, it suggests that, morally speaking, one should treat them as good people with utterly objectionable positions rather than as inherently bad people, that is, as irredeemable. (Liberal communitarianism should borrow from religions that hold that we are all God's children, and that one should hate the sin but love the sinner.) And, it follows, that if globalist policies are to gain ground, they will have to help nationalists to transition rather than condemn and further humiliate them. That is, empathy is called for, both for moral and for practical reasons. One should treat all people with dignity, even if one strongly disagrees with their viewpoints. (Needless to say, if they act on these viewpoints, such actions should be treated as any other violation of the law, or more severely, when they are expressions of hate, as the law calls for.)

One may argue in response that "these people," sometimes referred to as "white trash" or "rednecks"—or more indirectly as uneducated, working-class whites—cannot be reached. However, the record shows that people in all parts of America have changed their minds over the years, following moral dialogues, on these issues. For instance, Gallup polling found that in only eighteen years, from 1996 to 2014, support for gay marriage more than doubled from 27 percent to 55percent.[60]

Empathy is a major moral value, essential for communitarians. Globalists might benefit if they considered what they would feel if the government issued regulations that violate values and habits that they hold in high regard. The argument advanced here is not based on moral equivalency. It grants that a regulation that bans a particular prejudice has the moral high ground, one not accessible to a regulation that limits a right. However, in both cases, those affected feel challenged and threatened. To reiterate, extended dialogues, which provide time to grieve and time to adapt, are justified on both moral and prudential grounds.

One notes that by mid-2017 there were signs that some globalists were realizing that attacking nationalism head on may not be justified, and certainly not prudent. They hence indicated that what they objected to was "ethnic nationalism" or "white nationalism." As a next step they drew a distinction between patriotism, which is viewed positively, and nationalism, which is viewed as troubling.[61] For instance, E.J. Dionne, Jr. reports that "nationalism rankles, partly because of its association with the evils of Nazism and fascism."[62] American patriotism, on the other hand, "is not a loyalty to blood or soil. It is an embrace of a series of powerful propositions," a quality "central to our identity."[63] And according to Lawrence Summers, "What is needed is a responsible nationalism."[64]

Conclusion

Globalization (the free flow of goods, people, and ideas) combined with the promotion of human (i.e. globally applicable) rights is a factor that accounts for the rise of populism. In response, extolling the virtues of liberalism will not suffice. What is missing is recognition of the importance of communities, as small as families and as large as nations, for people's flourishing and their ability to resist demagogues. Hence, communitarian considerations are needed for both analysis and policy making. They help to understand how communities that are under attack can be maintained and shored up. However, given that communities can be oppressive, they need to be leavened with liberal principles: hence the merit of a liberal communitarian philosophy. At the same time, one cannot ignore that the two sets of principles cannot be fully reconciled. This chapter has provided several major examples of ways that liberal and communitarian principles can be combined and their differences curbed.

TWO

The privatization of force

The U.S. Constitution and much of statutory law seek to protect individuals from intrusions by the government. It is the government's coercive power that must be constrained. In contrast, private agents are assumed by most Americans to engage in voluntary transactions, transactions that are mutually beneficial as to the various parties and that serve the common good.[1] Thus, major segments of Western political and social philosophy, public disclosure, and policy making hold the private sector to be basically the realm of freedom—and the government as the power that needs to be checked and reined in. However, this chapter presents considerable evidence that in at least three major areas, the restraints on governmental power are circumvented on a very large scale by private agents carrying out—for the government—activities that government is banned from undertaking. These areas concern surveillance, policing, and military interventions overseas. The question hence arises: what suggested remedies can correct this major challenge to the basic conception that underlies the Constitution and the rule of law? After reviewing several remedies, this chapter asks whether a more profound reconceptualization is called for.

Privacy merchants

The right to privacy, like other rights, is first and foremost a right "against" the government. It protects Americans from undue intrusions by the state.[2] The first right to federal privacy was formulated in the mid-1960s. This right limited the power of the government to interfere in the reproductive choices of couples and women[3] (i.e., decisional privacy). Several laws have further limited the information the government may collect. Particularly important among these is the Privacy Act of 1974, which restricts government agencies, including the Internal Revenue Service (IRS) and Social Security Administration, from sharing with third parties the personal information they collect on individuals without their consent.[4]

The Fourth Amendment also provides a major source of privacy for individuals against government surveillance. This amendment affirms "[t]he right of the people to be secure in their persons, houses, papers, and effects, against unreasonable searches and seizures," as well as the requirement of "probable cause" for a search warrant to be issued.[5] The Supreme Court's Fourth Amendment jurisprudence limits how the government can collect information for law enforcement purposes, generally requiring a warrant for searches and seizures, but making exceptions for "exigent circumstances," government "special needs" and administrative searches, consent by the person searched, "minimally intrusive" searches, and searches in the absence of a "reasonable expectation of privacy."[6] These privacy protections are enforced in part by the exclusionary rule, which limits the admissibility of evidence obtained in violation of the privacy doctrine, providing a disincentive for law enforcement to do so. After 9/11, the surveillance powers of the government were greatly increased; however, these powers became subject to much concern, criticism, and reform, especially after the Snowden revelations in 2013, and were amended with the 2015 USA Freedom Act.[7]

Much attention has been paid to the collection of personal information by the private sector. Such collection has increased in the 21st century, thanks to advances in information technology, and continues to grow rapidly in terms of the quantity, breadth, and dollar value of data collected.[8] Broadly speaking, there are two kinds of corporations that track the activities and backgrounds of internet users. One category tracks user activity on its sites in support of its regular business, such as recording purchases and viewed products to help increase sales. Though these corporations may sell personal data to advertisers or others, it is not their primary line of business. A second category has as its primary business the collection of personal information, often in the form of detailed dossiers, and selling it in the marketplace to any and all comers. Such companies, termed "data brokers" or "privacy merchants,"[9] are the focus of this section.

A major industry

Privacy merchants, or data brokers, are defined by the Federal Trade Commission as "companies that collect information, including personal information about consumers, from a wide variety of sources for the purpose of reselling such information to their customers for various purposes, including verifying an individual's identity, differentiating records, marketing products, and preventing financial fraud."[10] As of 2012, one leading privacy merchant alone, Acxiom, maintained a database of over "500 million active consumers worldwide, with about 1,500 data points per person," including "a majority of adults in the United States."[11] Though no comprehensive list of privacy merchants exists, estimates of the number of companies active in this sector range from the hundreds to the thousands.[12] The industry generated $150 billion in revenue in 2012,[13] compared to $75.4 billion for the U.S. Government's fiscal year 2012 Intelligence Budget.[14]

Privacy merchants' collection of consumer information is not limited to "publicly available information such as home addresses and phone numbers."[15] Collection extends to such specific and private information as YouTube viewing habits, medical conditions, pet ownership, income, social media activity, financial vulnerabilities, and many other kinds of information.[16]

Although privacy merchants' actions have not elicited the same kind of alarm that surveillance by the government has engendered, critics express concern about privacy violations and call for greater regulation and transparency of these private actors. Some note that data brokers create lists of people who are victims of sexual assault, or have specific health concerns. These critics argue that "many of the lists have no business being in the hands of retailers, bosses or banks" and that "[w]e need regulation to help consumers recognize the perils of the new information landscape ..."[17]

The American normative assumptions are that if one is an innocent citizen, not suspected of anything, the government will know very little about that person. And whatever information the government gathers about such people will be locked into separate silos, not accessible to other government agencies. In contrast, private corporations know a great deal about people's preferences and behaviors, and may (and do) keep detailed dossiers on most Americans, though some areas are carved out as protected, especially medical information and, to a lesser extent, financial data.

Working for the government

Very little attention is paid to the fact that the distinction between the government and the private sector—which uses information for commercial purposes to improve customer service and make profit—is increasingly meaningless. Privacy merchants sell the information they amass and process to the government. The difference between the Federal Bureau of Investigation (FBI) assembling detailed dossiers on most Americans (which would shock many) and simply purchasing such a dossier from a company such as Acxiom and LexisNexis is increasingly trivial. The private data is but one check and one click away from the government.

The U.S. government in general, and law enforcement agencies in particular, have made substantial use of the services provided by data privacy merchants since the 1990s.[18] One leading company, ChoicePoint,[19] provided "services to 7,000 federal, state, and local law enforcement agencies" as of 2006.[20] These include "multimillion dollar contracts with at least thirty-five federal agencies, including the Internal Revenue Service and the FBI."[21] Privacy merchants provide services specifically tailored to law enforcement needs, offering to "identify a subject's neighbors, relatives and business associates" and "discern geographic or pathological patterns in criminal behavior."[22] In 2012, the U.S. Treasury Department began using the Work Number database, which is owned by data broker Equifax and includes data on "54 million active salary and employment records, and more than 175 million historical records" from "more than 2,500 U.S. employers," in order to determine eligibility for government benefits and reduce fraud.[23] Even before

9/11, "ChoicePoint and similar services ran between 14,000 and 40,000 searches per month for the United States Marshals Service alone."[24]

"[C]ommercial data brokers have built massive data centers with personal information custom-tailored to law enforcement agents,"[25] and the FBI now holds "voluminous records from commercial data collectors like Acxiom, ChoicePoint," and LexisNexis's Accurint database.[26] (ChoicePoint has since been purchased by Reed Elsevier, the parent company of LexisNexis.) Accurint alone claims to be used by "over 4,000 federal, state and local law enforcement agencies across the country" and to have access to "over 34 billion public and proprietary records."[27] Likewise, findings indicate that "[f]ederal agencies have long evaded the privacy standards in the Privacy Act of 1974 by using information from commercial databases."[28]

Privacy merchant activities are basically legal

The limits on personal information that privacy merchants can collect or disclose, compared to those on the government, are relatively few. One important limit on disclosure of private information is the Fair Credit Reporting Act (FCRA), which restricts consumer reporting agencies (CRAs) from disclosing information except to third parties who have a "valid need." These third parties include creditors, landlords, and employers.[29] Employers are required to obtain specific, written consent from their employee or job candidate before requesting their credit information from a CRA.[30] While CRAs may be considered privacy merchants, they make up only a small fraction of that industry; however, other privacy merchants are subject to the provisions of the FCRA, to the extent that they provide personal information used in "making eligibility decisions affecting consumers."[31] The 1996 Health Insurance Portability and Accountability Act (HIPAA) limits direct access to a substantial part of health information, though privacy merchants still collect data on "over the counter drug purchases; whether the individual purchased disability insurance; purchase history or interest in various health topics like medicine preferences and diabetes care; ailment and prescription online searches."[32] The Gramm-Leach-Bliley Act (GLBA) requires financial institutions to clearly display their privacy policies, and requires them to take appropriate measures to "safeguard" private financial information from unauthorized disclosure.[33] The Act also limits the extent to which these institutions can share select types of personal information with a list of third parties, and gives consumers the right to opt out of having their information shared in such cases.[34] However, privacy advocates describe GLBA's protections as minimal and note that opt-out provisions put the burden of protecting privacy on the consumer.[35] No federal law gives individuals the right to learn what information privacy merchants collect on them. Individuals have no way to opt out of having their information collected or analyzed, or to take action to remove their information from privacy merchants' records, even if that information is inaccurate or outdated.[36] Outside of the areas covered by statutes such as FCRA, privacy merchants are "largely unregulated for privacy" and "generally free to sell information as they please with little regard for accuracy, currency, completeness, or fairness."[37]

Not only does government business with data brokers not invoke the Fourth Amendment, but it is largely unregulated by statute. Christopher Slobogin, who has focused intensively on the Fourth Amendment, argues that, unlike direct physical or electronic surveillance by law enforcement, there is "far less regulation" of what has been called "transaction surveillance," the acquisition by the government of already existing records.[38] Even when the government seeks information directly from the original third party, federal law on transaction surveillance virtually never requires a warrant.[39] Rather, transaction surveillance at most requires a subpoena, typically based on the lax standard of "relevance" to an investigation, and in other cases a certification order or extrajudicial certification, which Slobogin argues are rubber stamps.[40] If instead the government obtains the same information from a privacy merchant rather than from the original third-party source, such as a phone company, it does not need even a subpoena. As a result, the aforementioned privacy restrictions can easily be circumvented. For example, the Privacy Act has an exception for law enforcement (though a written request is still needed to obtain information from another government agency), and at any rate does not apply to records held by the private sector. Even beyond the Privacy Act's explicit exceptions, if the government "obtains personal information from commercial data brokers but keeps the information outsourced and does not maintain that information in a government system of records ... the Privacy Act ... imposes few or no privacy constraints on federal agencies, and no constraints at all on the commercial data brokers."[41] Likewise, while a subpoena is needed for law enforcement to access medical or financial information covered by HIPAA or FCRA, respectively, the government does not need a subpoena to acquire that information from a privacy merchant.[42]

In short, the fact that the government can readily circumvent whatever limitations are in place on its surveillance of individuals by purchasing the information from privacy merchants raises the question: has the nation in effect sought to abolish privacy, or must the nation find new ways to limit the information that privacy merchants can amass and, above all, what they can share with the government?

Suggested remedies

Require prior consent

A major suggestion to deal with the issue at hand builds on the assumption that people own information about themselves and hence every secondary use should require the user to gain the consent of the "owner." That is, in effect, the position the EU takes with its Data Protection Directive (DPD). DPD asserts that any secondary use of personal information released by a person or collected about him or her requires the explicit *a priori* approval of the original individual "owner" of the information, and that granting this consent cannot be delegated to an agent or machine.[43] If such a rule were to be fully heeded, research would suffer greatly because of the great costs involved in seeking consent and the difficulties of securing a representative sample. Security would be hindered by having to ask for consent from those one needs to put under surveillance. And, given that such information is used many times a day, people would have to spend good part of their day reviewing requests for consent for such information use.

The European DPD hence provides a considerable number of exceptions to the consent, including for "journalistic purposes or for artistic or literary expression."[44] It also allows national laws to add further exceptions for reasons of national security, law enforcement, or "protection of the data subject or of the rights and freedoms of others."[45] Moreover, the DPD is not strongly or consistently enforced in those areas that are not exempted.[46]

Protect sensitive information

Sensitive information is defined as personal information whose disclosure violates a significant prevailing societal norm.[47] Much personal information is in effect already ranked by law as if the level of sensitivity were being taken into account. Thus, collecting and reusing medical information in the US is highly controlled, as it is considered particularly sensitive (and within that, information on HIV status is even more regulated); financial information is somewhat less sensitive—and less regulated; and non-sensitive information (such as purchases of most consumer goods) is much less regulated. To complete this approach, all remaining kinds of personal information would have to be regulated according to their level of sensitivity.[48]

Limit the information private parties can collect, whether or not it is sensitive

Several such restrictions are already in place, although critics argue that they have not kept pace with advances in technology. For example, the FCRA regulates CRAs, which sell information about people's residential and tenant history, employment history, and insurance claims to entities such as a landlords and employees. CRAs must provide an accessible means for consumers to find out what information the agencies have about them and if it has been used against them. Consumers may challenge the accuracy of that information and have inaccurate information deleted. Above all, CRAs may sell such information only to those with a "valid need."[49] Although this rule may deter privacy merchants from selling consumer data too broadly, it has little relevance to government purchases of data, as law enforcement officials have long been exempt from these protections for counterintelligence and terrorism investigations, and law enforcement access to credit reports was broadened by the USA PATRIOT Act.[50]

Public safety and private police

The number of private police has surpassed that of public police, yet private police are not held to the same standards and, furthermore, are accountable to their employers rather than to the public. The use of private police has dangerous implications for public safety and privacy. For example, there is often a lack of oversight with regard to the use of firearms by private police, a clear public safety concern. And the government has used private police as a way to exploit loopholes in the constitutional protections afforded to citizens.

What is the scope of the private police sector?

Citizens who are otherwise occupied may well assume that public safety, keeping people safe in their home and in public spaces, is the mission of the police. Actually, the role of the private sector in public safety has grown dramatically since the first Bush administration started. The private police sector[51]—those hired, trained, armed, and commanded by private parties ranging from corporations to neighborhood associations—has grown so much in the U.S. that it is now much larger than the public police.

While in the 1970s there were 1.4 private police for every public police officer, by the 2000s there were 3 private police for every public police officer, and 4 private police for every public police officer in California.[52] As for security guards in particular, estimates range from 1.5 to 2 of them for every public police officer.[53] Given that there were "more than 900,000 sworn law enforcement officers"[54] serving in the U.S. as of late 2014, the above ratios would put the number of private police in the U.S. at 2.7 million, and the number of security guards at 1.35 to 1.8 million (some sources count "1 million plus" security guards).[55]

Accountability

Private police provide a major way to circumvent the standards, oversight, and accountability to which public police are subjected. This is not to argue that all or even most private police are retained for this purpose. Nor does it mean that the public police are subject to sufficient accountability. Much national attention has recently been paid to abuses by the public police, particularly the number of people killed by police, and the fact that a highly disproportionate number of those killed have been unarmed African Americans.[56]

There are no federal training standards for private police. No state even "comes close to meeting the training standards recommended by the country's largest membership group for security guards."[57] Many states allow armed private guards to carry guns without firearms training, do not require them to undergo mental health examinations, do not check if they are under court order not to carry weapons, and do not require them to report the use of their weapons.[58] The same is true for a majority of states with regard to "proprietary guards," those employed by the guarded company rather than by a separate security company.[59]

Private police are usually not subject to constitutional limits. The criminal procedure law that restrains public police consists of a "vast set of interrelated constitutional doctrines," including "the Fourth, Fifth, and Sixth Amendments, made applicable to the states through the Due Process Clause of the Fourteenth Amendment, along with the Supreme Court's elaborate efforts to implement those provisions through rules of evidentiary exclusion and the restrictions on interrogations imposed by *Miranda v. Arizona* and its progeny."[60] (In *Miranda v. Arizona* (1966), the Supreme Court set forth guidelines for law enforcement, known as Miranda warnings, which specify that suspects being questioned must be informed of their rights, including the right to remain silent.[61]) Private police, like other private citizens, are restrained merely by "tort and criminal doctrines of assault, trespass, and false imprisonment."[62] This means in practice that "confessions extracted by private police without Miranda warnings and evidence obtained through unlawful searches conducted by private agents are not subject to exclusionary rules."[63] Thus, a move towards greater reliance on private police threatens to undermine the civil liberties gained over the twentieth century with respect to public police—limited as these gains may be.[64]

There are some exceptions to the immunity of private police from constitutional limits. Section 1983 of the U.S. Code provides a "cause of action" against "any person" who, acting "under color of" state law, violates a plaintiff's federal constitutional or statutory rights."[65] Individuals claiming to have been "detained, harassed, physically abused, or otherwise injured by private police" can use "section 1983 litigation when the private police act under color of law, for example by acting jointly with local police, by exercising police powers granted by statute or by the local police, and when private security is provided by off-duty police in their official uniforms."[66]

The Supreme Court, however, has "shied away from addressing the constitutional status of private police" while developing "an elaborate, notoriously muddled doctrine of state action" with unclear relevance to private police,[67] and the Court has not provided meaningful guidance to lower courts on the constitutional status of private police.[68] Moreover, public police benefit from "having a private arm that reports crimes, that may detain and search citizens, and that may even testify in court, admitting evidence that might otherwise be excluded."[69]

Since the 1970s, public police have increasingly relied on private security personnel "to obtain evidence that effectively circumvent[s] constitutional requirements under the Fourth, Fifth, and Sixth Amendments," which is a legal loophole "so long as a court can find that there was a legitimate private purpose behind the search."[70] This practice has been referred to as the "silver platter doctrine"; it suggests that current law and "new organizational forms of partnership create *incentives* that permit the circumvention of rules meant to constrain public police behavior."[71] Finally, it may be that "the greater the legal restraints on the public police, the more private police will be turned to for 'dirty work,' sometimes by the public police themselves."[72]

In short, public police conduct in a considerable number of cities is subject to criticism and concern. However, there are at least basic mechanisms in place for oversight, accountability, and reform. The private police, which often do not operate in high-crime areas and hence have less opportunity to commit abuse, are not subject to the same procedural checks as public police and may be available to carry out the public police's "dirty business."

What remedies?

Rethinking privatization

The U.S. should rethink how much policing we want to privatize at all.[73] Bringing public values to private policing, by holding private police to the same regulatory and constitutional standards as public police, is impractical. Furthermore, "there is virtually no political support" for stricter regulation or labor standards for private police,[74] or for significantly curbing private police work

Expand constitutional restrictions to cover private police

This approach is favored by those who argue that restrictions stemming from the Bill of Rights "should follow function over form: both official police and private police functioning as arms of the state should be held to constitutional standards because they have been legitimized, directly or indirectly, by the state, to fulfill a public demand for order and security."[75] However, the same approach may not be appropriate for "private mercenaries who fulfill merely a private demand for force unrelated to communal order and security."[76] Yet, attempts by courts to address the issues raised by private police are "vanishingly rare."[77]

Private military contractors (PMCs)

Many expect the military to be responsible for defending the nation against external threats. Thus, the state is often defined in terms of its "monopoly of the legitimate use of physical force within a given territory."[78] In reality, the private sector conducts much of the business of U.S. national defense, including the production of military assets and services and the training of personnel. Of $519 billion in federal spending on contracts in 2012,[79] the Defense

Department accounted for 70 percent, allocating 56 percent of its own budget on contracts. Private contractors provide vehicles, armor, weapons, transportation, logistical support, and many other goods and services; make up about a quarter of intelligence workers; and absorb "70 percent or more of the intelligence community's secret budget."[80] As with private police, defense contractors in addition often play a complementary role to the public military, with roles including protecting diplomats,[81] providing counterterrorism training, and supplementing U.S. military forces abroad.[82]

Problems with U.S. use of private military contractors

Concerns regarding the use of private military contractors by the United States fall into two categories. First, PMCs generally lack accountability. The contractors have more direct authority over their employees than the U.S. military does. Second, the measures that do exist for holding PMCs accountable lack consistency and effective application. The result has been serious human rights abuses committed by PMCs that often go unpunished.

PMCs are much less accountable

The last decade's wars in Afghanistan and Iraq witnessed extensive corruption and serious human rights abuses by PMCs. While uniformed military personnel were sometimes held accountable by military courts, PMCs and other contractors were rarely held responsible for wrongdoing.[83] According to the bipartisan Congressional Commission on Wartime Contracting in Iraq and Afghanistan (CWC), which issued a series of detailed reports between 2008 and 2011, the "limited jurisdiction over criminal behavior and limited access to records" that characterized the PMC sector contributed "to an environment where contractors misbehave with limited accountability."[84] Of the more than $206 billion spent by the U.S. on contracts and grants in Iraq and Afghanistan through 2011, between $31 billion and $60 billion was lost to waste and abuse.[85] Although some PMCs have been convicted of fraud or bribery,[86] accountability has been generally lacking.[87] While the details of this wartime fraud and abuse are covered extensively elsewhere,[88] it is worth briefly noting some of the abuses committed by PMCs in particular to demonstrate the relevance of their ambiguous legal status.

Perhaps the most notorious example of abuse of the 2003 Iraq War concerned the Abu Ghraib prison. Amnesty International and media organizations reported that U.S. personnel, including soldiers and PMCs, had engaged in "systematic abuse" of prisoners. This included torture, sexual abuse, and interrogation-related deaths.[89] These abuses were largely unpunished; 11 U.S. soldiers were convicted of crimes relating to the scandal, but these were "were mostly low-ranking soldiers and they generally received lenient sentences."[90] The PMCs involved in the scandal have evaded even this limited level of accountability, in part because the Justice Department has abstained from prosecution.[91] A class-action suit by former Abu Ghraib prisoners against one of the contractors involved, CACI International, was still ongoing as of 2016, after a series of contradictory court rulings over the justiciability of the case. In the most recent ruling, a district court again dismissed the detainees' claims, on the basis of the "political question" doctrine, which holds that "courts are not authorized or equipped to resolve certain matters—like some military decisions or aspects of foreign relations—and must leave them to the other branches of government."[92] In other words, PMCs working in Abu Ghraib, who "were involved in many of the very same incidents,"[93] were too close to the military to be prosecuted by U.S. courts, yet not close enough to be subject to the Uniform Code of Military Justice (UCMJ).[94]

Although PMCs may be bound by contractual arrangements with a customer, such as the U.S. government, military officers have no direct control over PMCs and lack "even the legal authority to order a contractor to do those services he or she was hired to perform."[95] This is because the "duty of disciplining contractors falls squarely on the contractors' corporate employer."[96] In such a situation, military officers must rely on "soft control,"[97] to keep contractors in line. According to the Congressional Budget Office, "[t]he military commander has less direct authority over the actions of contractor employees than over military or government civilian subordinates" and "limited authority for taking disciplinary action," as "[t]he contractor, not the commander, is responsible for ensuring that employees comply with laws, regulations, and military orders."[98]

The heavy reliance on contractors has troubling implications for democratic and constitutional constraints on the conduct of foreign policy. PMCs' lack of accountability provides a perverse incentive for future administrations to contract out "dirty work" such as torture. Use of PMCs can disrupt the balance of powers within the government. For example, "because Congress has less information about and control over the use of contractors than the use of troops," using PMCs can "speed policy making and limit the number and variety of inputs into the policy process" and so bypass "some of the constitutionalism said to be key to democratic policy making."[99]

Remedies to promote contractor accountability

Modify the legal status of PMCs

In the U.S., several efforts have been made to close the legal loopholes affecting PMCs, including amending the UCMJ and the Military Extraterritorial Jurisdiction Act (MEJA). The Civilian Extraterritorial Jurisdiction Act has also been introduced to complement MEJA, with the "strong support" of the DOJ.[100] This bill aims "to clarify and expand Federal criminal jurisdiction over Federal contractors and employees outside the United States," "supplement rather than replace" existing "provisions of federal extraterritorial jurisdiction," and deal with crimes including "federal violent, corruption, and trafficking offenses."[101] Amending international law to reflect the increasing prevalence of PMCs (e.g. by expanding or simplifying the definition of "mercenary") might be another way to increase accountability.[102] However, "if there is to be law reform in this area, it is important to bear in mind the difficulties with the existing conventional law,"[103] including lax enforcement and the emphasis in international law on the narrowly defined term "mercenary."[104]

Most of the bills intended to deal with PMC abuse and fraud failed to make any headway in Congress.[105] The MEJA Expansion and Enforcement Act was passed by the House in 2007, but not by the Senate, and made no subsequent progress.[106] Some provisions from the Comprehensive Contingency Contracting Reform Act of 2012, backed by Sen. Claire McCaskill and building on the recommendations of the CWC, were incorporated into the 2013 National Defense Authorization Act, but were "watered down over time or cut entirely."[107] While the role of money in politics is difficult to prove, this legislative inertia likely results in part from the influence of military contractors in Washington. Recent consolidation in the defense contracting industry,[108] the government's reliance on military contractors, and the millions of dollars the industry spends on lobbying combine to give military contractors substantial leverage to resist reforms.[109]

Strengthen the enforcement regime

While many experts on PMCs are troubled by their legal unaccountability, Laura Dickinson, who focuses her studies on human rights and international security, argues that the legal jurisdiction for holding contractors accountable is adequate, and the real problem is the lack of an effective "enforcement regime" for these laws. She thus makes three broad recommendations for organizational reforms. First, she suggests reforming government contracts with PMCs to include "public law values" (including human rights norms, norms against corruption and waste, and democratic processes)[110] as well stronger oversight and enforcement requirements, and an accreditation requirement for contractors.[111] Second, she calls for greater public participation in the design and implementation of such contracts.[112] And third, she suggests "reforming the organizational structure and culture of private security firms," which might include a greater supervisory role for judge advocates and military commanders, as well as the adoption of legal corps and stricter standards within private security contractors.[113]

While Peter Singer is more skeptical of existing legal accountability, he also makes suggestions for reforming the relationship between government and PMCs. Acknowledging that PMCs have proposed various self-regulation schemes, he argues that the public interest in the nature of their activities necessitates greater public scrutiny and regulation.

Reduce government reliance on PMCs

It may be wise to simply oppose privatization of security in general. Outsourcing of "essential or inherent functions" such as the armed forces and police both undermines the "capacity, effectiveness, and morale" of government and violates constitutional and democratic principles.[114] Another approach entails recognizing that PMCs do have some merits, but their use should be curtailed. This is the approach taken by the CWC, which argued that the U.S. was "over-reliant" on contractors and should consider reducing their use or the "the number, nature, and scope of the overseas contingency operations" for which they are needed.[115]

One way to reduce reliance on contractors would be to do so in particular areas rather than simply call for an overall reduction. For example, Singer argues that due to the lack of full command authority of military officers over PMCs, "wherever possible private security contracting should be kept out of critical battlefield areas," and that "when the military requires a service, it should be sure to examine first the possibilities offered within the force, across other service branches, and then to trusted allied forces."[116] Likewise, the CWC recommended that the government "phase out use of private security contractors for certain functions," particularly for guarding convoys or bases that are at risk of attack from enemy forces.[117]

Conclusion

The preceding three case studies suggest that the public–private distinction, a major normative and legal meta-conception that has framed much of public discourse and policy making over the last 200 years, is obsolete. Many of the statements most commonly made in public discourse about the government and the market, or the state and individual rights, view one of these two realms as virtuous and the other as problematic. Many Americans see the government as coercive and the private sector as the realm of freedom, and hence hold that the government should be checked and curbed and the private sector be free to follow its own course. Libertarians and civil libertarians similarly hold that the government is oppressive and that individual rights must be protected. In contrast, the left sees the private sector—particularly Wall Street—as the source of major societal deformations and seeks to use the government to check the private elites and promote social justice. However, the preceding case studies show that in at least these three major areas, the two sectors increasingly act as one, with the private sector carrying out government missions, and the government using the private sector to circumvent the limits imposed on it.

To provide but one more illustration of the extent to which the old but still-dominant framework is obsolete, take the following situation. In January 2009, the U.S. had about 34,400 troops in Afghanistan.[118] The U.S. military asked the White House to authorize a major increase in the level of troops committed to this country (known as the Afghan surge). The request was followed by an intensive, months-long debate in the White House, Congress, and the public over how many additional troops to commit. Some called for as many as 80,000, some for as few as zero.[119] The president settled for 30,000, and eventually the troop level peaked at 100,000 in August 2010.[120] During the debate, however, almost no one mentioned that at the same time the U.S. had deployed 74,000 PMCs in Afghanistan, many more than the additional troops.[121] In reality, a larger "contractor surge" occurred over the same period: the number of contractors increased to 107,300 in December 2009. Moreover, as the U.S. drew down troop levels in Afghanistan, beginning in 2011, it also undertook a *second* contractor surge with little fanfare: the number of contractors, which had fallen to 70,600 in September 2010, rose to 107,800 by March 2013.[122] This blind spot extends to casualty figures as well. When Obama spoke in 2015 about the "more than 2,200 American patriots who made the ultimate sacrifice in Afghanistan," for example, this did not include the 1,592 private contractors, 32 percent of whom were Americans, who were killed over the same period.[123] A reasonable debate should have encompassed the size of both public and private forces.

Any new approach need not hold that there are no differences between the private and public sectors, and hence treat privacy merchants as if they were agents of the National Security Agency (NSA), members of the private police as public cops, and private military contractors as troops. One promising approach focuses on what might be called the "degrees of separation." This approach suggests that private actors that are directly controlled by the government, have largely public missions, and are financed by the public (such as security guards hired to protect American diplomats) should be treated much more like public sector agents. In contrast, those who are private actors that mainly serve the private sector, who market their wares to one and all (the government included), and for whom the government is not a particularly large or influential client, should be granted much more leeway. Those in between these two extremes should be treated accordingly.

To avoid a misunderstanding: this chapter suggests that all private agents who carry out a government function—directly or indirectly—should be subject to more accountability and oversight, of a kind similar to that to which public agents are subjected. However, there should be a difference in degree, according to the extent that the private actors are autonomous from the government.

One analogue for the needed approach is the normative and legal response to the rise of the "on-demand" or "gig" economy, in which companies such as Uber use part-time contracts for jobs previously performed by employees. Recent court and administrative rulings have looked at the extent to which the rules that apply to the traditional employee–employer relationship should also apply to the relationship between on-demand services and their contractors, based on several different criteria. For example, in June 2015, the California Labor Commissioner's Office ruled that an Uber driver should be classified as an employee rather than an independent contractor, because Uber was "involved in every aspect of the operation" and played a controlling rather than merely facilitating role.[124] Likewise, in August 2015, the National Labor Relations Board ruled that companies such as McDonalds that used contractors and franchisees as intermediaries with their workers are still "joint employers" of those workers, which entitles unions representing these workers to bargain directly with the company as well as the contractor or franchisee.[125]

More broadly, the distinction between workers and contractors "has been the subject of intense legal battles for decades," resulting in federal agencies designating the criteria that should be taken into account, with the extent of control usually the most important.[126] Thus, the IRS lists three broad categories: "behavioral," in the sense of whether the company controls the worker's performance; "financial," in terms of whether the "business aspects of the worker's job" are controlled by the company; and "type of relationship," such as whether there is a written contract or long-term association and whether the work performed is a "key aspect of the business."[127] The difficulty of maintaining a sharp dichotomy between employees and contractors suggests that it would be productive to employ a nuanced approach that involves gradations in employee status and employer obligations. The same is true for privacy merchants, private police, private military contractors, and all other private actors who carry out missions historically carried out by the government.

In developing a new meta-doctrine to replace the sharp private/public distinction, several variables stand out as helpful in determining the degrees of separation between the government and its private agents. These include:

(a) Command and control. Does the government directly order the private agents about, daily, and in a tight formation, just like its own troops, or does the government define a mission and contract it out, but let private supervisors control the actual agents?

(b) Accountability. Does misconduct by the private agents harm the public as much as would direct misconduct by the government (e.g. the way enhanced interrogations soiled American reputation in the Middle East and elsewhere), or is that harm largely absorbed by the private actor (e.g. cost overruns, if charged to the company rather than the taxpayer)?

(c) Financing. Does the government finance the private actor completely or to a significant degree, and hence gain considerable influence over that actor? Or, is the government only one of the private actor's many customers, limiting its influence?

Surely other criteria might be developed, but these suggested criteria illustrate the approach that would govern private agents as if they were public ones, with varying levels of strictness according to the extent to which they are separated from the public architecture. The rise of private contractors in American government creates a need for new society-wide normative and legal doctrines[128] and a fundamental change in Western (and particularly American) thinking. This change is illustrated by the notion that the Fourth Amendment may apply to private actors and not just to government agencies. It makes little sense to lock the door (of the public sector) if one leaves the windows (of the private sector) wide open. For American society to uphold the values it seeks to implement, it requires normative positions, policies, laws, and institutions that apply to both sectors. Many of the remedies listed above are partial. Most are of merit, but nevertheless do not offer the kind of comprehensive new framework that the evidence suggests is needed. It will take an almost revolutionary effort to develop the needed comprehensive meta-conception and integrate it into the policy and legal worlds.[129]

THREE

Captured

Capture is a phenomenon where private interests gain control of major segments of government—especially those of lawmaking and law enforcement—and employ them to serve their own particularistic ends. It is typically discussed with regard to regulation and hence often referred to as regulatory capture. However, as we shall see, often much more than regulation is captured.

Liberals tend to favor regulations as expressions of the public will and serving the common good, as a way to protect minors, patients, and many kinds of consumers from abuse by unscrupulous actors in the private sector. Laissez-faire conservatives and libertarians tend to oppose regulations because they view them as an abuse of the government's power and as harmful to the economic well-being of the nation. Yet this form of the debate overlooks the phenomenon of regulatory capture which reveals that regulations work neither to promote the public good nor to undermine private actors. These observations have led some scholars to argue that regulations are useless or worse, and others to seek more effective forms of regulation.

The realities of regulation

The term regulatory capture is often associated with the work of the economist George Stigler and his frequently cited article "The Economic Theory of Regulation," in which he writes that, "as a rule, regulation is acquired by the industry and is designed and operated primarily for its benefit."[1] This work builds upon

Stigler's previous essay with Claire Friedland, "What can Regulators Regulate? The Case of Electricity,"[2] which takes up the question of the efficacy of regulation more generally and concludes that regulatory efforts rarely cause any deviation from market outcomes. Stigler's research on regulation influenced the work of a number of later scholars investigating the phenomenon of capture and applying the methods of public choice theory to regulatory issues.

In addition, the liberal–conservative debate represents a case of deficient generalization, in which various observers note incidents where the realities of regulation deviate from their core assumptions, but neither side has proved ready to draw conclusions from these numerous incidents, most of which point in the same direction. Thus, many liberals are quite aware of regulations that end up serving private interests rather than the public, but they still strongly favor regulations. For instance, they considered the enactment of the Dodd-Frank financial reform bill in 2010 to be one of the major achievements of the Obama administration, despite the fact that the law was in a sense doubly captured: prior to passage, the initial bill was greatly diluted by lobbyists working for the industries it is supposed to regulate. Also, the law, as enacted by Congress, is particularly open ended, leaving it to various agencies to shape the needed specifications, under conditions particularly favorable to lobbyists. Conservatives too are aware of incidents in which regulations serve those in the private sector, usually their allies, but nevertheless continue to stand strongly opposed to regulation in general.

Means of capture

Capture is achieved in several ways, briefly illustrated here. Arguably, these could all be diminished to make regulation serve its original goals.

Special interests compose the regulations

To give an example, Citigroup and other banks have had a direct influence on weakening financial regulations. In one instance, the

New York Times reported that "Citigroup's recommendations were reflected in more than 70 lines of the House committee's 85-line bill. Two crucial paragraphs, prepared by Citigroup in conjunction with other Wall Street banks, were copied nearly word for word."[3]

Diluting regulation

In the wake of the 2001 Enron scandal, Congress passed the Sarbanes-Oxley Act in 2002. Hailed in the *Economist* as "the most sweeping reform of corporate governance in America since the Great Depression,"[4] the law left it to the Securities and Exchange Commission (SEC) to work out the details of the new regulations. However, the SEC was subjected to extensive lobbying by the accounting industry, such that the regulations included a definition of auditing that created a loophole for auditors to continue practices initially targeted for prohibition, as they entailed a conflict of interest.

Sarbanes-Oxley was further weakened in 2006. Whereas it initially required auditors to investigate any accounting issues that have a "more than remote" chance of damaging a company's finances, the rules were revised to require auditors only to investigate issues that have a "reasonable possibility" of doing so. Moreover, in 2009 small businesses were permanently exempted from two of the Act's key provisions—the first requiring executives to confirm the integrity of their firm's internal accounting procedures, and another requiring an outside audit of these procedures. This gradual dilution of regulations is reflected in the size of the regulatory text of the law, which was reduced from 180 pages to a mere 65.[5]

Eliminating regulation

Since the Trump administration took office, many environmental regulations have been rolled back. For example, Donald Trump signed a bill into law that eliminated a rule designed to prevent coal mining from polluting streams—a rule strongly opposed by coal mining companies. And Scott Pruitt at the Environmental

Protection Agency eliminated a rule—unfavorable for oil and gas companies—that required the reporting of methane emissions.[6]

Weak enforcement

In 2012, the Federal Trade Commission (FTC) imposed a $22.5 million fine on Google for using tracking cookies on consumers' web browsers to collect data on their internet use. This represented an infringement on consumers' privacy rights by the web company, a charge which has been leveled at them before. However, it is doubtful that the FTC will do much economic damage to the web powerhouse. The tiny fine is less than what Google earns in a few hours.

The FTC also dropped its antitrust investigation into Google, choosing a settlement option with the company instead. Although the FTC exacted some concessions from Google, it was seen by many as a mere slap on the wrist.[7] The FTC's Bureau of Competition had written a 160 page report and recommended a lawsuit against the company, but at the beginning of 2013 FTC commissioners unanimously decided to discontinue the investigation.[8]

Gaming the regulators

Special interests affect the regulatory regime in their favor by switching regulations into a new jurisdiction (e.g. from state to federal) or by pitting the regulators against one another. According to the *Washington Post*, when mortgage lender Countrywide Financial felt "pressured" by the federal agencies charged with overseeing it, executives "simply switched regulators."[9] As a national commercial bank, Countrywide had been under the jurisdiction of the Office of the Comptroller of the Currency. As early as 2005, Countrywide executives engaged in talks with the Office of Thrift Supervision (OTS), known to be a much more "flexible" regulator. Less than two years later, Countrywide redefined itself as a "thrift" instead of a "national commercial bank" and thus became regulated by the OTS. Over the next two years OTS proved to be a very lax regulator of Countrywide's mortgage lending, as it also proved to be for IndyMac, Washington Mutual, and other major lenders.[10] It is worth noting that they also played a significant role in the financial crisis that followed.

Setting prices and rates

Regulators are often charged with limiting the profits gained by one industry or another; e.g. limiting the rate increases of utilities. However, in several major cases, captured regulations had the opposite effect: they bolstered the profits of a specific industry by setting higher prices and rates than the market would provide. An example of this can be found in the establishment of price ceilings on gasoline in some eastern Canadian cities. The imposition of price ceilings, which on the surface seemed to hedge against rising prices, actually artificially inflated gas prices in these areas and greatly slowed the pace at which these markets would respond to a general decline in the price of oil. These regulations helped to better entrench the position of otherwise inefficient firms already selling in these gas markets, and worked to discourage the entrance of newer, more efficient firms with higher overhead costs. Thus, the price ceilings served the narrow interests of entrenched firms while at the same time preserving inefficiencies in the market and artificially inflating prices.

Close relationships between regulators and industry

In the words of then-Senator Barack Obama, the U.S. Nuclear Regulatory Agency (NRC) is "captive of the industries that it regulates."[11] The NRC is indirectly funded by industry fees; however, since the fees are routed through the U.S. Treasury, an NRC spokesman maintained that "[i]t's not a case where the industry is handing us a check". The Union of Concerned Scientists has counted dozens of instances where the NRC allowed reactors to stay in operation, despite safety concerns.[12]

After the explosion at BP's Deepwater Horizon well in 2010 and the resulting oil spill in the Gulf of Mexico, there was widespread consensus that the federal agency responsible for regulating the well, the Minerals Management Service (MMS), had failed in large part because it had been captured. In the *Wall Street Journal*, Gerald P. O'Driscoll, Jr. wrote, "By all accounts, MMS operated as a rubber stamp for BP. It is a striking example of regulatory capture: Agencies tasked with protecting the public interest come to identify with the regulated industry and protect its interests against that of the public. The result: Government fails to protect the public."[13] The Interior Department's inspector general found that MMS officials responsible for overseeing drilling in the Gulf of Mexico were allowing oil and gas officials to fill out their own inspection forms, and some even considered themselves part of the industry they were tasked to regulate.

A challenge to capture

Despite there being a number of different avenues for private interests to capture regulations, it is worth noting that capture is rarely complete, and thus even regulations subject to capture can generate some public benefit. Consider again the case of Sarbanes-Oxley, which was in part a response to the actions of Enron Corporation and its accounting firm Arthur Andersen, which were found to have used irregular accounting practices to conceal a significant amount of Enron's debts and losses. As these practices came to light, Enron's stock plummeted from over $90.00 to less than $0.50 per share, forcing the company to declare bankruptcy, causing substantial losses to many thousands of investors, and leaving thousands of Enron employees without their retirement savings accounts and other benefits. Enron was not alone; similar scandals involved other major American corporations such as Tyco and WorldCom.

As noted above, Sarbanes-Oxley was significantly diluted during its creation and in the initial years of its implementation. Nevertheless, the law has achieved some of its goals. In his review of the Act, John C. Coates of Harvard Law School has concluded that Sarbanes-Oxley created significant incentives for firms to devote greater resources toward internal controls of their accounts.[14] Furthermore, the Act provides a number of long-term benefits, including greater transparency and accuracy concerning firms' financial data, which reduces risk of losses for investors. Finally, the Act requires that high-level executives sign off on their firms' financial statements, creating not just a paper trail but also a culture of increased accountability at the highest levels of corporate office. Thus, in spite of being significantly diluted, Sarbanes-Oxley can be seen as a somewhat successful attempt at regulation.

A new approach to regulation?

Recently, scholars have suggested a new approach to regulation, led by Cass Sunstein and Richard Thaler, who argue in favor of a benign paternalism that induces desired patterns of action through small incentives, opt-out programs rather than opt-in, and simple persuasion.[15] Rather than coercing desired outcomes through heavy penalties or regulation, Sunstein and Thaler, whose ideas were embraced by President Obama and Prime Minister Cameron, contend that the government should operate as a "choice architect" that "nudges" people in the right direction.[16] However, this new mechanism assumes a benign government, out to serve the public, and does not provide antidotes to capture.

The role of campaign contributions

There is considerable reason to hold that a major way capture is effected is by campaign contributions. The amount of campaign contributions granted to individuals who are seeking election or re-election to Congress has reached a level that seriously undermines the democratic system. Although some contributors argue that they give because they share the philosophical positions of the candidates, this defense should not be allowed to stand if they do not distribute their funds among those who seek election that share their position, and grant them only to those who provide them with benefits. This argument is particularly indefensible when contributors make contributions to elected officials who hold opposing philosophies on the matter at hand, but provide a benefit. This is far from a rare condition. During his presidential campaign, Donald Trump revealed: "I give to everybody. When they call, I give. And you know what, when I need something from them two years later, three years later, I call them. They are there for me."[17]

To further illustrate: Senators Orrin Hatch (R–UT) and Tom Harkin (D–IA) co-sponsored the Dietary Supplement Heath and Education Act of 1994, which defined supplements as food rather than drugs, allowing the supplements to be marketed and sold without the oversight and safety testing required of the latter. Since that time, they have continued to mobilize senators to vote against legislation to regulate the supplements industry. They pressured the Senate to vote down Sen. Dick Durbin's (D–IL) amendment to the 2012 Federal Drugs Administration (FDA) Safety and Innovation Act, which would have required supplements with potentially serious side-effects to be labeled, and Sen. John McCain's (R–AZ) 2010 Dietary Supplement Safety Act, which would have required supplement manufacturers to include all ingredients on the label and register with the FDA. They also pressured FDA officials to weaken their draft Dietary Ingredient Guidance.

Harkin and Hatch's efforts are a major reason why unregulated supplements suffer from poor quality control, with a 2013 study finding that herbal supplements often contain unlabeled fillers or contaminants and that a third "showed outright substitution, meaning there was no trace of the plant advertised on the bottle."[18] The two senators have been the top recipients of donations from this industry for decades.[19] This is only an example—there are numerous cases of such quid pro quo. One can argue that Senator Hatch, a conservative Republican, voted that way because he is opposed to regulation on ideological grounds. The same cannot be said about Senator Harkin, a liberal Democrat.

Some who defend the prevailing system argue that contributors are merely buying access and do not gain benefits. The Supreme Court has reinforced this claim in *Citizens United*. According to the opinion delivered by Justice Kennedy in that case, "Ingratiation and access … are not corruption."[20]

First, one should not ignore that gaining access is by itself a very valuable benefit. Second, in many situations, contributions lead to, or are followed by, very concrete benefits well beyond access.

Leading up to the repeal by Congress of the US oil export ban, some of the largest oil and gas companies contributed millions of dollars to the Senate Leadership Fund, a super PAC (political action committee) for Senate Republicans run by former aides to Senator Mitch McConnell. Specifically, "[i]n the second half of 2015, Senate Leadership Fund received $1 million from Chevron, $1 million from Petrodome Energy, $750,000 from Devon Energy Corporation and $500,000 from Freeport LNG CEO Michael Smith."[21] Congress passed the repeal of the oil export ban as part of a spending bill designed to prevent a government shutdown, and it was subsequently signed by President Obama.[22] "[F]or oil executives, [this] was the culmination of a long-sought goal."[23]

The 62 Senators who voted for the Keystone XL pipeline collectively received $31,754,343 from fossil fuel companies, compared to the combined total of $2,672,091 given to the 36 who voted against it.[24]

The fact that campaign contributions flow much more to committees that can dish out benefits, especially appropriations committees, and much less to committees unable to do so (e.g. foreign policy), and much more to chairs rather than their members, is indirect evidence of the connection between contributors and benefits.

Particularly suspect are benefits granted to contributors, individuals, or corporations that are not located in the districts of the members of Congress. This is far from a rare phenomenon. According to Anne Baker, between 2006 and 2012, "The average member of the House received just 11 percent of all campaign funds from donors inside the district."[25] *McCutcheon v. Federal Election Commission* is a case that highlights non-constituent contributions; Shaun McCutcheon, who had contributed to 16 federal candidates, filed a complaint because of his inability to contribute to 12 other federal candidates, as well as various political committees, because of aggregate limits. McCutcheon was a resident of Alabama and had contributed to congressional candidates across the country.[26] None of the 12 candidates he intended to contribute to was running for election from Alabama.[27] As Richard Briffault explains,

> By preserving the base limits while striking down the aggregate limits, McCutcheon enables an individual to give much more money but not any more money to any one candidate … Unless the donor wants to give money to many more candidates campaigning against

each other in the same electoral contest—which seems unlikely—the donor will give to more candidates in many different states and districts. By striking down the aggregate limits, McCutcheon directly promotes contributions by non-constituents.[28]

Briffault then tackles the Court's rhetoric in *McCutcheon* with regard to responsiveness, asserting that despite Chief Justice Roberts's "contention that striking down the aggregate donation cap will *promote* the accountability of representatives to their constituents," in fact it does no such thing. As Briffault points out, representatives may be responsive to contributors, but when these contributors are not constituents, it "undermin[es] the very responsiveness to the people that the Chief Justice rightly celebrates as 'key to the concept of self-governance.'"[29] In short, campaign contributions from non-constituents should face a higher level of scrutiny than those from constituents. They are particularly likely to lead to irrelevant benefits because interests served do not stem from the constituency that the given member of Congress has a duty to serve—and may well disadvantage them when the benefits flow to others.

Another issue is that of independent expenditures. The Supreme Court has ruled that independent expenditures[30] cannot be limited because they pose no threat of corruption, as they are not made in coordination with the candidate. Further, it decided that to impose limitations would amount to infringing on free speech. In *Citizens United*, the group Citizens United produced a negative documentary on then Senator Hillary Clinton with the intention of releasing it within 30 days of the primary election. However, the release of "electioneering communications" paid for by corporations and unions within 30 days of the primary was prohibited at the time. The Court overturned this restriction and opened the door to unlimited independent expenditures. The Court quotes *Buckley v. Valeo* to explain its rationale: "The absence of prearrangement and coordination of an expenditure with the candidate or his agent not only undermines the value of the expenditure to the candidate, but also alleviates the danger that expenditures will be given as a *quid pro quo* for improper commitments from the candidate."[31] Thus, the Court held that because independent expenditures are not made in coordination with the candidate, there is no risk of *quid pro quo* corruption. The ruling in *Citizens United* helped to lay the foundation for super PACs, the funnel through which individuals and corporations can make unlimited contributions.[32]

Actually, there are several ways that candidates and the so-called independent PACs sidestep anti-coordination regulations. First, Federal Election Commission (FEC) rules allow super PACs and campaigns to communicate directly; they may not discuss candidate strategy, but can confer on "issue ads" featuring a candidate.[33] Matea Gold writes that "it is now standard practice for candidates to share suggested television ad scripts and video footage online— materials that are then scooped up by outside groups and turned into television spots."[34] Second, it is very easy for those who spend the super PAC monies to note which points their candidate are flagging and run ads to support these, or prepare supportive campaign literature and so on.

Finally, many candidates fundraise for super PACs, and while the candidates themselves cannot ask for contributions over $5,000, the FEC issued an advisory opinion that allows campaign aides to raise greater amounts for super PACs.[35] Not surprisingly, these super PACs with ties to a specific candidate appear to gain most of contributions.[36] In the words of Rep. David Price (D-NC), "it amounts to a joke that there's no coordination between these individual super PACs and the candidates."[37] As election law attorney Robert Kelner puts it, "[i]f there's no separation between the campaigns and outside groups, then the logic of the *Citizens United* decision really falls apart."[38]

Remedies?

Various constitutional amendments have been proposed to address campaign financing. However, in 1997 and in 2014, the Senate rejected proposed amendments that would have allowed Congress to determine campaign spending limits in federal elections.[39] The other avenue for an amendment to the Constitution, which relies on an introduction by two-thirds of the state legislatures, is a very hard row to hoe, and little progress has been made.

The fact that almost all attempts to limit the flood of private monies into public hands by curbing what one can contribute to election campaigns have failed is evident in the continued growth of election spending. (Amounts spent have increased faster than would be expected, taking into account inflation and population growth.)[40] Between 2000 and 2012, the cost of each U.S. presidential election was greater than the last. The 1998 Congressional races cost approximately $1.6 billion ($2.4 billion adjusted for inflation), while in 2014 they cost $3.8 billion.[41]

Furthermore, although courts have held that corruption can be deterred through transparency and disclosure requirements, such measures are woefully insufficient. In *McCutcheon*, the Supreme Court stated, "disclosure of contributions minimizes the potential for abuse of the campaign finance system [and] may also 'deter actual corruption and avoid the appearance of corruption by exposing large contributions and expenditures to the light of publicity.'"[42]

It's true that super PACs are required to disclose their donors. However, because they may receive money from entities that are not required to disclose, the actual donors can easily remain anonymous. The Sunlight Foundation provides the following example to illustrate the issue at hand: "In 2010, a super PAC that was active in one of that year's marquee House races listed a single donor: a 501(c)(4) organization that does not have to disclose its donors. This is what is known among some campaign finance lawyers as 'the Russian doll problem.'"[43]

Section 501(c)(4) and 501(c)(6) organizations fall in the category of politically active non-profits, which can accept unlimited contributions and are typically under no obligation to disclose their contributors. In theory their political activity is limited, but in practice these limits are often unenforced. The prevalence of these organizations in federal elections has increased, and they are often associated with the term "dark money," since their funding sources are obscured.[44] As part of the reforms here suggested, disclosure should be mandatory for all organizations that spend in one way or another on political campaigns.

Furthermore, super PACs can have misleading or vague names that make it impossible to know which interests they are seeking to promote. How is one to tell that Americans for Progressive Action was started by a Republican and never supported any Democrat? That American Bridge 21st Century supports Democrats, while America Rising supports Republicans?[45]

In *Buckley*, the Court did recognize that disclosure may not be sufficient to prevent corruption, stating that "Congress was surely entitled to conclude that disclosure was only a partial measure, and that contribution ceilings were a necessary legislative concomitant to deal with the reality or appearance of corruption."[46] However, when Congress did act, the Court struck down practically all the limits Congress set on making contributions.

Needed: a new political force

The basic issue may not be a strictly legal one, that is, the problem may well not be that no one has been able to develop a law—able to pass the Court's muster—that would limit the flow of funds from private hands into the campaign chests of politicians. The main problem seems to be the lack of a political force strong enough to carry such a law forward in the face of fierce opposition from a large variety of powerful special interest groups.

There is no sign that a political party could mobilize such a force; the needed change may require a major social movement. Key examples of social movements that led to major changes are of national liberation, socialism, religious movements (such as radical Islam), and movements that seek to protect the environment. These movements differ greatly from one another, in particular with respect to the values they promote. They share, though, several sociological attributes, despite their major normative and historical differences: they can withdraw legitimacy and political support from a declining regime and lay the foundations for a new one, in the process affecting both the private and the public realms. The progressive movement is the most applicable model. Without such a force, much of American life must be expected to continue to be captured by special interests.

There is a connection here to populism. The masses involved correctly sense that the government all too often is not serving them. The trouble is that their justified anger is focused on the wrong address.

FOUR

Forging new legitimacy

Some see societies and their laws in Durkheimian ways. They view societies as communities that have shared moral cultures which are expressed in laws, supported by moral consensus. Others see societies and their laws in a Marxian way. They view societies as arenas in which different power groups clash. As I see it, societies combine both elements. We have seen, in the preceding chapters, the important role that private concentrations of power play in shaping public life, above all through lawmaking and implementation. This chapter examines the role of values and consensus in providing legitimacy to the social order and its laws, or withdrawing such legitimacy and forging a new one. When the old legitimacy is lost but no new one is formed, authoritarian regimes and/or populist movements are likely to follow.

Moral dialogues are social processes through which people form new shared moral understandings, the foundations on which new legitimacy can be constructed.[1] These dialogues typically are passionate, disorderly, and without a clear starting point or conclusion (in contrast to elections or debates in a legislature). However, moral dialogues often do lead to profound changes in the moral positions of those who are engaged in them. Although moral dialogues never change the values of all those involved, they often, as we shall see, change the moral positions of a sufficient number of people so that actions and policies that previously had little support (e.g. environmental protection), and actions and policies considered morally inappropriate by many (e.g. same-sex marriage), gain widespread moral approval.

Moreover, we shall see that when moral dialogues mature, the new shared moral understandings that arise have profound sociological effects well beyond changes in values and norms and attitudes. These new or changed moral understandings are embedded in new laws or lead to significant changes in law and, more importantly, lead to major changes in voluntary behavior. For instance, the shared understanding that we have a moral obligation to the environment led to the founding of a new U.S. government agency (the Environmental Protection Agency), scores of new laws and regulations, and considerable changes in voluntary personal behavior, including recycling, preferences for sustainable sources of energy (a factor in purchasing cars, appliances, and solar panels), donations, and voting. True, these changes were also effected by other factors, especially changes in economic incentives. However, the restructuring of these incentives reflects in part changes in shared moral understanding. This chapter focuses on the dynamics and effects of moral dialogues that lead to significant changes in shared moral understandings (SMU).

The following deliberations leave for future discussion the study of the effects of external structural factors on moral dialogues, such as differences in political and economic power, social inequality, race, and gender. They seek to introduce moral dialogues as distinct from reasoned deliberations, expressions of emotions, and culture wars, and leave for future examination the important effects of structural factors on moral dialogues.

One can readily envision moral dialogues within a family or a small community but may well wonder if a society that encompasses many millions of people can engage in a moral dialogue. We shall see below that such society-wide dialogues take place by linking millions of local conversations (between couples, in neighborhood bars, in coffee houses, car pools, next to water coolers at work, and so on) into a society-wide moral give and take.

In his book on democratic citizenship, *Citizen Speak*, Andrew Perrin describes the social interactions in which moral dialogues occur, though he does not use this term. He writes:

> In everyday political life, citizens do have the opportunity to deliberate, though not in the laboratory conditions of Ackerman and Fishman, nor in the

dramatic street battles of social movements. They can deliberate with friends, colleagues, fellow students, neighbors, members of organizations they belong to, anonymous others through letters to the editor, talk radio, Internet chat, and more ... I have called these contexts *political microcultures*."[2]

However, Perrin seems to wonder if such deliberations could lead to the equivalent of a SMU. In the face of conflicting values, he questions whether they might result in compromise rather than consensus.[3]

Since the advent of modern media, especially following the rise of social media, moral dialogues occur even on a transnational level. The suggestion that the "people of the world" can have moral dialogues may seem at first like one of those dewy-eyed notions held by naive idealists. Indeed, even in national dialogues, not all citizens participate, and the resulting understandings are not shared by everyone. Millions are preoccupied with basic needs, set back by a lack of education, or under the influence of mind-numbing substances, and in parts of the world by authoritarian regimes.

The attentive public,[4] deemed as those who are publicly aware and engaged, is growing, as education and access to the media are spreading through many parts of the world. The citizens of countries as different as Russia, China, Iran, and Saudi Arabia have more access to transnational communications than they had in 1980. Hence, transnational moral dialogues are able to have a greater reach than before.

The effect of transnational moral dialogues is reflected in new shared understandings regarding land mines, trading in ivory and antiques, whale hunting, norms against proliferation of nuclear weapons, armed intervention in the internal affairs of other nations, the responsibility to protect (against genocides), human trafficking, and—to a lesser extent—support of human rights and climate protection.

Before I proceed, I must note a meta point that underlies much of the following: escaping the curse of dichotomies. A good part of public discourse and quite a few philosophical and social science deliberations draw on dichotomies. For instance, for the last two centuries the people of many nations have been engaged in debates between those who champion the private sector and those who champion the public sector; about the merits of the market as compared to those of the government; between liberals and conservatives. These debates typically ignore a very large amount of social "business" conducted in the third sector, that of communities, voluntary associations, ethnic and religious groups, hundreds of thousands of not-for-profit corporations, and millions of families. This observation is particularly relevant for much that follows because moral dialogues occur largely in the third sector.

The curse of dichotomies is equally evident in the analysis of behavior as either rational or irrational, and of dialogues as either evidence based, drawing on facts and logic ("cold"), or passionate ("hot"), and hence irrational. Such dichotomies are particularly seductive because they do not tax the memory, are strongly favored by the mass media (which only rarely give voice to third positions), and allow one to split ambiguities and project positive traits and attributes onto one element of the dichotomy and negative ones onto the other.

Moral dialogues tend to follow a set pattern. I choose my words carefully. Not all moral dialogues follow all the stages next outlined; the pattern next unveiled should hence be viewed as an ideal type.[5] It serves as an analytic matrix for the study of various specific dialogues and the comparison of one to others. In presenting the pattern (some would call it a "natural history") I draw on illustrations from American experience, although its presence in other societies and transnational dialogues is self-evident.

Baselines

To assess the effects of any given moral dialogue, one must establish what the SMU was before the dialogue took place. For instance, to assess the effects of moral dialogues on our moral obligations to "mother earth," about our stewardship of the environment, one must start by noting that in the 1950s there was no shared sense of such a moral responsibility. People dumped garbage in lakes and streams, drove cars that emitted a great deal of pollutants, used coal as a major source of energy, without any concern about their environmental implications. In the same period, racial segregation was legally enforced and widely supported. Women were expected to be homemakers and submissive. Gay people were considered sinners and deviants. Smoking in public raised no moral issues. People felt obligated to do "all they could" for their loved ones until their heart and lungs stopped functioning. Researchers can readily find some academics, clergy, or visionaries that made a moral case against any one of these established mores. However, they did not start moral dialogues and did not have a significant effect on the nationwide SMU.

Sociological dialogue starters

Moral dialogues often start with the articulation of what might be called a "moral brief," akin to what lawyers file before they argue a case before the U.S. Supreme Court. It typically includes a criticism of the prevailing moral culture and society and a substantive statement of what a new SMU should contain. One should note in this context that some protest movements and organizations mainly provide a criticism of the prevailing order but contain little content—or only exceedingly vague content—about the core values to replace the old ones. They are more disruptive than transformative. Major changes in SMU require that briefs also include statements about the new SMU to replace the old one. (It is a point that was not fully taken into account by several groups that brought down old regimes during the Arab Spring.)

Betty Friedan provided such a brief for a moral dialogue about women's rights and status in her 1963 book *The Feminine Mystique*. Ralph Nader did the same for the consumer protection drive in his book *Unsafe at Any Speed*, published in 1965. In the words of Paul Offit, "What Harriet Beecher Stowe's *Uncle Tom's Cabin* did for civil rights legislation, and Upton Sinclair's *The Jungle* did for food and drug legislation, Rachel Carson's *Silent Spring* did for environmental legislation."[6] Other moral dialogues were started by a declaration, for instance Martin Luther's 95 theses, which prompted the Protestant Reformation. A Harvard committee provided a brief for changing the definition of death to one that occurs when there is a "brain death." Sometimes moral dialogues are triggered by an event rather than a brief, such as the Three Mile Island accident in

1979, which started a dialogue about nuclear safety. However, in all the cases examined, a brief followed.

In examining moral briefs, it is important to distinguish between *historical starters* ("first") and *sociological take-off points*. When a book or trial or event leads to a new moral dialogue, historians will often point out that rather similar ones have already been published or have taken place before. For instance, before *The Feminine Mystique*, other books on the topic had been published, including *The Second Sex* by Simone de Beauvoir in 1949. However, these previous starters were false starts; they did not start major moral dialogues that could lead to new SMU. For the purpose of studying changes in SMU, one must focus on those briefs and events that served to initiate the kind of dialogues and societal changes next described; that is, those that were followed by a dialogue that took off rather than remaining grounded.

Some studies refer to the selection of dialogue starters as "agenda setting," the process through which people attribute a higher importance to some issues as compared to others. According to H. Denis Wu and Renita Coleman, "For more than thirty years, the main concept in agenda setting theory has been the transfer of issue salience, or how media emphasis of certain issues raises their importance for the public."[7] A common finding is that the media largely determines the issues the public focuses on.

James Jasper describes what here are referred to as "starters," using the term "moral shocks." According to Jasper,

> "Moral shocks," often the first step toward recruitment in social movements, occur when an unexpected event or piece of information raises such a sense of outrage in a person that she becomes inclined toward political action, whether or not she has acquaintances in the movement. The triggers may be highly publicized public events such as a nuclear accident, or personal experiences such as the death of a child. They may be sudden, like an accident or public announcement, or they may unfold gradually over time, as in the realization by Love Canal's residents that they were living over a toxic waste dump. Similarly, the shock may come from a plan for something new or from new information

about something existing, which has already done unseen damage.[8]

The content of the brief, how well it is argued and presented, or the nature of the starting events, is often not the most important factor determining whether they will serve merely as a historical first or will lead to a sociological take-off. Much more important is whether or not the sociological conditions that would allow the changes to take off are in place. Thus, for instance, briefs for liberal democracy in societies of the kind the U.S. found in Afghanistan in 2003 are unlikely to lead to a take-off.[9] Kristin Luker's book *Abortion and the Politics of Motherhood* illustrates how a change in sociological conditions allowed for a moral dialogue to take off. Luker writes that

> the pro-choice activists started out being considerably more liberal than many Americans, but within a very short period of time, American public opinion had moved much closer to the pro-choice position. It is tempting to argue that the pro-choice people simply "persuaded" a great many fellow Americans to accept their point of view. To some extent they probably did; certainly the mere fact that they made the abortion issue a subject for public debate allowed many more people to become familiar with it and to form personal opinions about the merits of the case. It seems likely, however, that American public opinion was shaped more significantly by the large-scale social changes going on at the time—changes in the status of women, changes in traditional sexual morality, and an increasing concern with poverty.[10]

Similarly, looking at the feminist movement, it seems that *The Feminine Mystique* led to take-off not because it was more convincing than previous books on the subject, but partly because it was published after World War II, during which time many women worked in factories and (some) participated in the military and were thus open to suggestions that they were able and entitled to play roles other than homemakers (among other factors). The question of which sociological developments set the stage for this and other take-offs, and which failed, requires its own major study and is not explored in the following discussion.

Some starters that launch moral dialogues are events rather than briefs. For instance, Rosa Parks refusing to give up her seat and move to the back of the bus is widely recognized as *a* starter of the civil rights movement, among others.[11] The brief for the movement followed later, especially in the speeches of Martin Luther King, Jr., above all in *I Have a Dream*. This case illustrates my hypothesis that for moral dialogues to take off and reach their destination (a new SMU), all the elements are needed, but the sequence may differ from one dialogue to another.

Finally, one should note that many moral dialogues take off but then lose altitude and need to be relaunched if they are to lead to a new SMU. For instance, dialogues about inequality in the U.S. are following this pattern. Google Trends data shows no definitive spike in the popularity (relative to all other Google searches) of the search term "social inequality"—instead it oscillates with relative consistency.[12]

Moreover, some moral dialogues that do take off never produce a new or changed SMU. For instance, briefs that called for the formation of a global government, in particular the 1947 Montreux Declaration by the World Federalists as part of the World Movement for World Federal Government,[13] initiated a measure of moral dialogues, but these petered out without gaining a new SMU.

Megalogues

For a starter brief or event to lead to a new SMU, it must be followed by processes that would lead a large number of people to reexamine their moral values, giving up on what they long believed was right, and accept a new set of values as morally valid.

Some advocates of moral causes believe that if the president would make a powerful speech or conduct "fireside chats" as President Roosevelt did, this would lead to a new SMU and change the direction of the nation. President Kennedy's speech that urged Americans not to ask what their country can do for them but what they can do for their country is credited with engendering a historic change; however, although the speech is often quoted, there is scant evidence that, by itself, it had much of an effect. President Carter tried to make Americans treat the saving of energy as a test of their moral fortitude in his famous malaise speech—with mainly negative effects. President Obama spoke eloquently for many causes, especially for finding common ground, but the nation became more polarized. Such speeches can serve as sociological dialogue starters, but they must be followed by dialogues in order for them to have the sought-after societal effects. People who adhere to a moral value do not change their position because of just one speech, however eloquent.

Instead, when a topic takes off, or "gets hot," it becomes the subject of extensive discussion in personal settings (over dinner, at the water cooler, in bars) and in local meetings of voluntary associations and clubs (Rotary, parent–teacher associations, places of worship). These, in turn, are amplified and linked through national organizations during their meetings (such as the American Israel Public Affairs Committee, League of Women Voters, National Association for the Advancement of Colored People, Sierra Club, Conference of Catholic Bishops, National Council of Churches, etc.), and through the media (call-in shows, commentaries and debates on TV and radio) and social media.

To illustrate, in 2015–16 a subject that was only sporadically discussed in previous years became a focus of a nationwide moral dialogue in the U.S., namely the rights of transgender people. Google Trends data shows that the search term "transgender bathrooms" had little relative popularity in the United States for roughly 10 years, but then experienced a surge of interest after 2015.[14]

Distinct attributes

Moral dialogues differ sharply both from expressions of emotions and from rational deliberations. In effect, they constitute a hybrid that has qualities of its own, different from the composite elements. Moral statements contain emotions in contrast to sheer statements of facts or logic. At the same time, these statements contain justifications—that is, they are intellectually accountable—in contrast to emotions. When one discloses that one hates or loves, or declares any other emotion, it suffices to state "because this is what I feel."[15] In contrast, if one states that a given condition is immoral, say not fair, one is expected to spell out the reasons and give a basis for this statement. And one may be challenged with arguments that such a statement is inconsistent with previous ones, or violates a general ethical position to which the person subscribes, or with still other arguments—and one is expected to justify one's moral judgment or modify it.

The discussion now turns to elaborating these points, comparing the three kinds of expression (rational, emotional, and moral) and the related group processes.

Moral statements differ from rational statements that are focused on facts, as well as from logical conclusions that can be drawn from these facts. People are invested *emotionally* in moral statements, and hence when new facts arise or new arguments are made based on evidence, people will not change their positions readily. True, much has been written pointing out that facts and values cannot be completely separated and they often bleed into each other. Still, there is a clear difference between what have been called *is* versus *ought* statements. Reasoned deliberations are about *is*, moral dialogues are about *ought*.

To illustrate, one may argue whether or not a death penalty is justified on empirical-logical, rational grounds by comparing crime rates in states that have death penalties versus those that do not. Or, before and after such sentences were carried out in states that either dropped or adopted this penalty. In contrast, if one holds that it is morally wrong for the state to deliberately take a life, statistics about the effects on crime rates will matter little (or only if one can show that the result leads to a higher loss of lives).

Quite a few previous discussions of the attributes of dialogues suffer from the curse of dichotomies. The main case in point is the growing recognition that the assumption that people are rational creatures, able to collect and process the information needed to make rational choices, is a false one.[16] It is assumed *ipso facto* that therefore people are irrational, unable to make sensible judgments, because the analysis started from a binary position. If not A, then it must be B. Actually, as Talcott Parsons pointed out long ago, there is a whole third realm, that of the non-rational. This realm includes "other worldly" matters which deal with questions and views about the afterlife, deities, the meaning of life, why we were born to die, and with the selection of moral values, especially when two or more of these values are in conflict.

The same holds for group deliberations. Thus, according to James Kuklinski and his associates, "In a democratic society, reasonable decisions are preferable to unreasonable ones; considered thought leads to the former, emotions to the latter; therefore deliberation is preferable to visceral reaction as a basis for democratic decision making."[17] James Q. Wilson writes about, "the contrast [James] Madison draws between opinions and passion, since opinion implies a belief amenable to reason whereas passion implies a disposition beyond reason's reach."[18]

Moral values and deliberations are either ignored or explicitly "reduced" to irrational emotions. According to Ernest R. House, "Values might be feelings, emotions, or useless metaphysical entities."[19] Cheryl Hall notes that an "endemic problem for deliberative theory stems from the supreme value it places on calm rational discussion, to the exclusion of both emotionally laden speech and passionate protests." [20] Some advocates of deliberative democracy have suggested supplementing deliberation "with more obviously emotional forms of communication."[21] However, Hall argues that deliberative democracy is "more reliant on passion than either advocates or critics acknowledge," criticizing the assumption that reason and passion must be in opposition in deliberation. All these statements assume a dichotomous world, limited to "cool" rational deliberations or "hot" emotions.

Jonathan Haidt, in his nuanced analysis, ultimately still holds that people are basically driven by emotions, and make up post hoc reasons to justify them.[22] Thus, if one seeks to persuade them, one must appeal to their emotions. If this were true, moral arguments would make no difference, ethical deliberations would have no effect.

The stark opposition between rational and emotional group processes does not recognize a third realm of moral statements and dialogues—in which people engage each other's values. Reasoning concerning moral differences, the kind of deliberations that ethics texts provide, is different from reasoning that deals with facts. True, the two realms bleed into each other. Nevertheless the distinction stands. Thus, to argue against the death penalty because one believes that the state should never deliberately take a person's life falls into the first category, while the argument that the death penalty is not effective in suppressing crime falls into the second.

The following serves as an illustration of this third realm of moral statements. For generations, Americans have been strongly opposed to governments running high deficits. Indeed, many American states and municipalities are legally required to balance their budgets each year. This position is mainly based on moral values, such as "one should not live beyond one's means," and not "burden our children with debts," and that it is morally wrong to be in debt. It is sinful. In German, the same word is used to describe guilt and debt. The factual harms that deficits cause are a rather complex question and there is considerable evidence that balancing the budget each year (rather than over a cycle of recessions and prosperity) is a poor policy.

I am not arguing that rational deliberations and moral dialogues do not affect each other. However, when one examines particular dialogues one can, as a rule, readily determine which statements are mainly moral versus largely factual, and see differences in give and take between those that are evidence centered and those focused on moral issues.

We can gain some insight into the issue from mental experiments. A father finding out that his young son smokes may merely yell at him, demanding that he stop (sheer emotion), or strongly express, in emotive terms, his concern for his son's health, and also explain the risks involved to him and others around him. For the purposes of moral dialogues, it matters not in this case if the argument that the father made was merely a rationalization that followed his emotions or one that he developed on the basis of information he garnered and understood. What matters is if his son is less likely to be swayed when exposed to sheer emotion as compared to emotion accompanied by reasoning. Moral dialogues, it follows, draw on both emotional expressions and reason. Otherwise they are shouting matches, guilt trips, or expressions of blind love, shame, and other such emotions.

Some accord a great role to the media as a moral persuader. For instance, when it shows a graphic picture following an earthquake or typhoon, millions of donations flow to the people in the devastated area, based on the emotions the picture evokes. However, on closer inspection, one notes that the picture does not so much shape one's moral disposition as direct where it is applied. One can determine this by noting that large donations will come from Americans because voluntary donations are part of the American moral tradition. In some other countries, the same pictures will lead to greater demands on the government to act. And in still others, very few donations will be forthcoming. Bernard Cohen made this point well when he observed that "[the press] may not be successful much of the time in telling people what to think, but it is stunningly successful in telling its readers what to think *about.*"[23]

In further deliberating on the question at hand, one can draw on firsthand experience in moral deliberations. Thus, when we serve on a committee which considers whether or not to disclose to the public or the authorities some unethical conduct or acts that might be illegal—for example, bullying or unconfirmed reports about inappropriate advances made by a coach—we note that our emotions are surely engaged but that we also take into account moral arguments.

Moral dialogues resolve differences and are thus able to lead to new SMUs in their own ways, a far cry from relying on new empirical evidence. One often-used procedure in moral dialogues is *to appeal to an overarching value* that the various parties to the sorting-out process share. Robert Goodin in effect is using this rule when he seeks to pave the road for a community that must sort out a course between the rights of non-smokers and those of smokers.[24] At first, this may seem as a typical clash between two values: the rights of one group versus those of another. However, Goodin points out that *both* groups are committed to the value that one's liberty does not allow that person to violate the "space" of the other. In popular terms, my right to extend my arm stops when my fist reaches your nose. Goodin argues that that value applies because non-smokers, in their non-smoking, do not penetrate the smokers' space, while smokers do violate non-smokers' space in public situations, thus non-smokers' rights should take priority. Using such arguments, American communities reached the SMU that lies at the foundation of the new restrictions on smoking in numerous public spaces. (The fact that these new regulations met very little opposition shows that they were based on a thoroughly shared moral understanding, unlike Prohibition.)

Another procedure is to bring a *third value into play when two diverge or clash*. For instance, those who tried to restore the Black–Jewish coalition of the 1960s in the United States argue that both groups share a commitment to liberal causes. Additionally, attempts to create an interfaith coalition pointed to the shared commitment to fighting poverty, as the participants struggled to work out a joint position.[25] Groups that strongly support pro-life public policies and those that strongly support pro-choice ones agreed to work together to improve the care of children, which both groups cherish.[26]

"Culture war" is a term that was used originally between social conservatives and liberals about issues such as abortion and divorce. More generally, it is used to refer to "a conflict between groups with different ideals, beliefs, [or] philosophies."[27] It implies persistent, unresolved value differences such as between Protestants and Catholics in earlier eras, Shias and Sunnis, and secular and Ultra-Orthodox Jews more recently. One may view culture wars as failed moral dialogues, in part due to higher levels of emotional involvement as compared to moral dialogues. However, one should note the findings of an excellent study by historian Stephen Prothero that shows that, over time, even these dialogues often lead to new SMUs, for instance with respect to same-sex marriage, the use of contraception, and divorce.[28] This may even be true about gun control; however, in this realm SMUs have not yet reached a level where they can lead to significant changes in voluntary behavior or the law.

Dramatization

So far the analysis of moral dialogues has focused on communications; on members of a community, however small or large, exchanging moral viewpoints, discussing moral issues with one another, reexamining their moral positions, and reaching (often) common ground. One should not ignore, however, that *all* such dialogues also contain acts that serve to dramatize the moral issues under discussion, such as sit-ins, demonstrations, occupying administrative buildings on campuses and corporations, sit-downs in traffics lanes, and spilling blood on fur coats (by animal rights activists). Court cases such as the Scopes Trial, Congressional hearings regarding Joseph McCarthy, and the confirmation of Associate Justice Clarence Thomas also serve to dramatize the issues.

These dramatizations serve two main purposes. One is to nurture the dialogues. Following dramatizations, especially those with novel rather than merely routinized elements, one finds a spike in dialogues. The importance of dramatization has risen since the advent of TV. Pictures are highly evocative, while verbal dialogues rarely lend themselves to dramatic footage. Hence, dramatizations are a particularly effective means to promote moral dialogues, to keep the issues under discussion in the public eye, and to evoke participation.

Second, dramatizations engage people's emotions, while verbal give and take relates more to intellectual accountability elements. Dramatization thus helps to ensure that people who may be swayed by an argument will also refigure their emotional commitments accordingly.[29]

Closure

Many moral dialogues lead not only to significant changes in the moral positions of millions of individuals—which are essential for bringing about changes in prevailing SMUs or to form new ones—but also engender significant changes in behavior and laws. When moral dialogues are advanced successfully, they lead to the formation of new shared moral judgments or to changes in moral positions (values, norms, and attitudes). For example, as far as one can determine, there was no significant shared moral commitment to the environment in 1950. By 2016, "74% of U.S. adults said the 'country should do whatever it takes to protect the environment.'"[30] Furthermore, "Seventy-three percent of Americans say they prefer emphasizing alternative energy, rather than gas and oil production, as the solution to the nation's energy problems."[31]

To reiterate, even when successful, the change in SMU encompasses merely a large segment of the people who engaged in these dialogues; there always remain some who do not change their moral position. Moreover, some moral dialogues fail, e.g. between the pro-choice and pro-life groups. Many take off, slow down, and are relaunched before a significant level of SMU is reached (e.g., the dialogue on inequality). However, when these dialogues take off and mature, they change the moral positions of large segments of the population, often ending with new moral majorities.

More importantly, the great significance of SMUs is that they lead to voluntary *changes in behavior—well beyond changes in attitudes.* Thus, people who acknowledge that they have a moral obligation to the environment are much more likely than others to recycle, use recycled paper, bike and walk, buy low-emission cars that use fuel efficiently, support public policies that protect the environment, use solar panels, and so on. True, these behaviors are also affected by changes in economic incentives and legislative acts. However, for reasons next outlined, it makes a very great difference (a) if the changes in behavior are mainly voluntary, due to changes in what people consider the right behavior, versus mainly due to economic and legal incentives, and (b) if the changes in incentives and laws are supported by SMUs, or not.

To call attention to the significant role of SMU in engendering significant voluntary changes in behavior is not to suggest that the social change effected by SMU cannot be supplemented or manipulated when combined with economic and legal incentives or disincentives and social arrangements such as "nudges." [32]

The role of SMU in affecting behavior rather than just attitudes is of great significance and hence deserves some elaboration. In a very extensive study of what motivates people,[33] a study whose findings were replicated and augmented many times,[34] Amitai Etzioni showed that people can be motivated to engage in pro-social behavior that they would not otherwise have engaged in, in three ways. They can be coerced; motivated by economic incentives or disincentives; or convinced of the moral rightness of changing their behavior.

The study shows that people resent being coerced, and will try to deviate from forced patterns of behavior whenever they believe they can get away with it. Hence compliance will be costly, unreliable, and far from satisfactory.

People who are *paid* to behave—to read a book,[35] come to class,[36] work, etc.—will be less alienated than those who are coerced, but they will also seek to gain the incentives while giving as little as possible in return, as they feel they can because their preferences are not compatible with what they are paid to do.

In sharp contrast, people who find that what they are asked to do is *morally compelling* will feel ennobled when they carry out their tasks and will seek to carry them out well, even if they are not supervised. (Those in hybrid situations will act accordingly; e.g., the feelings and behaviors of physicians paid to take care of their patients, but also convinced that they are doing good, will fall somewhere between those responding only to economic incentives and those who feel morally compelled.)

There are those who hold that each person is out to pursue his self-interest, and, famously, that an invisible hand will ensure that as a result the economy will thrive and all will do well. Whether this is true or not for the economy need not be examined here; however, this certainly does not hold true for society. The problem of social order, as Dennis Wrong put it,[37] is that people need to be motivated to engage in pro-social behavior. However, no society can provide for a sufficient number of police, accountants, or border patrolmen, etc. to coerce a satisfactory level of pro-social behavior. Moreover, such enforcement is costly, as the U.S. discovered when it incarcerated people en masse, spending more on prisons than on higher education, trying but failing to curb substance abuse. Last but not least, such enforcement faces the often-cited challenge: who will guard the guardians? Many enforcement agents are corrupt and engage in anti-social behavior themselves.

In contrast, to the extent that most people, most of the time, do most of what needs to be done—go to work, take care of their family, pay taxes, avoid polluting, and so on—it's because they hold that the expectations that they will act responsibly are legitimate, are morally compelling. When this is true, compliance will be high, costs low, and inclination to rebel minimal. An interesting example is tax compliance. It has been shown that if people believe that taxes are fair and legitimately used, they pay more of the taxes owed.[38]

When SMUs are formed, they enable a society to limit coercive enforcement and rely much more on self-regulation. For example, when public smoking bans were enacted, they caused little opposition and resulted in general compliance because they followed public education (especially on secondhand smoke risks) and moral dialogues.[39] On the other hand, Prohibition failed miserably because public consensus on the issue was lacking; the law was not backed up by a SMU.[40]

Although the main benefits of new SMUs (or the reworking of an old, obsolete one), as we have just seen, are an increase in voluntary adherence to social norms that define pro-social behavior, SMUs also lead to new *laws and regulations* or to changes in them. That is, the new SMUs tend to become legally embedded and reinforced. This is the case because (a) many social functions cannot rely only on moral persuasion and voluntary compliance (or economic incentives); (b) even if only relatively few people defy the social norms and their rebellion is ignored, it is likely to unravel voluntary compliance over time because those who adhere to the norms will feel that they are being taken advantage of or treated unfairly, like "suckers." Thus, if a growing number of people speed or park illegally with impunity, more and more will follow. Hence, mature SMUs are best expressed not only in changes in voluntary behavior but also by being embedded in laws. Thus, the rise in the SMU that we have a stewardship over the environment led to the formation of the Environmental Protection Agency and scores of laws limiting pollution. The rise in SMU that African Americans were treated unfairly led to Affirmative Action, the formation of Equal Employment Opportunity Plans, and court cases banning several forms of segregation, among other such moves.

Those who tend to favor enacting moral changes should note that in many cases gaining new SMU *precedes the enactment of laws* that express and undergird the values agreed upon. Dialogue about women's rights advanced before Title IX became the law of the land. The same is true about gay rights before the U.S. Supreme Court ruling which made same-sex marriage legal across the country, and before legal segregation was struck down.

Case study

Baseline

The moral dialogue about same-sex marriages is a subset of a much more encompassing moral dialogue on homosexuality, a dialogue not here examined. In 1970, no U.S. state allowed same-sex marriages. Even civil unions for same-sex couples did not exist as an alternative. According to the Supreme Court, it was not even a substantial federal question (implying that same-sex marriage was not something to be considered)—a statement the Court made in 1972 when refusing to hear a case on the issue. Over a decade later, in 1986, as a result of the Supreme Court's decision in *Bowers v. Hardwick*, states maintained their ability to criminalize gay sexual relations.[41] In 1996, the Defense of Marriage Act (DOMA) was passed with 79 percent approval in the House[42] and 85 percent approval in the Senate,[43] which declared that for federal purposes, marriage was between one man and one woman.[44] It was signed by President Clinton, whose statement on DOMA declared that "I have long opposed governmental recognition of same-gender marriages and this legislation is consistent with that position."[45] In terms of public opinion, a 1996 Gallup poll found that 68 percent of respondents thought same-sex marriage should not be valid.[46] Data from the Pew Research Center taken from the same year shows a similar figure of 65 percent.[47]

Sociological dialogue starters

There were several "historical starters," such as the 1993 case in which the Hawaii Supreme Court suggested that it may be unconstitutional to reject same-sex marriage.[48] However, this prompted a backlash, and "[b]y 2001, thirty-five states had passed laws limiting marriage to a union of one man and one woman [including Hawaii]."[49] One should not mistake this legislation as a reflection of a new SMU but, rather, see it as a codification of the status quo, which was previously seen as unnecessary. Vermont's recognition of same-sex civil unions in 2000 can be viewed as a "sociological starter," though it provided an alternative to same-sex marriage rather than a redefinition of marriage.

A take-off point was reached when Massachusetts was the first state to legalize gay marriage, in 2004.[50] As such, because of the DOMA provision denying federal benefits to same-sex couples, it put state and federal law at odds.[51] The decision in Massachusetts prompted a backlash of state constitutional amendments banning same-sex marriage.[52] California voted for Proposition 8 in 2008, which banned same-sex marriage in the state. But "advocates could show the nation that allowing gay and lesbian couples to marry had no negative consequences."[53]

Billion-hour buzz

The legalization of same-sex marriage by Massachusetts in 2004, with the media portraying happy gay and lesbian newlyweds, helped to trigger a national debate on the subject. For instance, a search of *New York Times* articles containing the phrase "gay marriage" from 2000 through the end of 2003 turns out about 230 results, while from 2004 through the end of 2007 there are over 1,500.

In 2004, 2005, and 2006, proposed amendments to the Massachusetts state constitution were discussed at "constitutional conventions." "Each convention generated extensive local and national media coverage, and drew large crowds of demonstrators on both sides."[54] Ultimately no amendments were made, and same-sex marriage remained legal.[55] During this time, marriage equality remained a salient issue across the country. In order to gauge public opinion after Proposition 8 in California, there were focus groups, roundtables, and 30 groups created a survey together.[56]

In Maine, same-sex marriage was legalized in 2008, repealed by voters in 2009, and then was supported on a ballot measure in 2012. To prepare for the 2012 referendum, a new type of canvassing was introduced, one that involved "in-depth conversations, in which the canvasser asked open-ended questions designed to invite respondents to share their experiences."[57] Over 200,000 such conversations took place, and it is estimated that these conversations changed the stance of 12,500 Maine voters.[58] One of the televised political ads in Maine at the time closed with the statement: "This isn't about politics. It's about family and how we as people treat one another."[59]

Television played a key role in moral dialogues on marriage equality. The portrayal of gay and lesbian characters in the media has increased,[60] and there is evidence that this had an impact on public opinion. "According to a 2012 *Hollywood Reporter* poll, 27% of people who had changed their minds about gay marriage from anti- to pro- in the last decade said that they made their decision after watching gay characters on shows like *Modern Family* and *Glee*."[61]

When President Obama came out in support of same-sex marriage in 2012, it had a significant impact on the amount of conversation taking place.[62] On blogs there was a more than 60 percent increase in statements on same-sex marriage after Obama's announcement, and the number was even greater on Twitter.[63] "For the week of May 7–11 [2012], Obama's comment on May 9 in favor of same-sex marriage was the No. 1 topic on blogs and the No. 3 subject on Twitter." Furthermore, "There have been nine previous weeks [since 2009] when the subject [same-sex marriage] was among the most discussed on blogs or Twitter."[64]

In 2013, the Human Rights Campaign (HRC) introduced an image of a pink equal sign against a red backdrop in support of marriage equality as part of a social media campaign in connection with the Supreme Court's consideration of *Hollingsworth v. Perry* and *United States v. Windsor*, two cases that had implications for marriage equality. The logo went viral, with many people replacing their Facebook profile pictures with one that included it, prompting news headlines such as "How the Red Equal Sign Took Over Facebook."[65] HRC provides the following description of phenomenon of the red logo:

> The red marriage equality logo first appeared on HRC's Facebook page at 2 p.m. on March 25, 2013. Within 24 hours, HRC's Facebook post to encourage digital activists to change their social media profile pictures to a red and pink version of its ubiquitous logo received 189,177 shares, 95,725 likes, appeared over 18 million times in Newsfeeds, created upwards of 10 million impressions worldwide, and inspired countless memes. Facebook recorded a 120 percent increase in profile photo updates, and they deemed the effort the most successful campaign in their history.[66]

Pew Research Center did a study of news coverage both leading up to and during the Supreme Court hearings; the study looked at 500 stories about marriage equality during an eight-week time frame, concluding that the coverage indicated "strong momentum for same-sex marriage."[67] Although this number is by no means inclusive of every relevant news story during the selected time frame, it serves to give an idea of the extent to which marriage equality was being discussed. Pew also noted that the "Gay Voices" microsite of the *Huffington Post* "produced so much coverage that it was examined separately from the rest of the news media."[68]

Dramatization

The movement for same-sex marriage used court cases to dramatize the issues at the heart of the moral dialogue. Protests kept attention on the issue. For example, after Proposition 8, protests were widespread in California,[69] which kept the issue in the media; 2,500 protesters gathered at the Sacramento Capitol, and other large protests occurred outside of religious institutions that had supported the measure to ban same-sex marriage.[70] Same-sex marriage was also supported in Pride Parades in many cities. In 2013 DOMA was ruled unconstitutional by the Supreme Court decision in *United States v. Windsor*,[71] which furthered the momentum of the pro-same-sex marriage movement.

Closure

In June 2015, the U.S. Supreme Court decision in *Obergefell v. Hodges* recognized a constitutional right to same-sex marriage.[72] It applies to all 50 states, though some states still have laws on the books that ban same-sex marriage, and now seek to obstruct it in other ways. A month prior to the decision, a Gallup poll showed that 60 percent of respondents thought same-sex marriage should be legal.[73] The tide had turned, and Justice Kennedy recognized that Americans had reached a new SMU. He wrote that "new insights and societal understandings can reveal unjustified inequality within our most fundamental institutions that once passed unnoticed and unchallenged."[74]

The roles of law in moral dialogue

There are many ways law and moral dialogues interact, and they often overlap. First, and most often, *laws reflect and ensconce new SMUs*. An example is deregulation policies in the 1970s and 1980s. Following the liberal 1960s, the U.S. experienced a considerable conservative backlash. One of the many expressions of this change in the moral consensus was a growing support for a smaller state, including for deregulation. One of the first major steps in this direction took place in 1978. That is when President Carter signed the Airline Deregulation Act into law, after it was passed in Congress with wide bipartisan support. At that point the President stated: "When I announced my own support of airline deregulation soon after taking office, this bill had few friends. I'm happy to say that today it appears to have few enemies. Governors, mayors, consumer advocates, all supported the bill."[75]

Second, often the development of SMU and laws is akin to someone walking on two legs—one leg advances first, followed by the other, and only then is more progress made on either front. For instance, as support for women's rights grew, in moral dialogues triggered by the suffragists, women gained the right to vote. After more dialogues they gained a right to credit in their own name, equal opportunity in federally funded education programs, and so on. Currently the moral dialogue about equal pay for equal work is maturing, but has yet to be enshrined in law.

Third, *laws can trigger or nurture moral dialogues*. For instance, laws in North Carolina nurtured moral dialogue on transgender rights. In March 2016, House Bill 2 (HB2), also known as the Public Facilities Privacy and Security Act, was passed by the General Assembly in North Carolina. HB2 requires people to use public restrooms in accordance with the sex listed on their birth certificate. It was enacted to preempt the expansion of Charlotte's nondiscrimination ordinance passed by the city council, which allowed people to use restrooms that correspond with their gender identity. The passage of HB2 triggered a storm of protests which further fed the massive dialogue on the subject. PayPal cancelled its plans to open a new operations center in the state as a result of the law.[76] Musicians cancelled performances, the National Basketball Association chose to relocate the All-Star game,[77] and over 100 business executives from companies such as Starbucks, Citibank, and eBay signed an open letter calling for a repeal of the new law.[78] The law received widespread media coverage, was the subject of many op-eds, panel discussions on radio and TV, and millions of people turned to social media to discuss it.

Fourth, *law can serve to express a moral position, the result of a moral dialogue.* In effect, most laws both express a moral position and operate as tools for enforcement. Other laws are almost entirely moral expressions. Cass Sunstein writes:

> There can be no doubt that law, like action in general, has an expressive function. Some people do what they do mostly because of the statement the act makes; the same is true for those who seek changes in law. Many debates over the appropriate content of law are really debates over the statement that law makes, independent of its (direct) consequences. I have suggested that the expressive function of law has a great deal to do with the effects of law on prevailing social norms. Often law's "statement" is designed to move norms in fresh directions.[79]

For instance, he notes, "Many people who oppose capital punishment would be unlikely to shift their position even if evidence were to show that capital punishment does have a deterrent effect. They are concerned about the expressive content of capital punishment, not about its ineffectiveness as a deterrent ..."[80]

Examples of laws with a primarily expressive purpose include French Good Samaritan laws, which require people to help others under certain circumstances. Here, the moral position is clear and the fact that people are rarely charged with failing to help shows that the main function of these laws is expressive.

Many states have decriminalized, but not legalized, marijuana. They seek to be less punitive but still signal that the state does not approve of such usage. Alexandra Natapoff writes that "decriminalization is a powerful form of normative recalibration, an opportunity to adjust criminal rules when they violate popular understandings of what should be punished and by how much."[81]

A related point is that "Law can function as an attitude signal of what most other people approve or disapprove."[82]

Fifth, *law can be ahead of a moral consensus, and thus trigger change.* When President Eisenhower issued Executive Order 9981 to desegregate the military, the nation was far from a consensus on civil rights for all, but the order "was an important precursor to *Brown v. Board of Education of Topeka.*"[83] As we have seen in the discussion of same-sex marriage, state laws that permitted same-sex marriage well before the Supreme Court's ruling took place contributed to the moral dialogue that resulted in a shift of public attitudes in favor of same-sex marriage. In the same vein, Richard McAdams writes that

> In a democratic society, legislation and other law can change what people believe about the approval patterns in their community or society; the law operates as a signal of popular opinion. Because people value approval, intrinsically or instrumentally, such beliefs influence behavior. Updating one's beliefs to account for the law, an individual will infer the prospect of greater disapproval costs from behavior the law condemns ...[84]

Community building and power structures

When moral dialogues mature, they also serve as a major source of community building and nurturing. Communities are not merely places where people bond and have affection for one another, but they are also places where they have a shared moral culture, and share values from which specific norms are derived.[85] However, these moral cultures are continually challenged by technological, economic, and international developments, among others. Moral dialogues recast these cultures in response. These dialogues also serve to shore up as well as revise the core values needed to prevent communities from disintegrating as a result of various factions pursuing their own subset of values.

Social scientists and social philosophers long worried that the social transformation that accompanied the Industrial Revolution, which entailed moving many people from villages, which were communities, into cities, where people were "atomized," caused people to lose their essential social moorings. The thesis is often referred to as a shift from *Gemeinschaft* to *Gesellschaft*.[86] True, we have since learned that one can find communities in industrial societies, for instance in ethnic neighborhoods like Chinatown, Spanish Harlem, the Village, and in gated communities, in which many millions of Americans live.[87] However, there is still considerable evidence that a large number of people are missing the social bonds that are essential for their flourishing; hence, the call for rebuilding communities. Moral dialogues are one major process for such a communitarian reconstruction.

Major liberal scholars hold that each person should define the good and the state should be morally neutral. Hence some suggested that the state should stop issuing marriage licenses altogether and leave the various religions' functionaries and civic bodies to determine what marriage is. Moreover, liberals feared that even if the state remains morally neutral, as long as the society forms strong SMUs, these will be embedded in laws.[88]

In contrast, communitarians pointed out that social order requires a core of shared values. Some of the reasons have already been cited, notably the need for much of the order to rest on voluntary compliance. Other reasons are that in order for various factions (that have different interests and different values) to be able to form shared public polices and to limit conflicts from turning into unresolved stand-offs, if not violence, society needs a core of substantive values as well as a belief in procedures to resolve differences. SMUs are the process that can keep these essential core values intact, or allow them to adapt rather than unravel in times of change.

I refer to a set of "core" values because the difference between core and other values is crucial for several reasons. First, much attention has been paid in recent years to the polarization of American politics, reflected in more and more people identifying themselves with either a conservative or a liberal position and fewer and fewer as somewhere in the middle—as well as a growing adamancy in the positions held by both camps. Polarization is viewed as a key reason why the government is in gridlock and held in low regard by the overwhelming majority of the American people. From a communitarian viewpoint the main question is whether the polarization concerns secondary values, and hence differences can be settled by appealing to core values, or is holistic, leading to irreconcilable differences. If the breakdown of moral consensus is holistic, either moral dialogues will fail to lead to SMUs, or they will restore the needed consensus by leading to the formation of a new core of shared values.

The same difference is also highly relevant to the ways immigrants and minorities are treated. The U.S. has long recognized the value of diversity and pluralism, but holds that these are best bounded by a shared framework. This issue comes into sharp relief when the ways immigrants should be treated are debated. France seeks complete assimilation. In the U.S., some advocates called for bleaching out all traces of previous moral commitment to one's country of origin and its culture. At the opposite extreme, a British commission concluded that, due to the diversity of the UK, the government should not promote a national identity.[89] There are numerous intermediate positions. Particularly relevant for the discussion at hand is an approach that might be referred to as diversity within unity. It holds that there is no reason to oppose or see as threatening the social order if various members of society pray to different gods, maintain a distinct subculture, and secondary loyalties to their country of origin—as long as their first loyalty is to their new country, they accept the democratic regime as the way to resolve differences, learn the nation's language or languages (while, if they wish, maintaining their original one), and abide by the laws (but these laws ought to tolerate differences, say, in the ways animals are slaughtered and marriages are performed).[90]

SMUs serve to sort out which moral values fall into the diversity category and which into the unity one. Above all, they help to recast the whole framework when societal changes call for it to be recast. And SMUs serve to sort out what are considered to be core values and what are diverse ones that enrich rather than threaten the social order.

A major subject that is not treated in this chapter, because it requires a major study all by itself, is the role of power in structuring communications in general and moral dialogues in particular. It is sufficient to note that not all people have equal access to the media (e.g., the digital divide); the media is owned and managed in ways that favor some groups and viewpoints over others; and whether or not the results of dialogues are implemented is clearly affected by the prevailing power structure.

One should note, though, that moral dialogues differ from other communications and deliberations in their relation to power. I advance the hypothesis that in effect these dialogues favor those who otherwise are less privileged. Appealing to values is often the strongest societal change resource to which they have access. Indeed, a study of American history, I hypothesize, would show that major societal changes that came about were the result of social movements in which the formation of new SMUs played a key role. These include the movements that championed civil rights, women's rights, the protection of the environment, gender equality, and the progressive movement. In all of these movements, moral dialogues played a key role.

There are thus two major dynamics: power struggle and the quest for legitimacy. Societies function best when the power hierarchy is relatively flat—all major interests, as well as concerns for the common good, get their day in court and a fair share of whatever assets there are. Currently both factors are out of order: the common good and the needs of many are neglected as special interests capture many of the levers of power, resulting in a loss of legitimacy. One major cause of populism is the combination of a sense of impotence and being unfairly treated.

Part Two
Rights and the Common Good

FIVE

The common good

Much of the power struggle that affects laws can be viewed as merely a contest among various special interests, with the legislature acting mainly as the site for this tug of war. Or it is viewed as a tug of war between special interests and the common good, something the legislature supposedly embodies but often neglects. I have already tried to show that moral dialogues often do result in wide SMU as to what is legitimate and what is not. Demonstrating that a given act is serving a common good is a major source of legitimacy. I now turn to show that the concept of common good is a valid one, and then (in the following chapter) the ways that differences between competing interests (and individual rights) and the claims of the common good can be worked out. The common good (alternatively called "the public interest" or "public goods") denotes those goods that serve all members of a given community and its institutions, and, as such, includes both goods that serve no identifiable particular group, as well as those that serve members of generations not yet born. It is a normative concept with a long and contested history. Philosophers, theologians, lawyers, politicians, and the public have arrived at distinct understandings about what the common good entails, how it should be balanced against individual goods, and if and by whom it should be enforced. Though there are many critics of the concept of the common good (discussed below), it has survived as a meaningful concept for well over two millennia, and continues to serve as a very significant organizing principle of civic and political life.

The common good in philosophical and religious thought

The common good has deep roots in the history of philosophical and religious thought. For Plato "the good" was objective, defined as that which "every soul pursues [...] and does whatever it does for its sake."[1] Arriving at knowledge of the good within a community would create unity, which is "the greatest blessing for a state."[2] In this conception there is no tension between the private and public good, as individuals are thought to attain happiness (a private good) through the pursuit of justice (a public good). For Aristotle, "a polis exists for the sake of a good life," and human beings, as political animals, lead a good life by contributing to the good of the community.[3] He asks: What sort of people do we want society to form, and how should we structure society to accomplish this? This question presupposes a society that has a shared end that both is separate from and actively shapes the good of the individual. The ancient Roman philosophers had a similarly robust conception of the common good. Cicero, writing around 50 BC, defined a "people" or "republic" as "not any collection of human beings brought together in any sort of way, but an assemblage of people in large numbers associated in agreement with respect to justice and a partnership for the common good."[4]

Often drawing on Greek and Roman tradition, Christian theologians have explored the common good. In *The City of God*, Augustine takes up Cicero's definition of a republic as a people joined by their pursuit of the common good, and specifies the content of that good from a Christian perspective: the good is none other than God, and to pursue the common good is to render unto God the love and worship that is His due. Thomas Aquinas maintains a theological conception of the common good: "God's own goodness ... is the good of the whole universe."[5]

Economics and the common good

The place of the common good in modern (neoclassical) economics has its origins in the Enlightenment conception of society as existing "in order to further the goals of individuals, neither asking where the goals of individuals come from, nor inquiring into the processes by which individuals are formed in society."[6] In neoclassical economics, the common good is not an objective goal to be discerned and pursued but, rather, the aggregation of individual goods. This idea was first articulated by Adam Smith, who posited that man, in pursuing his own personal gain, unwittingly "promotes that of the society more effectually than when he really intends to promote it."[7]

In this view, the common good—the summation of all private goods—arises naturally from economic exchanges, and no state efforts are needed to promote it. Indeed, attempts to guide the preferences of individuals towards a common goal are seen, at best, as paternalism, and at worst, as the first step on the road to totalitarianism, as was famously argued by Friedrich A. Hayek in *The Road to Serfdom*.[8]

Economists, though, have introduced exceptions to this rule for situations in which the invisible hand is unable to provide "public goods" that benefit society at large. The market's inability to produce such goods reflects what economists call a "market failure" (an instance where the market is unable to achieve an efficient allocation of resources) and thus government intervention in the production of these goods is tolerated. Examples of public goods include defense, basic research, and public health (e.g. fluoridation and vaccinations). Thus, Kenneth J. Arrow wrote that "we expect a free enterprise economy to underinvest in invention and research (as compared with an ideal) because it is risky, because the product can be appropriated only to a limited extent, and because of increasing returns in use. This underinvestment will be greater for more basic research."[9]

Pluralist critiques

The pluralist tradition of political science, which largely adopts the assumptions of neoclassical economics, has little room for a robust notion of the public interest, and in some cases criticizes such a notion as implicitly anti-democratic. Pluralist thinkers, drawing upon their theory's economic underpinnings, argue that in a free and robust democracy competition among interest groups—which reveal and are guided by the preferences of individuals (i.e. private goods)—gives rise to a public policy that maximizes general welfare. The representative function of such a political system is preserved both because all individuals are free to associate with any number of these groups, and because each group can exercise pressure equivalent only to its popular support. Political scientists in the pluralist tradition readily criticize top-down notions of the public interest and the common good as inviting authoritarianism at the expense of procedural democracy. Thus, Frank Sorauf argued that the tug of war between private interest groups produces public policy superior to anything that would be reached by the state enforcing its own formulation of the public interest.[10]

Critics argue that discrepancies in wealth, power, and social status give groups varying degrees of leverage over the government, and as a result public policy—based on interest-group politics—does not maximize social welfare (i.e. aggregation of individual goods), much less reflect a robustly defined common good, but rather serves the interests of the politically and economically powerful. Moreover, interest-group pluralists fail to properly incorporate notions of the public good into their normative framework.

In less individualistic societies—many of them non-Western—the value of the common good is rarely questioned. However, the normative status of the common good—unlike that of rights—is far from self-evident to many in the West. The use of the term "the common good" is contested on a number of fronts. First, there are those who argue that it does not exist at all. Ayn Rand wrote that

> "Since there is no such entity as 'the public,' since the public is merely a number of individuals, the idea that 'the public interest' supersedes private interests and rights, can have but one meaning: that the interests and rights of some individuals take precedence over the interests and rights of others."[11]

A communitarian conception of the common good

Communitarians counter that the common good does not merely amount to an aggregation of all private or personal goods in a society. Contributions to the common good often offer no immediate payout or benefit. It is frequently impossible to predict who the beneficiaries will be in the long run. Still, members of communities that support the common good invest in it not because it will necessarily or even likely benefit them personally, or even their children, but simply because they consider it a good that ought to be nurtured. They consider it the right thing to do—by itself, for itself. This explanation surprises only those who claim that, even when we act in clearly altruistic ways, we always have an ulterior, self-serving motive. For everyone else, examples of such common goods are readily apparent: in addition to national defense and basic research, discussed above, public health and environmental preservation are widely accepted examples of common goods. The non-self-interested nature of these measures stands out especially when serving the common good entails not merely some minor costs to the individual (e.g. taxes) but the existential risks of certain forms of service, such as fighting for one's country.

Protecting the environment, preventing climate change, and developing sustainable energy sources are all costly projects that will pay off only over the longer run, and then only to unknown, unpredictable beneficiaries. The millions of people who are working towards these goals today cannot be sure that they will be alive to see the full impact of their work. Self-interest-maximizing individuals would gain a much better rate of return on their money if they invested in readily available financial instruments such as stocks and bonds, and then used the dividends to purchase air conditioners and sunscreen.

Several academic communitarians, in particular Michael Sandel and Charles Taylor, argue that any conception of the good must be formulated on the social level, and that the community cannot be a normative-neutral realm. Moreover, unless there is a social formulation of the good, there can be no normative foundation for resolving conflicts of value between different individuals and groups. Such an overriding good (e.g. the national well-being) enables persons with different moral outlooks or ideological backgrounds to find principled (rather than merely prudential) common ground.

Communities are the most likely source of particular specifications of the common good. Some have argued that the term "community" is so vague that it cannot even be defined. In contrast, communitarians hold that community can be clearly defined as a group of individuals that possesses two characteristics. The first is a web of affect-laden relationships which often crisscross and reinforce one another (rather than merely one-on-one or chain-like individual relationships). The second characteristic shared by the individuals of a community is some commitment to a core of shared values, norms, and meanings, as well as a collective history and identity—in short, a particularistic moral culture. Liberal communitarians hold that community is basically a major common good in itself as well as a major source of other common goods; "basically," because, like all goods, community can take on dysfunctional forms, especially when its social bonds, culture, or political structure are oppressive. Hence the special import of balancing the community as a value with commitments to individual rights.

To state that a given value is a common good of a given community does not mean that all the members subscribe to it, and surely not that they all live up to its dictates. It suffices that the value be recognized as a common good by large majorities and be embodied in law and in other institutions. At the same time, a value to which members merely pay lip-service cannot qualify. We shall see below that it is essential for solid analysis to consider the extent to which values are institutionalized as a continuous variable rather than as a dichotomous one. Some values are relatively highly institutionalized, e.g. marriage in the U.S. in 1950s. Others are merely aspirational, e.g. the belief that U.S. should promote democratic regimes overseas. The common good may be promoted and enforced by the state, but this is not necessarily the case. Indeed, often the core values are promoted by informal social controls, by peer pressures, and by communities.

Particularly important and challenging is the observation that references to the common good should be read as if the emphasis is on the "common" and not on the "good". For the following discussion, the main issue is whether a value is widely shared and institutionalized—not whether a particular ethicist would judge it to be morally good. Thus, for example, a society may define as a common good giving precedence to economic development over political development, or expect that all members adhere to a particular religion. Many may not consider it a good society, but it is the good that the given society has formulated as its common good.

Rights versus the common good

Several scholars have made strong arguments against an approach that attempts to balance rights and the common good. They argue that rights are a common good, and that hence the very opposition of the two goods—rights and the common good—that the balancing analysis presupposes is a false one. This view is held particularly with regard to freedom of speech, taking inspiration from Justice Holmes' dissent in *Abrams v. United States* (1919)[12] that the "ultimate good," both for the individual and society, is "better reached by free trade in ideas." It is expressed in the Federal Communications Commission's opinion that "the public interest is best served by permitting free expression of views." Likewise, Scott Cummings points out that many believe that "strong protection for individual rights is itself advancing the public interest."[13]

At first, it may seem that one can resolve this issue by granting that common goods are a right. For instance, instead of referring to security as a common good, one can recognize a right to be safe, or a right to life.[14] However, such redefinition does not vacate or obviate the balancing question. It merely moves it from asking about the balance between a good and a right to the balance between adhering to two rights that command different public policies and behaviors. One can speak about the difference between what the right to privacy and the right to safety call for, but this change in wording leaves standing the question toward which right the nation is tilting in a given period, and where it ought to tilt.

One next notes that many common goods are not recognized as rights either in the U.S. Constitution or the Universal Declaration of Human Rights. There is no right to national parks, historical preservation, or basic research. One can of course aspire to add these rights, but until they are recognized as such, one had best not dismiss the normative claims for these goods because they are "merely" common goods and not individual rights.

Last but not least, some common goods cannot be reasonably defined as individual rights. The National Archives in Washington DC houses the original copy of the Constitution. That is a clear common good. However, to argue that individual Americans have a right to have the Constitution preserved is stretching the concept of a right to the point that it becomes meaningless and has no foundation either in American core normative concepts or in legal traditions.

In response to this account of the common good, libertarians have developed elaborate arguments that explain why people invest in these common goods that do not necessarily benefit them, without giving up on their assumption that people are rational utility maximizers. For example, Anthony Downs, Gordon Tullock, and William Riker all wondered why a rational actor would vote. These social scientists assumed that "the voter calculates the expected utility from each candidate's victory, and naturally votes for the candidate whose policies promise the highest utility."[15] Yet the probability that any one voter's ballot will affect the outcome of all but the closest elections is virtually zero. As voting always imposes at least some costs, costs that almost always outweigh the expected benefit, Downs et al. argued that people vote because they believe that the results will be close and hence their one vote could decide the election—a personal benefit that would offset the individual cost of their effort. However, it turns out that many millions vote even when elections are known not to be close.

Moreover, the evidence shows that the most important factor that explains whether a person will vote is the extent to which the person considers voting his or her duty as a citizen. André Blais writes that "about half the electorate ... vote out of a strong sense of moral obligation, because they believe it would be wrong not to vote; they do not calculate benefits and costs."[16]

Another criticism of the common good comes from those on the left who hold that the concept—as manifested, for instance, in the call to serve the "fatherland" or "mother church"—serves to conceal class differences in economic interests and political power so as to keep those who are disadvantaged from making demands on the community. These critics are correct in asserting that this concept can be abused in this way. However, the fact that a concept is abused—a common fate of compelling concepts—does not mean that it is without great merit. Otherwise, we would have to do away with such concepts as science, rationality, and community, all of which have been misappropriated. That said, one best considers what particular goods the calls to serve "the" common good seek to serve.

SIX

Rights *and* responsibilities

I started this book by suggesting that the language of human rights is morally incomplete, that it must be complemented by considerations of community and the common good. I noted from the outset that these two sets of moral claims cannot be made fully compatible, although the tension between them can be reduced. I turn next to ask how these contested claims are often dealt with and how they are best sorted out.

The advocacy model

Deliberations about lawmaking and public policy often follow the advocacy model characteristic of the American courts. According to this model, interested parties are divided into antagonistic ideological camps, with each side (and there are only two) presenting its respective interpretations of the facts in the way that will most strongly support its brief. Following the notion that one ought to "zealously" defend one's client, each side feels free to make emotive points, provide stretched interpretations and selective facts, and advance particularistic normative arguments favorable to its case. The implicit assumption is that the proper judgment (if not "the truth") will arise out of the clash of two extreme advocacy positions. The American judges act as neutral referees, and the jury is kept mum during the proceedings.

In public discourse, the advocacy model is reflected in the increasingly polarized debates between liberals and conservatives over numerous issues, including the role of government, gun control, abortion rights, and even climate change.[1] Liberal communitarianism and other intermediary positions are often barely heard over the noise from the resulting clash.

The case of Chelsea Manning, previously known as Bradley, who was charged with leaking hundreds of thousands of secret military documents to WikiLeaks in 2010, illustrates this mode of deliberation.[2] The defense presented the young soldier as "naïve but good-intentioned."[3] To Manning's champions in the media and on the left, Manning is a heroic whistleblower and a victim of government overreach.[4] By contrast, the government contended that Manning is a traitor, guilty of aiding the enemies of the United States.[5] The prosecutor asserted that Manning "used his military training to gain the notoriety he craved."[6]

These positions reflect the state of the debate over government secrecy more broadly. Law Professor David E. Pozen notes that,

> for every governmental assertion of leaks "that have collectively cost the American people hundreds of millions of dollars, and … done grave harm to national security," one finds the rebuttal that "there has not been a single instance in the history of the United States in which the press's publication of a "legitimate but newsworthy" government secret has gravely harmed the national interest"—indeed, that there have been few destructive leaks anywhere in the world.[7]

Many public policy deliberations follow the same pattern of strong, often extreme, one-sided advocacy between two conflicting positions. Key examples include the debates between pro-life and pro-choice advocates,[8] those who favor gun control and those who defend an individualized right to own guns,[9] and free market champions and those who favor strong regulations.[10] Data show that American media and politics have become more polarized in recent years. That is, they are drawing more on the advocacy model and focusing less on finding common ground, forging compromises, and devising "third way" solutions.[11]

In public discourse, the give and take about freedom of the press and the way publishers ought to handle leaks has taken a particular turn. In the media, which usually seeks[12] to keep news reporting separate from editorializing, coverage of the recent leak investigations has been loaded with emotive terms criticizing the way these investigations have been conducted. News reports concerning the Department of Justice's investigations into James Rosen and its seizure of Associated Press (AP) phone records include such editorializing terms as "unprecedented,"[13] "sweeping,"[14] and "aggressive."[15] Further, the editorial pages of many newspapers and magazines have been particularly partisan in their rhetoric. They refer to a "war" on free speech,[16] contend that the Rosen investigation is "as flagrant an assault on civil liberties as anything done by George W. Bush's administration,"[17] and declare that the Obama administration "uses technology to silence critics in a way Richard Nixon could only have dreamed of."[18] The editors of the *New York Times* assert that "the Obama administration has moved beyond protecting government secrets to threatening fundamental freedoms of the press to gather news."[19] Nick Gillespie of the *Daily Beast* writes that the Obama administration's crusade "declares 'war on journalism' by essentially criminalizing the very act of investigative reporting."[20] At the *San Francisco Chronicle*, the editors write, "The feds seemed to have conflated journalism with espionage."[21] Ron Fournier claims in the *National Journal* that "the leak inquiry threatens national security."[22]

The media has given little room, even on the op-ed pages presumably set aside for views opposed to those of a newspaper's own editorials, for articles that explain, let alone seek to justify, the government's viewpoint. One of the media's own, former NBC anchorman Tom Brokaw, noted that "many of the same reporters who are tough on the gun lobby when it comes to second amendment rights, run behind the shield of the first amendment, without doing it in a way that is qualitatively analytical, and not just a knee-jerk reaction."[23] Similarly, *Washington Post* reporter Walter Pincus lamented the "circling of the media wagons."[24] In response to the White House Correspondents' Association's statement that "our country was founded on the principle of freedom of the press and nothing is more sacred to our profession,"[25] Pincus wrote, "I worry that many other journalists think that last phrase should be 'nothing is more sacred *than* our profession.'"[26]

In contrast, the government has been unusually ambivalent in defending its position. At first, Attorney General Eric Holder stated that the leak to the AP "put the American people at risk," and that trying to determine who was responsible "required very aggressive action."[27] However, soon thereafter he struck a conciliatory tone, saying in an interview with the *Daily Beast* that "while both of these cases were handled within the law and according to Justice Department guidelines, they are reminders of the unique role the news media plays in our democratic system, and signal that both our laws and guidelines need to be updated."[28] President Obama stated that "we must keep information secret that protects our operations and our people in the field."[29] But in the same speech, he also said that he was "troubled by the possibility that leak investigations may chill the investigative journalism that holds government accountable"[30] and that "journalists should not be at legal risk for doing their jobs."[31]

The government's hesitant defense of its actions seems to reflect several factors: The administration is highly vulnerable to criticism from the press;[32] it faces pushback from both sides of the political and ideological spectrum;[33] there exists a high level of distrust in the government;[34] and Americans have long been suspicious of the federal government's accumulation of power at the expense of individual rights.[35] As a result, the government seems wary of picking a fight with those "who buy ink by the barrel."[36] All said and done, in this case public discourse is hampered not merely by the advocacy approach but also by the fact that the voice of one of the two sides, that of government speaking for national security, is muted.

A liberal communitarian approach

The liberal communitarian philosophy holds that the advocacy model is flawed in that it assumes that the clash of two strong one-sided views will lead to a just conclusion, reasonable judgments and sound public policies.[37] The liberal communitarian approach favors the model exemplified by the *agora* in ancient Greece,[38] the *jirgas* of Afghanistan,[39] and the U.S. Senate in earlier decades.[40] This model is one of dialogue, in which opposing sides engage in a civil give and take and commit to finding a course acceptable to all concerned. [41]

In contrast to the advocacy model, this chapter draws on a liberal communitarian philosophy, which assumes that as a nation we face two fully legitimate normative and legal claims: protecting national security and the freedom of the press. Neither can be maximized nor fully reconciled, as there is an inevitable tension between these two claims. It thus follows that some balance must be worked out between the conflicting claims. That is, the liberal communitarian model assumes from the outset that the nation is committed to both individual rights and the advancement of the common good, and that neither should be assumed *a priori* to trump the other.[42] The liberal communitarian philosophy is dedicated to achieving a balance between individual rights and social responsibilities, which emanates from the need to serve the common good.[43]

The Fourth Amendment provides an important text for the liberal communitarian philosophy when it states that "[t]he right of the people to be secure in their persons, houses, papers, and effects, against unreasonable searches and seizures, shall not be violated."[44] By banning only *unreasonable* searches and seizures, it recognizes that there are *reasonable* ones—those that serve the common good (or, to use a term more familiar to the legal community, the public interest).

Liberal communitarians thus take it for granted that deliberations about legitimate public policy ought to start with the assumption that the public's "right to know" and the freedom of the press must be balanced with concern for national security, rather than from the position that limitations on the press are *ipso facto* a violation of a basic right or freedom.

Within history

Achieving a communitarian balance, however, does not mean invariably opting for the *same* golden middle ground between rights and responsibilities, or freedom and security. Rather, it requires consideration of how changes in historical conditions might shift the equilibrium point. The September 11, 2001 attacks against the United States heightened the country's need to attend to homeland security. One can argue over the severity of the threat that terrorism now poses and how far the government should reach while seeking to protect the United States from future attacks. However, one cannot deny that the combination of less-than-fully secured nuclear arms in Pakistan and Russia and the existence of many thousands of people around the world who seek to harm the United States continues to pose a security risk.[45]

A second set of factors that affects the historically appropriate balance between national security and freedom of the press is the technological developments that have taken place since the advent of the "cyber age" around 1990.[46] This revolution in computing technologies has made classified information more broadly accessible, retrievable from remote locations, and easily transferrable.[47] Bradley Manning, a young soldier stationed in the middle of the desert in Iraq, was able to download and share many thousands of top secret documents, undetected by his superiors.[48] In the age of ink and paper, such a feat would have been physically impossible. Moreover, the internet and the 24-hour news cycle put pressure on reporters to publish as soon as they receive a story. In times past, a newspaper that received classified information had time, at least until printing the next edition, to weigh whether or not to publish and to consult with the authorities. Today the same newspaper, fearing being "scooped" by the competition, often posts the story online, where it becomes instantly available not only to a domestic audience but also to declared enemies of the United States.

These developments seem to justify *some* re-balancing. A liberal communitarian holds that deliberations should focus both on the extent of this recalibration and on ensuring that corrective measures are neither excessive nor irreversible as historical and technological conditions change again.[49] However, to simply ignore these new historical developments seems unreasonable. We have not reached the point where we can declare, with regard to the campaign against terrorism and the need to protect the United States from future attacks, "mission accomplished".

SEVEN

Privacy vs. security

This chapter applies liberal communitarianism to explore the issues raised by the tensions between the right to privacy and national security, a perpetual issue that has gained more attention since the 2001 attacks on the U.S. homeland. To proceed, I draw on a liberal communitarian philosophy I helped to develop[1] that assumes that nations face several fully legitimate normative and legal claims, and that these claims can be neither maximized nor fully reconciled, as there is an inevitable tension among them. It follows that some balance must be worked out among the conflicting claims rather than assuming that one will always trump the others. This chapter applies this approach to the balance between security and privacy.[2]

In contrast to this balancing approach, contemporary liberals tend to emphasize individual rights and autonomy over societal formulations of the common good.[3] And at the opposite end of the spectrum, authoritarian communitarians (mainly in East Asia) privilege the common good a priori and pay heed to rights mainly to the extent that they serve the rulers' aims. Hence, when Gregory Ferenstein writes in the *Daily Beast* that communitarians grant priority to the common good over rights, he is both correct and mistaken.[4] He is correct if he has in mind the likes of Bilahari Kauskian,[5] but not when he attributes this position to those who have endorsed the responsive communitarian platform.[6]

The Fourth Amendment text provides a strong expression of the liberal communitarian philosophy, which is particularly relevant to privacy. It states that "[t]he right of the people to be secure in their persons, houses, papers, and effects, against unreasonable searches and seizures, shall not be violated."[7] By banning only *unreasonable* searches and seizures, it recognizes, by extension, that there are reasonable ones, namely those that serve the common good or, to use a term more familiar to the legal community, the public interest. Liberal communitarianism is based upon the same fundamental premise. When it comes to the give and take over what qualifies as legitimate public policy, liberal communitarianism starts with the assumption that the public's right to privacy must be balanced with concern for national security (and public health, among other common goods) rather than from the position that any breach of privacy contravenes an inviolable basic right.

The advocacy model, in which there are only two sides, and each side presents its interpretation of the facts in the way that most strongly supports its position,[8] has been applied to the question of how to strike the proper balance between privacy and security—an issue that has gained renewed front-page attention following the revelations in mid-2013 that the government has been collecting the phone records of millions of Americans and, via a program referred to as PRISM, the electronic communications and stored data of foreigners from major internet companies such as Google and Facebook.

The public discourse on the subject following the disclosure of the PRISM and phone-records programs took an unusual form: instead of the common clash between conservative and liberal camps, major voices sharply critical of the government emerged from both the right (especially libertarians, whose following has been growing in recent years)[9] and the left (especially civil libertarians), and these voices were supported by editorials in the mainstream media and other outlets. At the same time, the government and those who supported the need for security were rather tongue tied, especially compared to others in this particular public discourse.

Thus, on the right, Rush Limbaugh declared that the PRISM program revealed the "totalitarian nature" of the Obama administration. Senator Rand Paul (R-KY) suggested that the snooping demonstrated that the president "views our Constitutional 'right of the people to be secure in their persons, houses, papers, and effects' as null and void."[10] On the left, *The Nation* agreed, reporting on the PRISM program under the headline, "A Modern-Day Stasi State,"[11] while Al Gore quipped, "Is it just me, or is secret blanket surveillance obscenely outrageous?"[12] The *Atlantic*'s Conor

Friedersdorf argued that, thanks to PRISM and the collection of phone records, "the people in charge will possess the capacity to be tyrants—to use power oppressively and unjustly—to a degree that Americans in 1960, 1970, 1980, 1990, or 2000 could've scarcely imagined." Friedersdorf emphasized that "it could happen here, with enough historical amnesia, carelessness, and bad luck."[13] On the pages of the New York Times, Jennifer Stisa Granick and Christopher Jon Sprigman described the mass surveillance programs as "criminal."

On the other side of the debate, there were few in the media who forcefully stood up for the need of enhanced security against terrorism. National Review's Andrew C. McCarthy dismissed the "caterwauling of privacy activists,"[14] arguing that the collection of metadata fell well within the bounds of what is permitted by the Fourth Amendment[15] and stating that concerns about the PRISM program were "overblown."[16] Similarly, the editorial board of the Wall Street Journal argued that "Mr. Obama is conceding too much to the folks who imagine the government is compiling dossiers on citizens and listening to calls à la 'The Lives of Others.'"[17]

Senator Dianne Feinstein led the government's charge, but did so with very short statements such as, "I think people want the homeland kept safe to the extent we can,"[18] and "It's called protecting America."[19] In contrast, President Obama, rather than advocating on behalf of the security side, spoke in favor of a communitarian-like balance:

> I think it's important to recognize that you can't have 100 percent security and also then have 100 percent privacy and zero inconvenience ... And in the abstract, you can complain about Big Brother and how this is a potential program run amuck, but when you actually look at the details, then I think we've struck the right balance.[20]

In comparing the advocacy and the liberal communitarian approaches to public discourse, one notes that intermediary or third positions (not necessarily compromises) find little room in the former. Moreover, the advocacy approach does not take into account the basic tenets of the balancing approach of the

Constitution, especially the Fourth Amendment. Typical pro-privacy arguments run as follows: There is a right to privacy that is important both in its own right and as a necessary means for realizing various other values such as democracy, creativity, and the flourishing of the self; the government is violating this right by this or that act; thus, the government should be made to desist. The implicit assumption is that the whole normative and legal realm is the domain of the right and any consideration of other values, such as security, constitutes an "intrusion." When Nadine Strossen served as the president of the ACLU, she was asked if she ever encountered any security measure of which she approved; she first responded with a firm "no" and then corrected herself and approved of fortifying the doors of commercial airliners that separate the pilot's cockpit from the cabin holding the passengers.[21] Similarly, the ACLU objected even to the use of handheld computers at Transportation Security Administration (TSA) checkpoints— describing them as "a violation of the core democratic principle that the government should not be permitted to violate a person's privacy, unless it has a reason to believe that he or she is involved in wrongdoing"—even though these computers were using the same data as all the other computers, and were simply reducing the distance that agents had to travel to review the data. In other words, the handheld computers merely added a bit of convenience, not a new intrusion.[22] However, the Fourth Amendment and the liberal communitarian approach that it reflects divide searches between those that are reasonable and those that are not, *and hence reasonable searches do not constitute an intrusion and are not a violation of privacy.* In other words, the normative and legal realm is divided between segments in which security ought to take precedence and those in which privacy should take precedence—and the discourse ought to be about where the boundary lies. Hence, it is misleading to argue as if the whole domain were that of privacy and any attention to security entailed a diminution of privacy. The "turf" is divided between these two concerns from the very beginning. (Therefore, it is just as untenable to argue that the realm is one of security only and any concern for privacy *ipso facto* entails a diminution of security.)

The balance between privacy and security that the liberal communitarian paradigm seeks must be constantly adjusted as historical circumstances change (e.g., following the 2001 attacks on the US homeland) and technological developments occur (e.g., improvements in facial recognition technology). Thus, a society ought to afford more leeway to security measures if there are valid reasons for thinking that the threat to the public has significantly increased—and give less leeway once the threat has subsided. The chapter now turns to examine the criteria that can serve in sorting out where the balance lies in a particular historical situation.

Finding the balance

The liberal communitarian approach draws on four criteria to identify a proper balance between the competing values of security and privacy for a given nation in a given time period.[23] First, a liberal democratic government will limit privacy only if it faces a *well-documented and large-scale threat* to national security, not merely a hypothetical or limited threat to a few individuals or localities. The main reason why this threshold must be cleared is because modifying legal precepts—and with them the ethical, social, and public philosophies that underlie them—endangers their legitimacy. Changes, therefore, should not be undertaken unless there is strong evidence that either national security or privacy have been significantly undermined.

The 9/11 attacks constituted a significant change in historical conditions, revealing the serious threats posed by non-state actors determined to strike within the borders of the United States. Because there have been no significant new attacks within the country since 2001, there is a growing tendency to call for a re-balancing to oppose enhanced security measures (e.g., surveillance by the NSA and special judicial proceedings for suspected terrorists by the Foreign Intelligence Surveillance Act (FISA)), and to call for more attention to privacy concerns (e.g., by relaxing the standards of TSA searches and restricting the use of surveillance technologies such as drones). However, although the United States has done much to disrupt al Qaeda and other terrorist groups, the threat of terrorism still seems considerable. There are many hundreds of thousands of people around the world who deeply hate the United States and what it stands for, who consider it to be the "Great Satan" and wish it harm, and who believe that using violence against it constitutes an act of martyrdom. It seems reasonable to assume that some of these individuals will act on their beliefs. At the same time, al Qaeda has regrouped and established new affiliates in Africa,[24] the Arabian Peninsula,[25] and other parts of the world.[26]

Worse, there is a significant danger that these hostile groups might get their hands on a weapon that is capable of inflicting far more damage than the planes that brought down the Twin Towers (i.e., a nuclear weapon). Both Russia and Pakistan have less-than-fully secured nuclear arms within their borders.[27] The situation in Pakistan seems to pose a particular threat, as the government has so far been either unable or unwilling to combat terrorists within its borders and has experienced at least six serious terrorist attempts to penetrate its nuclear facilities.[28]

In 2009, Najibullah Zazi, a Denver cab driver who was trained in explosives by al Qaeda, was caught constructing bombs that he planned to detonate in the New York City subways.[29] The NSA intercepted an email between Zazi and an al Qaeda operative that tipped off the government to the plot and prevented it from being carried out,[30] apparently only days before Zazi and his accomplices planned to carry out the attack.[31] At the same time, the government's surveillance foiled a similar plot to bomb the New York Stock Exchange.[32] Overall, United States intelligence officials claimed in 2013 that the PRISM program and the collection of phone company metadata had disrupted 54 terrorist plots, one-fifth of which were to be carried out within the borders of the United States.[33] This number does not include all those plots that were foiled by more traditional methods or those that were successfully carried out, such as the Boston Marathon bombing.

To conclude, it is impossible to reliably measure the scope of the terrorist threat, even for those who have full access to all the intelligence that is available. However, it seems that the time has not yet come to re-balance by reducing security measures.

Second, once it has been established that national security needs shoring up, one should determine if this goal can be achieved without introducing new limits on privacy. For instance, this balancing criterion could be satisfied as follows: data could be encrypted, locked up in computers, and made accessible only with a court order, allowing the data to be available on very short notice if one needs to track the movements and whereabouts of a particular individual. This is a procedure reportedly followed by those overseeing and carrying out the NSA program that holds American phone records.[34]

Third, to the extent that privacy-curbing measures must be introduced, they should be *as non-intrusive as possible*. For example, in 2013 the TSA gave up its use of body scanners that revealed almost-nude images and replaced them with scanners that produce "cartoon-like" images that mark the places where hidden objects are detected.[35] In this way, the TSA is able to carry out the same thorough search in a way that is far less intrusive than full-body pat-downs or scanning that revealed every contour of the traveler's body.

Fourth, measures that *ameliorate undesirable side-effects* of necessary privacy-diminishing measures are to be preferred over those that ignore these effects. Thus, to the extent that those engaged in counter-terrorism searches are instructed to ignore misdemeanors, such as minor drug offenses or vandalism, this criterion is met.

Another way to think about balancing is to compare the security benefits yielded by a given measure with the tangible harms it inflicts. Thus, the evidence suggests that enhanced surveillance has led to the disruption of 54 terrorist activities.[36] At the same time, even Hendrik Hertzberg, the *New Yorker*'s liberal political commentator, notes:

> The threat that [the NSA's programs] pose to civil liberties, such as it is, is abstract, conjectural, unspecified. In the roughly seven years the programs have been in place in roughly their present form, no citizen's freedom of speech, expression, or association has been abridged by them in any identifiable way. No political critic of the Administration has been harassed or blackmailed as a consequence of them.[37]

But Hertzberg refers only to the NSA programs. And there have been some abuses of other surveillance programs. For example, government surveillance has been used to target political dissenters.[38] But this does not mean that all surveillance programs ought to be canceled or that they no longer serve an important anti-terrorism purpose. Instead, the measures that curb such abuses need to be enhanced.

When presented with the preceding statement, strong privacy advocates often argue the following:

- this evidence is based on information that is released by the government, and the government cannot be trusted; and
- even if enhanced surveillance programs have caused little harm so far, they may do so in the future and hence should be avoided.

(In fact, some privacy advocates go as far as calling for all enhanced programs to be all but canceled, not merely curbed and closely scrutinized.)[39]

The next two sections address how to verify these claims and how to further reduce the extent to which future security measures harm privacy.

Narrowing the gap

Generalized searches are legal and legitimate

The privacy model most often employed by privacy advocates is that of probable cause and individualized search. These advocates argue that before the government searches anyone it must, as required by the Constitution, present to a court of law evidence demonstrating that there exists strong reason (enough to convince a judge) for believing that the particular person is likely to be a terrorist. Only then, according to these advocates, can a person be subjected to surveillance.[40]

The courts, however, have long established (employing, in effect, a rather similar line of analysis to the liberal communitarian analysis outlined above) that when there is both a clear public interest and a small privacy intrusion, "general searches" (i.e., of masses of people) without individualized causes are legal and are needed.

This ruling has been applied to airport screening,[41] sobriety checkpoints,[42] drug testing of those whose jobs involve public safety,[43] and the screening of mail and internet communications.

This endorsement of general search has been supplemented by other rulings legitimating the government's power to conduct generalized searches.

General search was further legitimized by section 215 of the USA PATRIOT Act and the National Security letters that it authorizes. This legislation allows the government to conduct surveillance without first identifying some individual as a suspected terrorist while also granting the authority to search through third-party databases without notifying suspects, as long as the "information is relevant to a terrorism investigation."[44]

Computers do not violate privacy

The incontrovertible fact that privacy and security pose conflicting demands and, hence, must be balanced, does not mean that one cannot find ways to reduce the conflict between these two core values. One major way is to draw a sharp line between what is stored in and processed by computers and what is revealed to human agents. *Computers per se do not violate privacy.* They do not gossip. They see no evil, hear no evil, and speak no evil. They can vastly facilitate the violation of privacy, but only as perpetrated by human agents. Indeed, with respect to much of the data collected by the NSA, "[t]hey park stuff in storage in the hopes they will eventually have time to get to it or that they'll find something that they need to go back and look for in the masses of data ... most of it sits and is never looked at by anyone."[45] Hence, those who are concerned with finding a reasonable balance between security and privacy should focus on the interface between computers and human agents, and ensure that once the computers flag particular individuals, this information is revealed only to law enforcement authorities and used by them in legal and accountable ways.

A very telling example is the way the government is reporting that the collection of metadata on phone records is set up. The government collected from Verizon—and, thus, likely from other companies as well[46]—records of the numbers dialed by Americans and the length of the call, but not the content of the calls, as claimed by some critics.[47]

The government did not listen to the calls, both because it did not collect the content of the calls and because it would require at least the labor force of the United States and Canada to listen to all of the calls. It reported that the storing of documents about calls is done so as to have rapid access to the information when needed and to stitch together various data. (For some reason, the government failed to stress that the phone companies keep the records for only short periods of time,[48] and security concerns require longer storage.)[49] If and when there is a suspect, the government reports that it requires a court order, which is in line with the particular individualized standard to which civil libertarians demand the government adhere. To the extent that this pattern is followed for United States persons (defined as citizens of the United States, permanent alien residents, corporations that are incorporated in the United States, and unincorporated associations with a "substantial number of members who are citizens of the U.S. or are aliens lawfully admitted for permanent residence"),[50] the tension between privacy and security would be much reduced. Whether this operating procedure ought to be followed when dealing with non-United States persons overseas is beyond the purview of this chapter.[51]

Further, using metadata for pattern recognition should not trouble rights advocates as long as the patterns are relevant to security. The *Wall Street Journal* correctly noted the paradox of data mining:

> [T]he more such information the government collects the less of an intrusion it is. These data sets are so large that only algorithms can understand them. The search is for trends, patterns, associations, networks. They are not in that sense invasions of individual privacy at all.[52]

Thus, computers can pull out all those who purchased a one-way ticket, paid with cash, and got the ticket at the last moment. It is far from clear, at least to this sociologist, that finding such patterns can suffice to identify terrorists. However, such searches could suffice to lead to closer computerized scrutiny (e.g., to see if those who drew attention have also made calls to areas where terrorists train, traveled to these parts, or visited al Qaeda websites) and, if suspicious activity is found, the computers could then flag a human agent.

Private is not secure

Numerous discussions of the issues at hand focus on the government as the threat to privacy and pay little heed to private actors, including corporations such as ChoicePoint,[53] Axiom, and RapLeaf, that have built very detailed dossiers on most Americans.[54] However, as the author has documented elsewhere, private data banks are generally just a click and a money order away from public authorities. In fact, the government has contracts with a number of companies that have been building dossiers on millions of private citizens.[55] ChoicePoint, for example, had at least 35 contracts with various government agencies, including the Department of Justice (which, by extension, made its data available to the FBI).[56] Those who fear that the government's data banks could, in the future, be used for nefarious purposes even if they are not presently—and, hence, oppose their creation even if they serve to enhance security—should note that, as long as these private data banks exist in the private sector (which the Constitution does not ban), they are just as open to abuse as if they were held by the public sector. Thus, if a tyrant were to take over the United States government tomorrow, or merely if J. Edgar Hoover were to be reappointed as the head of the FBI, it would matter little whether dossiers were kept by corporations or the government. To protect against abuse, one must look elsewhere rather than merely oppose the government's having what is already banked by corporations.

Trust but verify

Curb abuses

Critics have strong reason to hold that, once the government is granted the power to collect information about the private lives of individuals, these powers will be abused. The critics have identified the following abuses:

- using data to find and prosecute people of opposing political views—what some have called the Nixon effect;[57]
- using data to stigmatize people whose conduct violates established norms but not the law (e.g., information about adulterous affairs, abortions, or unusual sexual preferences. This type of information is sometimes referred to as the Scarlet Letter effect);
- using data to keep information that, in the past, would have been slowly forgotten, allowing people to develop new identities (e.g., the person whose "conviction of graffiti vandalism at age 19 will still be there at age 29 when [they're] a solid citizen trying to get a job and raise a family"[58]); and
- using data to go after crimes other than terrorist acts.

There is no question that, in the past, all of these abuses have taken place. One should also note that they are not one and the same. The Nixon effect and Scarlet Letter effect are clearly troubling, and one must discuss, as this chapter next does, how to curb and deter them. The status of a right newly minted by privacy advocates—the right to be forgotten—is much less clear because evidence shows that erasing the past much more often leads to people who continue to abuse children; to doctors who continue to practice medicine after killing patients due to their drug and alcohol abuse; and to con artists who continue to abuse the elderly—rather than people who start new constructive lives.[59]

Regarding other crimes, a serious question of balance is raised. On the one hand, there is reason to hold that the extraordinary powers granted to the government to counter the special threat of terrorism should not be used for other purposes. On the other hand, in a society in which over 35 percent of homicide cases go unsolved, with the number rising to nearly 60 percent for cases of forcible rape and almost 90 percent for instances of burglary and motor-vehicle theft, some extension of powers to enhance public safety might be justified.[60] Sorting out this particular balance, between privacy and public safety other than counterterrorism, is beyond the purview of this chapter, but it deserves much more attention than it has gained so far.

The discussion next turns to the question of what measures can be taken to further ensure that the counterterrorism powers will not be abused in any of the ways that they have been abused in the past. That is, instead of arguing that there is no need to re-balance security and privacy to minimize future terrorist attacks, the challenge now, given the assumption that a re-balancing is called for (for a defined period), is to determine what measures can be added to those already in place to ensure that the enhanced powers will be employed only for legitimate purposes.

The reason why the challenge is worded in terms of what measures should be "added" rather than which should be "employed" is because many are already in place. The executive branch has layers upon layers of supervisors, who are the first line of accountability. In addition, there are Inspectors General and Privacy Officers who often serve as quite forceful critics of the practices of concern here.[61] Congress has various committees charged with oversight, and there is also the investigative Government Accountability Office (GAO).[62] The courts, too, play an important checking and balancing role. The media frequently acts as a major guardian against abuses. Investigative bodies such as Pike and Church Committees—as well as the 9/11 Commission—also serve to review and vet the government's claims and behavior. In the past, all these institutions served to reveal abuses when they occurred and acted to curb them, but often only after considerable delay. Furthermore, the fact that abuses occurred at all suggests that there is reason to further enhance scrutiny of the government and establish additional precautionary measures.

Accountability vs. transparency

In searching for measures to enhance scrutiny, one ought to make a sharp distinction between two major ways of proceeding. The first approach entails enhanced transparency, in which more information about counterterrorism measures is provided to the media and, hence, to the public, as well as to members of Congress in general (rather than only to a select few with security clearance who serve on specialized committees). Following the revelations of the NSA programs in 2013, there was a very considerable demand for such disclosures for increased transparency. The president emphasized that the programs were transparent,[63] with aides stating that they were going to try to be even more transparent,[64] and additional information was released by the government,[65] on top of the continued stream of leaks. At the same time, more than one quarter of the Senate has urged the White House to be more transparent about its surveillance practices.[66]

The second approach entails increasing the power of, and adding layers to, institutional accountability and oversight. Although both might be called for, there are strong reasons to rely more on enhanced accountability and oversight than on much enhanced transparency. The distinction reflects the well-known difference between direct democracy (which is the idea behind transparency—the people will know all the details and judge the merit of the programs) and representative democracy (a good part of the judgment will be made by elected representatives, and the public will judge them).

Significantly higher levels of transparency present two kinds of serious problems. One problem is well known and plagues all efforts for direct democracy. There are sharp limits in the capacity of the public, who are busy making a living and leading a social life, to learn the details of any government program and evaluate it— especially given that, in the end, they cannot vote any program up or down, but have only one "holistic" vote for their representatives based on all that those representatives favor and oppose. Second, high transparency is, on its face, incompatible with keeping secret that which must be kept secret.

Moreover, when the government responds to calls for more scrutiny with the release of more information—so as to demonstrate that the secret acts did, in fact, improve security and did not unduly violate privacy—these releases encounter several difficulties. First, each piece of information released potentially helps the adversaries. This is, in effect, the way intelligence work is often done: by piecing together details released by various sources. Thus, the publication of information about which past terrorist operations were disrupted by the government could allow those groups to find out which of their plots failed because of U.S. government interventions versus those that failed because of technical flaws, the weakness of their chosen agents, or some other reason. Second, it is next to impossible to spell out how these cases unfolded without giving away details about sources and methods. (That is, unless the government releases misleading details. But, sooner or later, some whistleblower would likely expose the ploy, undermining the whole enterprise, which was meant to build trust in government.) Thus, one intelligence official reports that the leaks regarding the NSA snooping programs have already led to terrorist groups "changing their communications behavior based on these disclosures," meaning that we might "miss tidbits that could be useful in stopping the next plot."[67]

Moreover, however much information about specific cases the government releases, skeptics are sure to find details that need further clarification and documentation. (This is the reason why public relations experts urge those whose misdeeds are under public scrutiny to "tell all" right from the start, a strategy that may well serve politicians who cheat on their spouses, but not those who deal with combating terrorism.) Thus, following the uproar over the PRISM program, technology companies sought to "reassure users" by releasing reports on the frequency of government data requests. According to the *New York Times*, the result was that "rather than provide clarity, the companies' disclosures have left many questions unanswered."[68] When NSA Director General Keith Alexander released details about how the agency's surveillance programs had thwarted terrorist plots, the media immediately asked for more.[69] Moreover, there is no way for the media to determine whether the released cases are typical or were chosen because they reflect well on the government.

In contrast, a representative democracy approach suggests that one ought to search for ways to enhance the accountability and oversight power of various institutions, including Congressional committees, the FISA appeal court, the GAO, various Inspectors General, and privacy officers. Greatly increasing the use of audit trails is called for.

Briefing many more members of Congress may not be the best way to proceed. First, many members of Congress do not have the security clearance possessed by the members and key staffers of the congressional intelligence committees. Second, many members of Congress are known to be notorious leakers themselves. And third, the public's trust in Congress is at a historical low point.

Rather, the media and the public would benefit from a regular review conducted by an independent civilian review board. Such a board would be composed of the kind of people who served on the 9/11 Commission: bipartisan, highly respected by the public, able to work together, not running for office, and possessing the necessary security clearance. While not everyone agreed with the 9/11 Commission's conclusions, it was still well respected and largely trusted, with many of its recommendations eventually being implemented.

The new board would issue reports, say annually, that would state whether the government collected information for political reasons (as opposed to security concerns) in the pursuit of minor crimes rather than terrorists, or for other legitimate and legal goals.

However, instead of revealing detailed case studies, the civilian review board would provide statistics. For example, if it reported that there were a large number of cases in which serious threats were averted, such as the planned attack on New York City's subways, the public would learn that the threats to national security warranted increased efforts to enforce anti-leak legislation. If, on the other hand, the board reported that many cases involved fairly minor threats, this would tilt the consensus the other way.[70] (If the current Privacy and Civil Liberties Oversight Board were to be properly staffed and funded, and its powers increased, it might serve in such a function.)

Can we trust the government?

A common claim among civil libertarians is that, even if little harm is presently being inflicted by government surveillance programs, the infrastructure is in place for a less benevolent leader to violate the people's rights and set us on the path to tyranny. For example, it has been argued that the PRISM program "will amount to a 'turnkey' system that, in the wrong hands, could transform the country into a totalitarian state virtually overnight. Every person who values personal freedom, human rights and the rule of law must recoil against such a possibility, regardless of their political preference."[71] A few things might be said in response.

First, all of the data that the government is collecting is already being archived (at least for short periods—as discussed above) by private corporations and other entities. Second, if one is truly concerned that a tyrant might take over the United States, one obviously faces a much greater and all-encompassing threat than a diminution of privacy. And the response has to be similarly expansive: (1) One can join civic bodies that seek to shore up democracies; (2) one can work with various reform movements and public education drives; or (3) one can join groups that prepare to retreat to the mountains, store ammunition and essential foods, and plan to fight the tyrannical forces. But it makes no sense to oppose limited measures to enhance security on these grounds.

EIGHT

How liberty is lost

In the wake of numerous recent changes made in American law and that of many other countries following the September 11, 2001 terrorist attacks, civil libertarians, libertarians, and many others have raised concerns that the nations involved are sacrificing their liberty to enhance their safety. Senator Patrick Leahy expressed concern that the United States was "shredding [its] Constitution."[1] Civil libertarian organizations such as the ACLU have described the government's penchant toward obtaining new powers after September 11 as an "insatiable appetite," characterized by government secrecy, a lack of transparency, rejection of equality under the law, and "a disdain and outright removal of checks and balances."[2] Articles in the popular press express similar sentiments. Writing in the *American Prospect*, Wendy Kaminer expressed the fear that, "Give the FBI unchecked domestic spying powers and instead of focusing on preventing terrorism, it will revert to doing what is does best—monitoring, harassing, and intimidating political dissidents and thousands of harmless immigrants."[3] In short, it has been argued that in order to protect ourselves from terrorists, democracy may be endangered, if not lost.

The question, "Under what conditions is democracy undermined?" has been the topic of considerable previous deliberations, especially by people who have studied the fall of the Weimar Republic and the rise of the Nazis in Germany. However, for the last decades, much more focus has been on the question of how to help democracy grow in countries that have had little previous experience with this form of governance (for instance, some former communist states and a fair number of developing nations), rather than on how democracy might be lost. Given the recent events and claims, the latter question deserves to be revisited. This question is particularly germane because, if it were true that in order to survive future waves of terrorist attacks (including ones using weapons of mass destruction) we must turn our free societies into garrison states, many members of free societies might well be reluctant to accept such a trade-off.

Fortunately, the empirical basis for such a study of the conditions under which democracy is actually lost is very limited because democracy—once firmly established—has almost never been lost due to internal developments (as distinct from occupation by an invading force). Democracy seems to be an odd plant: it has been very difficult for it to take root, especially in parts of the world where it has not been "naturally" found, but where various efforts have been made to seed it. Once it buds, it often faces great difficulties and frequently dies on the vine, or at least suffers numerous setbacks before it grows properly. But after it firmly takes root, it tends to withstand numerous challenges well and is rarely lost. Indeed, one key example of democracy lost comes to mind, that is the already mentioned Weimar Republic—and it is arguable whether democracy was even well established there.

Before the discussion proceeds, a word on definition: if one defines "democracy" very lightly, such as a nation that holds regular elections, one finds that none of the preceding statements holds. Elections are held all over the world, including in nations in which there is only one political party, one candidate, a legislature which rubber stamps whatever the government proposes, a press controlled by the government, and where individuals' rights are not respected. Such "democracies" come and go, at the whim of the military or some other power elite. Democracy, here, is taken to mean a polity in which there are regular, institutionalized changes of power, in line with the preferences of the people, freely expressed. It entails a whole fabric of institutions: two or more political parties, some measure of checks and balances among the various branches of the government (although, of course, these may differ from the American setup), courts that effectively protect individual rights, and a free press. While some scholars draw important conceptual distinctions between liberal (rights-based) polities and democratic ones, and others focus on the definition of liberty, here we treat all of these as key elements of a democratic polity. To remind the reader of this fact, I will use the phrase "constitutional democracy"; our democracy is ensconced in a framework of rights that are not subject to majority rule.

The slippery slope hypothesis

The civil libertarian's narrative about how democracies are lost is basically as follows. First, the government, in the name of national security or some other such cause, trims some rights, which raises little alarm at the time (e.g., the massive detention of Japanese Americans during World War II). Then a few other rights are curtailed (e.g., the FBI spies on civil rights groups and peace activists during the 1960s). Soon more rights are lost and, gradually, the whole institutional structure on which democracy rests tumbles down the slope, with nobody able to stop it.

If one fully embraces this argument, one cannot in good conscience support any significant adjustments in the ways we interpret the Constitution, its Bill of Rights, the powers allotted to public authorities, and other key features of a democratic polity. If one fears setting foot on the slope because he may end up on his backside at the lower end of the slope, there is only one alternative—to remain frozen at the top, opposed to all changes. Indeed, during a debate about the USA PATRIOT Act (which includes numerous post-September 11 changes in U.S. laws to enhance the war against terrorism, including trimming some rights and redefining others), Nadine Strossen, president of the ACLU, was repeatedly asked whether there were any changes in public policies relevant to safety that she would find acceptable. She refused to endorse any. (When Katie Corrigan, legislative counsel with the ACLU's Washington office, testified before Congress she noted that the ACLU has supported some post-September 11 changes, including the fortification of cockpit doors, matching baggage with passengers, and limiting the number of carry-on bags passengers may bring on planes, a rather limited list.)

In contrast, I have argued that one should be able to make notches in the slope. In other words, before setting foot on it, one needs to and can clearly mark how far one is willing to go and what is unacceptable, to avoid slipping to a place one is not willing and ought not to go. A detailed examination of the changes introduced after September 11 in the United States finds some of them very reasonable (e.g., roving wiretaps) and others quite unacceptable (e.g., the military tribunals as originally conceived). The distinction between these changes suggests that, rather, than refusing to adjust, we need to examine more closely the various new measures that are being advanced. Indeed, very few would seek to leave the Constitution as originally formulated, according to which non-Europeans do not count as full persons, there is no right to privacy, and free speech is much less protected than post-1920 interpretations (led by the ACLU to its credit) made it. In short, changes in the ways we view individual rights do not signify the ending of a democratic form of government. Indeed, as I shall try to highlight in the next section, the relationship runs the other way around: when democratic institutions and policies do not provide an adequate response to new challenges, they are undermined.

Post-September 11 lessons

Did our constitutional democracy lose support after September 11 and, if it did, under what factors? The data cited next suggest that during the period immediately after the attacks, when the public was most concerned about its safety (fearing further attacks from sleeper terrorist cells on short order), people were most willing to support a strong government, including one that would set aside many basic individual rights.

However, in the subsequent period, as the government did take numerous and varying measures to enhance public safety and no new attacks occurred, the public gradually restored its commitment to the rights-centered, democratic regime. What endangered it was not curtailment of rights, but fear that the public would not be protected. And as the government vigorously enacted measures to protect the public, the public's support for constitutional democracy was reaffirmed. That is, the U.S. experience in the months following September 11 helps to support the suggested hypothesis by providing a case with a profile opposite of the Weimar one. When the government reacted firmly to a major challenge, support for constitutional democracy was sustained rather than undermined.

Public fears in the U.S.: 2001–02

To put the hypothesis that is being explored here in more formal terms, one may state that we seek to assess whether the size of a challenge (in this instance the September 11 attacks) minus the impact of new measures undertaken to enhance public safety will correlate with the extent to which the public will support a rights-based, constitutional democracy. (Correlate rather than equal, because other factors will affect the dependent variable.) For the purposes at hand, no distinction is made as to whether the public's concerns are realistic, overblown, or underestimating the danger. (We know from crime studies that the public's fear of crime and the actual level of crime do not necessarily go hand in hand.) The reason for this approach is that democracy will be endangered if the public's fears rise above a certain level, regardless of whether their concerns are realistic or not. The same holds for safety measures. If putting armed guards in airports adds little to public safety, but helps to reassure the public, then armed guards will serve to reduce anxiety and help to undergird public support for our form of government.

A reasonable measure of the initial scope of the public's safety concerns and the extent to which they declined after September 11 is provided by statistics on domestic airline traffic within the United States, based on behavioral data—which are considered more reliable than attitudinal data, to which I will have to turn shortly. Airline traffic fell precipitously in the period immediately following the attacks, and gradually recovered, but it had not returned to the pre-September 11 level by the end of the period for which information was available (through February 2002).

Prior to September 11, airlines were experiencing a slight increase of a little under 1 percent in enplanements over the year 2000; in August 2001, passengers boarding flights increased by 3.1 percent over the previous year (a year-high 56.1 million passengers boarded U.S. carriers for domestic flights in August 2001; 54.4 million did so in August 2000). In September 2001 (which includes the 10 days before the attack) enplanements dropped 34 percent from September 2000 (when 47.7 million passengers boarded planes, as compared to the 31.4 million who did so during the month of the attacks, when airports across the country were shut down).

Traffic began a slow but steady increase during the remainder of the year, though enplanements remained considerably less than they had been during the same months in the year 2000. In October, air carriers experienced 21.2 percent fewer enplanements over the previous year (a decrease from 50.5 million to 39.8 million). As the highly traveled holiday months approached, the drop in enplanements continued to recede. In November, there were 18.5 percent fewer enplanements than the in same month the previous year (a decrease from 50.9 million to 41.5 million), and December saw a 13.4 percent decrease over the 2000 holiday season (down from 46.7 million to 40.5 million).

The first two months of the year 2002 follow the same pattern, showing people slowly but steadily returning to air travel. January 2002 enplanements were down 13.0 percent as compared to 2001 (a decrease from 43.8 million to 38.1 million), and February saw 10.8 percent fewer enplanements as compared to February 2001 (a decrease from 47.6 million to 42.4 million).

In short, as numerous new airline safety measures were introduced, one new attack (by the so-called shoe-bomber) was successfully foiled, and no others took place, the public's confidence in airline travel was gradually being restored.

Commitment to constitutional democracy: attitudes

We can see a base line of sorts in the following data on perceptions about personal freedoms (Table 1). A year before the attacks, 54 percent of Americans were not concerned that the government threatened their own personal rights and freedoms, while two months after the attacks the figure rose to 67 percent, encompassing two-thirds of all Americans. (By that time several measures to enhance safety had been introduced and public fears were beginning to subside. Regrettably, no data is available for the same question immediately after the attacks.)

Table 1: Governmental threats to personal rights and freedoms

Do you think the government threatens your own personal rights and freedoms, or not?			
	Yes	**No**	**Don't know**
November 2001	30%	67%	3%
June 2000[a]	46%	54%	_[b]

Notes: [a] National Public Radio/Kaiser/Kennedy School of Government;
[b] Less than 1 percent.

Source: National Public Radio/Kaiser/Kennedy School Poll on Civil Liberties, October 31–November 12, 2001.

When people were asked explicitly, "Would you be willing to give up some of the liberties we have in this country in order for the government to crack down on terrorism, or not?" their responses tell the same story. Shortly after the bombing of the Murrah Federal Building in Oklahoma City in April 1995, a hefty majority (59 percent) favored giving up some liberties. Given a month, the numbers began to subside to 52 percent in May 1995, only to zoom to about two-thirds (66 percent) of Americans on September 11, 2001.

The same sentiments are revealed in another poll that asked, "What concerns you most right now? That the government will fail to enact strong, new anti-terrorism laws, or that the government will enact new anti-terrorism laws which excessively restrict the average person's civil liberties?" While 44 percent were concerned that the government would enact laws that would restrict civil liberties in 1995, about one-third (34 percent) expressed such reservations in September 2001.

The willingness of people to give up rights in order to fight terrorism, and their perception of whether or not they will need to give up some of their own rights, is also tied to their level of fear. As Table 2 shows, a clear majority (59 percent) of Americans were willing to give up some liberties after what was, in retrospect, a small attack, the bombing of the federal building in Oklahoma City in April 1995. When the same question was asked a mere month later, people had already begun to calm down, and their willingness to support reductions of liberty had declined to 52 percent. After the 2001 attacks on America, two-thirds of Americans were willing to sacrifice some liberty in order to fight terrorism. (When the question was worded differently, the percentage was even higher—78 percent).

Table 2: Willingness to give up civil liberties

Date	Question	Willing	Not willing	Don't know/ no opinion
April 1995[a]	Would you be willing to give up some of the liberties we have in this country in order for the government to crack down on terrorism, or not?	59%	24%	10%
May 1995[a]	Would you be willing to give up some of the liberties we have in this country in order for the government to crack down on terrorism, or not?	52%	41%	7%
August 1996[b]	Would you be willing to give up some civil liberties if that were necessary to curb terrorism in this country, or not?	58%	23%	6%
September 2001[a]	Would you be willing to give up some of the liberties we have in this country in order for the government to crack down on terrorism, or not?	66%	24%	7%
January– March 2002[c]	You are now more willing to give up certain freedoms to improve safety and security than you were before September 11th.	78%	22%	

Source: [a] ABC News/Washington Post Poll, September 11, 2001.
[b] Los Angeles Times Poll, August 3–August 6, 1996. This poll was conducted a few weeks after the explosion of TWA flight 800 and the bombing at Centennial Olympic Park during the 1996 Summer Olympics in Atlanta. The poll also contained the response "it depends," chosen by 13 percent of respondents (which is not included in Table 2).
[c] Gallup Poll, 28 January–22 March 2002. Responses to the question included "strongly agree" (29.5 percent), "agree" (48.8 percent), "disagree" (13.6 percent), and "strongly disagree" (8.1 percent).

Questions about "necessity" instead of willingness to give up liberties (Table 3) reveal a similar pattern. More than 6 in 10 Americans agreed that it was a necessary to give up some rights immediately after September 11. Two months later, the number fell to a little over 5 out of 10 Americans.

Table 3: Necessity to give up liberties

Date	Question	Necessary	Not necessary	Don't know
September 2001[a]	In order to curb terrorism in this country, do you think it will be necessary for the average person to give up some liberties or not?	61%	33%	6%
November 2001[b]	In order to curb terrorism in this country, do you think it will be necessary for the average person to give up some rights and liberties, or do you think we can curb terrorism without the average person giving up rights and liberties?	51%★	46%★	3%
November 2001[b]	Do you think you will have to give up some of your **OWN** rights and liberties to curb terrorism, or not?	58%★★	39%★★	3%

Notes: ★ Responses include "necessary for the average person to give up some rights and liberties" and "we can curb terrorism without the average person giving up rights and liberties."

★★ Responses include "yes" and "no."

Source: [a] *Los Angeles Times* Poll, September 13–14, 2002.
[b] National Public Radio/Kaiser/Kennedy School Poll on Civil Liberties, October 31, 2001–November 12, 2001.

In response to questions about specific measures, the picture is completely consistent: as fear subsided, support for safety, even at the cost of liberty, remained very high (as warnings about more attacks, including ones with dirty bombs and bioterror agents were standard diet), but declined over time with regard to all of the 10 specific measures the public was asked about. Indeed, on seven

Table 4: Law enforcement and civil liberties

Here are some increased powers of investigation that law enforcement agencies might use when dealing with people suspected of terrorist activity, which would also affect our civil liberties. For each, please say if you would favor of oppose it.

		Favor	Oppose	Not sure/ decline to answer
Expanded undercover activities to penetrate groups under suspicion	September 2001	93%	5%	1%
	March 2002	88%	10%	2%
Stronger documents and physical security checks	September 2001	93%	6%	1%
	March 2002	89%	9%	2%
Stronger document and physical security checks for access to government and private buildings	September 2001	92%	7%	1%
	March 2002	89%	10%	1%
Use of facial-recognition technology to scan for suspected terrorists at various locations and public events	September 2001	86%	11%	2%
	March 2002	81%	17%	2%
Issuance of a secure I.D. technique for persons to access government and business computer systems to avoid disruptions	September 2001	84%	11%	4%
	March 2002	78%	16%	6%
Closer monitoring of banking and credit card transactions, to trace funding sources	September 2001	81%	17%	2%
	March 2002	72%	25%	2%
Adoption of a national I.D. system for all U.S. citizens	September 2001	68%	28%	4%
	March 2002	59%	37%	5%
Expanded camera surveillance on streets and in public places	September 2001	63%	35%	2%
	March 2002	58%	40%	2%
Law enforcement monitoring of Internet discussions in chat rooms and other forums	September 2001	63%	32%	5%
	March 2002	55%	41%	4%
Expanded government monitoring of cell phones and email, to intercept communications	September 2001	54%	41%	4%
	March 2002	44%	51%	4%

Source: Harris Poll, March 13–19, 2002 and Harris Poll, September 19–24, 2001

out of the 10 measures, more than two-thirds of Americans were initially willing to sacrifice the specific rights listed.

When the same issue was raised in a different manner the results were similar. Table 5 shows that the percentage of Americans who held that the government went too far in restricting civil liberties to fight terrorism remained consistently small, but increased from eight percent to 12 percent as America experienced no new attacks and numerous new safety measures were introduced. The percentage of those who believed that the government did not go far enough declined somewhat.

Table 5: Government excess in restricting civil liberties

Based on what the Bush Administration has done so far and is proposing to do in response to terrorism, do you think they are going too far in restricting civil liberties in this country, not far enough, or are handling the situation just about right?				
	Too far	**Not far enough**	**Just about right**	**Don't know**
September 2001	12%	23%	59%	6%
November 2001	11%	14%	72%	3%
February 2002	8%	17%	72%	3%

Source: Newsweek Poll, January 31–February 1, 2002.

In responses to overarching questions (such as, "Overall, how confident do you feel that U.S. law enforcement will use its expanded surveillance powers in what you would see as a proper way, under the circumstances of terrorist threats?"), we see the beginning of a shift, the decline in those who are very confident that law enforcement will use such powers properly, which is less problematic than a significant increase in those who are not confident at all. While in March, the percent of people who felt "very confident" fell to almost one-third of what it was in September (from 34 percent to 12 percent), those who were "not confident at all" increased by a mere 2 percent (from 4 percent to 6 percent), well within the margin of error for such polls.

As far as one can rely on attitudinal data that vary according to how the question is phrased, the data support the thesis that the higher the fear, the greater the willingness to curtail liberty in order to protect safety; and that as new safety measures are introduced, and no new attacks occur—when the government's response seems effective—fear subsides and support for democracy beings to re-grow. The fact that the support for strong anti-terrorist measures remains high reflects the fact that all of the data were collected within nine months of the September 11 attacks and under frequent warnings about imminent attacks, new threats, and so on. The thesis would lead one to expect that if the panic subsides some more, the proportion of those supporting a curtailment of rights will further decline. This may seem obvious, but it surely is not so obvious to those who hold that democracy is lost by introducing new safety measures that entail some curtailment of rights. These are core elements of what protects the public and reassures it.

Lower crime rates—More support for liberty

Beyond the scope of this presentation is another relevant source of data—the correlation between the public support for "tough" elected officials and law enforcement personnel who favor restrictive and punitive policies that entail curbing individual liberties. Some informal evidence to this effect is available for the mid-1990s.

Following a series of high-profile violent crimes, including a rampage that killed five passengers on a Long Island railroad and several murders of European tourists in Florida, the public became highly fearful of violent crime and sought get-tough measures. In the mid-1990s the public cited crime as the biggest problem facing the country (19 percent), with an additional 2 percent identifying guns as the biggest problem, followed by the economy (14 percent) and unemployment and jobs (12 percent). In 1996, crime and drugs were identified as the biggest problem by nearly a quarter of respondents. In contrast, four years earlier, in January 1992, 54 percent of Americans cited economic issues as the most important issue facing the country, while only 2 percent cited guns or violence.

In the mid-1990s, Americans overwhelmingly favored treating juveniles who commit violent crimes the same way as adults, as opposed to more leniently (by nearly a three to one margin). They also supported more extreme measures such as caning, following American Michael Fay's such punishment in Singapore for vandalism. A 1994 poll shows that less than half of Americans felt that caning is too harsh a punishment for assault (44 percent), robbery (48 percent), and drug dealing (36 percent). Nearly 60 percent of Americans favored the "surgical or chemical castration of men repeatedly convicted of rape or child molesting."

During this same time period, demagogues advocated "street justice" and "shoot first, ask questions later." Former Los Angeles Police Chief Daryl Gates publicly made comments to this effect. For instance, at a news conference about the rioting that occurred after the beating of Rodney King by Los Angeles police officers, Gates was quoted on the front page of the *Los Angeles Times* as saying,

> "Clearly that night we should have gone down there and shot a few people. In retrospect that's what we should have done. We should have blown a few heads off. And maybe your television cameras would have seen that and maybe that would have been broadcast and maybe, just maybe, that would have stopped everything. I don't know. But certainly we had the legal right to do that."[4]

That wasn't the only time Gates made such comments. A few years later, in *USA Today*, Gates stated, "No matter how you use that club, people are going to criticize."[5] Law enforcement personnel were not alone in expressing their support of "street justice." Other public officials, including legislators, expressed similar views. For example, in 1995, a former member of the Georgia State Assembly introduced a bill (which garnered support, but failed to become law) dubbed "shoot first, ask questions later," which would have allowed homeowners to shoot intruders in their homes.

As the decade came to a close, these sentiments faded away to some degree. A poll conducted in 2000 shows the change in the public's perception of crime. The proportion of those who believed crime in the country was "very bad" or "bad" fell from 90 percent in 1996 to 80 percent in 2000. Even more to the point, among those who felt crime was a problem in the country, less than one quarter (23 percent) characterized crime as "very bad' or "bad" in their own community in 2000, as compared to the almost one-third (31 percent) who characterized crime as "bad" or "very bad" in 1996.

Polls conducted in the late 1990s also showed that people believed there was less crime in their neighborhoods. (In 1998, 48 percent of Americans thought there was less crime in their area than a year ago.) Also, in the latter half of the decade, fewer people believed that crime in the country had increased over the previous year. (In 1998, 52 percent of Americans thought crime had increased in the country over the previous year, as compared to 64 percent who thought crime had increased in 1997, and 87 percent who thought crime had increased in 1993.)

By the end of the 1990s, as public authorities succeeded in curbing violent crime, fear of crime subsided and there was less talk of get-tough, extra-legal measures and less support for harsh but legal measures. By the end of the 1990s and in the year 2000, when polls showed that the public perceived crime as less of a problem, the statistics on violent crime corroborated their feelings. For instance, in 1998 there were 1.5 million violent crime offenses, and by the year 2000 offenses had decreased even further to 1.4 million, a stark contrast with the much larger number of offenses in the mid-1990s (1.9 million violent crime offenses in 1994 and 1.8 million in 1995).

To the extent that one can draw conclusions from the evidence at hand, some of it being historical, some behavioral, and some attitudinal, it seems to support the thesis that democracy is endangered not when strong measures are taken to enhance safety, to protect, and reassure the public, but when these measures are not taken. In short, the "correlation" between strong safety measures and democracy is just the opposite of what civil libertarians argue: It is positive rather than negative. This, of course, does not mean that any and all new safety measures are needed, but that, in general, effective enhancement of safety (and more generally, those measures which respond to public needs) is crucial for democracy to be sustained. Once safety is restored, the measures can be gradually rolled back, without endangering public support for constitutional democracy.

Part Three
Supranational Overreach

NINE

Undermining genocide prevention

The Westphalian order and state sovereignty

Many hold state sovereignty to be the most profound foundation of the international order.[1] In contemporary thought and practice, sovereignty has been largely understood in association with the Westphalian principle that forbids armed interference by one state in the internal affairs of another.[2] Respect for international borders is a crucial part of this order. They are the markers that separate that which is fully legitimate and that which most assuredly is not. If the troops of a given state are positioned within its boundaries, the international community considers them to be a legitimate part of an orderly world composed of states. The international community holds that the same troops crossing a border with hostile intentions is a severe violation of the agreed-upon world order; should this occur, the international order and the invaded state are inclined to respond violently. There are countless reports that people in very different parts of the world feel personally aggrieved, insulted, and humiliated when they learn that their state's sovereignty has been violated, even if another state's troops have simply crossed some minor or vague line in the shifting sands.[3] That millions of people have shown that they are willing to die to protect their state's sovereignty is an indication of the depth of their commitment to this precept. Indeed, even when a state violates another's sovereignty to bring aid to the latter's population, strong loyalty to the sovereignty paradigm persists.

The same normative idea is also tied to the strongly held precepts of self-determination that played a key role in dismantling colonial empires and establishing independent nation-states. The right to state sovereignty is trumpeted by the governments and citizens of both autocracies and democracies—all of which tend to decry foreign intervention into their affairs on nationalist grounds. The respect for sovereignty[4] is ensconced in a great many international laws and institutions, such as the International Criminal Court (ICC) and, most notably, the Charter of the United Nations.[5] For example, the Preamble as well as Articles 17 and 53 of the Rome Statute, which established the ICC, identifies the Court's jurisdiction as complementary to the jurisdictions of its member states, which means that the ICC may pursue only those cases that states are unable or unwilling to prosecute themselves.[6] Article 2 of the United Nations Charter, meanwhile, states that the United Nations is based "on the principle of the sovereign equality of all its Members."[7]

A communitarian approach to sovereignty

Proponents of sovereignty as responsibility sought to fundamentally shift the role played by the international community in the internal affairs of states by establishing an *a priori* category of conditions that, if met, would cause states to forfeit their sovereignty. As such, states that called for armed humanitarian intervention would not need to justify interventions in principle but, rather, would need to merely show that a state had not fulfilled its responsibilities. States that manifestly neglect their responsibilities to prevent mass-atrocity crimes forfeit their sovereignty, and the international community has the responsibility to intervene with coercive measures, including military intervention.

Contemporary international theory and practice is largely departing from the view that sovereignty is absolute and is instead adopting the idea of conditional sovereignty—that is, that sovereignty is contingent upon states fulfilling certain domestic and international obligations. This is largely a communitarian approach, and it is one built on a communitarian notion of citizenship. In other words, it recognizes that states (like individuals) have not only rights but also responsibilities; they are entitled to self-determination and self-government, but must also demonstrate their commitment to the common good by protecting the environment, promoting peace, and refraining from harming their populations.[8] Recent humanitarian crises have further called into question the inviolability of sovereignty. The international community widely accepts that states have a responsibility to refrain from committing (or allowing) mass atrocities against their citizens (for example, genocide), and that in failing to uphold such responsibilities they forfeit their sovereignty. This understanding is manifested in the Responsibility to Protect (RtoP), as adopted at the World Summit in 2005.[9] Francis Deng and his associates, in a 1996 book entitled *Sovereignty as Responsibility*,[10] argued that when states do not conduct their domestic affairs in ways that meet internationally recognized standards, other states have not only a right but a duty to intervene. Deng forcefully stated this modification of the Westphalian norm and, at great length, defended his thesis that:

> The sovereign state's responsibility and accountability to both domestic and external constituencies must be affirmed as interconnected principles of the national and international order. Such a normative code is anchored in the assumption that in order to be legitimate, sovereignty must demonstrate responsibility. At the very least that means providing for the basic needs of its people.[11]

The International Commission on Intervention and State Sovereignty further developed the idea in its 2001 report *The Responsibility to Protect*, and centered its proposals on sovereignty as responsibility. It held that:

> The Charter of the UN is itself an example of an international obligation voluntarily accepted by member states. On the one hand, in granting membership of the UN, the international community welcomes the signatory state as a responsible member of

the community of nations. On the other hand, the state itself, in signing the Charter, accepts the responsibilities of membership flowing from that signature. There is no transfer or dilution of state sovereignty. But there is a necessary re-characterization involved: from *sovereignty as control* to *sovereignty as responsibility* in both internal functions and external duties.[12]

In 2004 the UN Secretary-General's High-level Panel on Threats, Challenges and Change (the "High-level Panel") advanced this view in its report, *A More Secure World—Our Shared Responsibility*, which argues that:

> Whatever perceptions may have prevailed when the Westphalian system first gave rise to the notion of State sovereignty, today it clearly carries with it the obligation of a State to protect the welfare of its own peoples and meet its obligations to the wider international community.[13]

Here, again, the report implies that a state's willingness and capacity to fulfill its basic responsibilities and obligations preconditions its sovereignty. RtoP reaches even further; it not only holds that states must fulfill their obligations to protect their citizens from mass-atrocity crimes in order to maintain their sovereignty but also holds that *other states* have the *obligation to intervene* if a state fails to uphold its responsibility to protect.[14]

Before the advent of RtoP, the United Nations Security Council had authorized interventions rarely and on an ad hoc basis—for example, in Somalia and Haiti; it had not developed a general case for downgrading state sovereignty. RtoP codified a specific set of criteria that would justify violating a state's sovereignty—and thus significantly "walked back" the Westphalian norm. Since the United Nations General Assembly endorsed RtoP unanimously in 2006,[15] "numerous resolutions by the Security Council and General Assembly" have referenced the concept, which has ascended to a place of prominence in the international debate and has been invoked by a wide range of state and non-state actors.[16] RtoP has also suffered setbacks, however, notably due to its invocation as the rationale for the 2003 invasion of Iraq and the 2011 NATO intervention in Libya, both of which weakened its support.[17] Accordingly, some of RtoP's normative grounding— namely, conditional sovereignty—has been similarly eroded.

Responsibility to protect—not regime change

As I see it, intervention for the purpose of regime change and nation building should be limited to non-lethal means, that is, it should exclude the use of force. Neither adding to the set of responsibilities a state must fulfill to guarantee its sovereignty nor demanding a certain form of government under the threat of armed intervention is justified; these matters should be the purview of the people of the states involved. Intervention over these issues often results not in a free regime but, rather, in new forms of authoritarianism, anarchy, or civil war.[18] Pushing RtoP toward regime change threatens the fragile international consensus on intervention. Russia and China—both states that have, in the past, strongly endorsed the Westphalian norm[19]—have in part come to accept armed interventions for humanitarian purposes, provided that those interventions do not advance other causes.[20] For example, in 2006 China's then ambassador to the United Nations endorsed RtoP as it pertains to "genocide, war crimes, ethnic cleansing and crimes against humanity," but insisted that "it is not appropriate to expand, willfully to interpret or even abuse this concept."[21] Pushing for too expansive a challenge to sovereignty might, thus, sour China on the more limited responsibilities outlined above.

RtoP is a major "globalist," liberal achievement. It can be reconciled with nationalist respect for communities' need to self-determination if it is not used to excuse coercive regime changes. This, in turn, does not mean that one needs to ignore oppressive, authoritarian regimes. One can support the citizens who seek reforms with non-lethal means.

TEN

Nationalism as a block to community building

A large number of observers view Britain's leaving the EU (Brexit) as an expression of populism, akin to the election of Donald Trump, the rise of Marine Le Pen and so on. Actually, Brexit is rather different from these other political and sociological developments. I illustrate this first by one 2017 development and then turn to outline the underlying forces at work.

In May 2017, after Emmanuel Macron defeated Le Pen and was elected as the President of France, he called for concentrating more power in the hands of "Brussels," that is, in the hands of the European Commission. This is despite the fact that Britain is leaving the EU because of popular rebellion against violations of national sovereignty by Brussels. One cannot have ever more economic and administrative integration on the EU level as long as the primary loyalty of most EU citizens is to their nation and not to the EU. The line "millions are willing to die for their country, but no one is willing to die for the EU" says it all.

I am not denying that it would be better if Poles and the French, Greeks, Finns, and Hungarians would all wake up tomorrow and see each other as brothers and sisters, or at least as dedicated citizens of a United States of Europe. However, this is not happening. On the contrary, EU overreach is alienating more and more Europeans. The EU did well when it stuck to opening borders to trade, a move that benefited all (albeit not equally). It was well tolerated when it arranged for numerous low-key forms of administrative coordination among the nations, for student and scholar exchanges, and set minimum standards to which all industries and commerce had to adhere. However, once it introduced a shared currency, affected the budgets of its member nations, opened the borders to the free movement of labor, and pushed for the absorption of a large number of immigrants—it intruded on national identities and the particular values of the various member nations.

As a result, the EU is now trying to stand between two steps. It seeks an ever higher level of economic and administrative integration. Macron calls for introducing a banking union, an integrated budget to be formulated by the EU and which all member nations will be required to follow domestically, to be overseen by an EU finance minister. At the same time the EU is maintaining a low level of political integration, while a higher level is needed if people are to be willing to make the kind of sacrifices for each other and changes in their national policies that a much thicker unified EU policy requires. In other words, true community building is severely lagging behind economic and administrative integration. The EU now must either move up—by integrating more politically—or scale back its economic and administrative integration. Regrettably, there are many indications that it will be forced to scale back rather than move up. Nations are restoring border controls, ignoring instructions from Brussels, and public opinion polls show that increasing majorities are seeking less integration, not more. (They love "Europe" but not the EU.) In this situation, to call for more economic integration will very likely lead to more nationalism and alienation from the EU, following ever higher levels of premature supranational community building.

The difficulties experienced by the EU, and in particular the 17 members of the eurozone, highlight a major challenge faced by many nations that are not in the EU. These nations face a communitarian paradox: On the one hand, they need a significantly higher level of transnational governance, which, as I shall attempt to show, can be provided only if the expansion of such governance is paralleled by a considerable measure of transnational community building. On the other hand, this communal expansion encounters nationalism, which acts as an overpowering communitarian block by standing in the way of building more encompassing communities, ones comprised of nations. The nations involved must either find much more effective ways to overcome this block (a very challenging undertaking) or limit the level of supranational governance (that is, the scope of the EU must be scaled back).

The communitarian march

A popular narrative sees the course of human history as a movement from numerous small communities (traditional villages) to more encompassing social groupings (city-states and feudal fiefdoms) to still more encompassing groups (nation-states), leading next to regional communities (such as the EU), and ultimately, some argue, to global governance and community. Theodore Lowi illustrated this narrative using Europe as an example:

> There were approximately 500 political, state-like units [in 1500]. By 1800 there were "a few dozen" [...] After World War I, the census of states was 23, having been reduced significantly by the absorption of many states into the Union of Soviet Socialist Republics (USSR) and others by the new Yugoslavia. By 1994 there were 50 states, arising out of the collapse of the Soviet Union and Yugoslavia. There is now a movement to reduce that number by 27, in a new megastate called the European Union.[1]

In *Bounding Power*, Daniel Deudney finds that over the past 500 years "all human political communities, initially isolated or loosely connected, have become more densely and tightly interconnected and subject to various mutual vulnerabilities in a manner previously experienced only on much smaller spatial scales."[2] Deudney sees "security-from-violence" as the primary driver behind this trend.[3] People were safe in small units in the days of bows and arrows but needed increasingly more encompassing social entities once gunpowder was invented, until finally intercontinental missiles and weapons of mass destruction pushed them toward a global community.[4] Other scholars point to different motivators, including trade, population growth, and irrigation and access to water.[5] A 2008 analysis by Jürgen Klüver predicts that "the social future of mankind is probably a global society based on the traditions of Western societies with local adaptations."[6]

Actually, very few attempts have been made to form communities using nations as building blocks—they have all collapsed. These included the United Arab Republic (1958–61) and the West Indies Federation (1958–62). (It is not clear if the social entities that were combined to make the USSR and Yugoslavia were full-fledged nations by the definition presented below. In any case, they too disintegrated). The EU is by far the most advanced attempt to form a community made up of a large number of well-formed nations. Its difficulties are, therefore, particularly illuminating for those who seek to study the communitarian march toward ever more encompassing social groupings.

Matters of terminology

For the purposes of the discussion at hand, it is essential to distinguish between states and nations. In defining nations, I follow others who have defined them as communities invested in states; that is, nations have the attributes of communities, albeit imagined ones.[7] People in well-formed nations see themselves not merely as citizens who pay taxes, are entitled to services, follow public affairs, and vote, but also as members of a national community. They have a strong sense of affinity for, and loyalty to, one another and to the good of their nation, and their identities are deeply invested in the nation. On major (albeit select) issues, loyalty to the nation trumps other loyalties. They tend to have a shared moral culture (although not one necessarily shared by all citizens), a sense of a shared history, and often a sense of shared destiny, or at least of a joint future. For the sake of brevity, I shall refer to these beliefs as the ethos.

Some scholars distinguish between nations and nation-states; the former may exist within or beyond the boundaries of a state and may precede it, while the latter describes cases in which the boundaries of the nation and state are congruent. This valid distinction can be set aside here because it does not directly affect the issue under consideration—the factors which prevent the communitarian march from moving to the next supra- or post-national level.

Enter nationalism

If one employs the terms just laid out to re-examine the communitarian march, one finds that in earlier ages, there was indeed a strong overlap between the state and the community—when people lived in small tribes and villages.[8] In the subsequent stages, during much of history, the state grew in terms of both people and the territory it encompassed, but the community remained localized. For instance, during the Middle Ages in Europe, most citizens lived in pre-nation-states, in the sense that they had a parochial rather than cosmopolitan viewpoint.[9] Their cognitive maps of the world were largely limited to their immediate environment, often to their village. This localism was enforced by the rigidity of divisions of the estates, such as the aristocracy, the bourgeoisie, and the peasantry, which stifled identification with those outside one's immediate social sphere.

As a result, state realignments engendered by the various monarchies—even those that resulted in territorial reallocations (through either treaty or conquest)—mattered little to the peasantry. Thus, when the Prussian army was defeated in 1806, its fate was met with apathy by the populace, so detached were they from "the personal instrument of the crown."[10] Similarly, the French peasantry frequently demonstrated the "self-absorbed indifference [...] on which two Napoleonic dictatorships had rested."[11]

In sharp contrast, with the rise of nationalism in Europe in the nineteenth century, the great community lag was overcome; state and community overlapped again in well-formed nations. The citizens of nations personally followed national developments or were linked to their peers, leaders, or opinion makers who did. Most citizens became deeply invested in the nation. National achievements and humiliations, whether real or perceived, were experienced as individual gains and insults. The mere suggestion of making territorial concessions to other nations often resulted in sharp emotional responses. The bitter contests between Israelis and Palestinians and between Serbs and Kosovars are two cases in point.

Several historical developments enabled the transformation of the state into an imagined community—into a nation. These include the spread of education, the expansion of the mass media, and increased geographical and status mobility. Economic factors also played a role. In the pre-nation era, those in power could secure the military they needed by hiring mercenaries or drawing on the aristocracy. Local politicians (say, Chicago aldermen or New York City politicians) could gain the votes they needed by doing material favors for their constituents, by handing out money or jobs.[12] However, as the escalating demands of warfare came to require the mobilization of millions—and the same held for winning elections—those in power found that appealing to peoples' sentiments and ideals was much more economical than providing them with material goods. Appealing to national values thus became a major resource for those who sought to win wars and elections.

I keep referring to "well-formed nations" as a reminder that the depth and scope of the communal commitment to the state that nationalism entails are contiguous and not dichotomous variables. Some national communities are weak, some are growing, and others have reached a high level of integration. Thus, many of the states initially forged by colonial powers, which cut across tribal and confessional communities, resulted in weak nations. For instance, Afghanistan still has a particularly weak national community, and its citizens have strong allegiances to tribes such as the Pashtun, Tajik, and Hazara. Iraq is divided among confessional (Shia and Sunni) and ethnic groups (Arabs, Kurds, and Turkmen). Both the United States and France are examples of states formed well before their national communities developed. In the case of the United States, this development occurred mainly after the Civil War.

The closing of the communitarian gap following nationalism, after which communities again become co-extensive with the state, is evident in large segments of the world; in the nineteenth century, empires (a form of a state without a strong community) were torn apart to form national states. The process manifested itself first in Latin America, as Portugal lost Brazil and Spain hemorrhaged colonies. It then showed itself in Europe, with the dismembering of the Austro-Hungarian Empire after World War I, and in the Middle East with the parceling out of the Ottoman Empire. It was followed after World War II by the collapse of the remaining European colonial powers and the birth of scores of nations in Asia and Africa.

The point of all these observations is to note that once community caught up with the state, under nationalism, a qualitative change occurred in the relationship between the citizens and the state. Once a nation was well formed, the people (and not just the ruling classes) strenuously resisted forming more encompassing communities and jealously guarded the rights, privileges, boundaries, identity, and culture—the ethos—of their nation. Thus, nationalism is standing in the way of what is considered the "natural" or "much needed" next step in the development of the transnational order.[13]

The end of nationalism?

The thesis that powerful nationalism stands in the way of extending communities beyond state borders differs sharply from the argument that, far from presenting a formidable, potentially immutable block, the nation-state has ceased to be an effective form of social organization and is being steadily and inexorably eroded. This erosion is said to be both external (due to globalization) and internal (due to pluralization).[14] Adherents to this view—sometimes referred to as post-nationalists—maintain that economic globalization has created markets that are beyond the capabilities of traditional nation-states to regulate.[15] And immigration is said to have led to heterogeneous nations in which ethnic minorities maintain transnational diaspora cultures, divide national self-identities, and further weaken a vital source of social cohesion undergirding the nation-state.[16]

Moreover, post-nationalists view this erosion of the nation-state as heralding a liberation of sorts from a "barbaric nationalism," and point to an international political successor. Jürgen Habermas, for instance, holds that major functions must be transferred to supranational institutions, such as handling international trafficking in drugs and arms, and ecological threats.[17] This is not to suggest that the post-nationalists expect states to simply disappear.[18] Rather, they hold, we must actively construct a post-national democracy oriented around civic solidarity. Gaining the citizens of nation-states as voluntary partners in the construction of a post-national system would enable state actors to cede power to supranational authorities.

Skeptics of this approach dismiss it as chimerical, doubting the possibility of constructing a "post-national polity through deliberation and attachment to civic values."[19] They are dubious of the viability of an EU-wide citizenry, arguing that nation-states are "the largest communities within which the identitarian (membership, belongingness) aspect of citizenship still makes sense."[20]

True, nations are buffeted by forces beyond their borders that they often cannot control. The list of challenges that cannot be handled by the nations on their own is all too well known (the spread of weapons of mass destruction, economic contagions, pandemics, global warming, etc.).[21] However, so far no bodies have emerged that have proven capable of handling major problems that nations cannot—or at least, that can match the nations in this regard. Nations continue to be the relevant decision makers in all matters concerning war. For instance, although the 2011 campaign in Libya was labeled a NATO operation, the key decisions—and commitment of resources—were made by France, the United Kingdom, and the United States, and were opposed by Germany and Turkey. Nations also continue to be the main players in the global economy, as was evident during negotiations regarding the financial crisis in the eurozone. The main actors were Germany and France on one side, and Greece, as well as Italy, Ireland, Spain, and Portugal, on the other; granted, the European Central Bank did play a role as well.

Transnationalism with limited community building

Faced with both the need for more transnational governance and the communitarian block that stands in the way of forming more encompassing social groupings, nations developed various adaptations that seek more transnational governance without building a parallel community. In a previous publication, I reviewed such attempts on a global level, including the roles played by civil society bodies, networks of government officials from different countries, and a few supranational bodies (e.g., the ICC and ICANN). I showed that these bodies do not and cannot provide more than a fraction of the needed additional global governance.[22]

The following analysis is focused on the EU. Although it is but a regional body, it is by far the most advanced attempt to generate a major transnational source of governance without building a thick supranational ethos (or demos)—without building a European community that has the kind of attributes that nations now command. (I write "thick" because various social scientists have pointed out that some groups within the various European nations have formed some transnational identifies and affinities, and that many Europeans have acquired some measure, however weak, of identification with Europe. However, these are far too thin to carry the weight of supporting the kind of transnational governance that the EU has put in place and is expanding.)

The EU: the test case

The EU is by far the most successful, albeit troubled, attempt to forge a major regional source of governance that has many of the features of a state, including a parliament, an executive branch, courts, and select reinforcement mechanisms (though mainly non-coercive ones). The European Commission, the main driver of the EU, has issued thousands of directives and forged a very large number of regulations, it sets standards and harmonizes policy, and it collects revenues and subsidizes projects—all across national borders.[23]

Moreover, the EU is a particularly important natural experiment for the thesis of this chapter: that there are steep limits to the extent to which one can advance the development of transnational administrative, legal, and economic integration with little community building.[24]

The Commission's progress was made possible with rather little community building (as the term is used here), by drawing on several political and sociological mechanisms.

a.   The Commission introduced measures that benefit the various EU members (even if not equally) and hence gained their support, most clearly in removing barriers to the movement of goods.[25] The Commission standardized technical specifications for technology and products such as railroads, medical devices, and toys.[26]

b. Instead of seeking to make all members adhere to the same standards and rules, the Commission qualified nations and their industries and services, colleges, hospitals, and much else on the basis of minimum compliance. That is, although the various national providers could vary a great deal in their level of competence, achievements, and reliability, they qualified as long as they met basic standards. This is much less sociologically taxing than if the Commission were to insist that they all meet the same exact standards.

c. Numerous small measures were introduced under the radar; for instance, by being buried in complex legal documents and treaties.[27]

d. The Commission tolerated a high level of violation of its rules and policies (sometimes referred to as the compliance gap). Even before eastern enlargement, implementation of EU policy within the 15 original member states was inconsistent and weak. Gerda Falkner and Oliver Treib analyzed over 90 implementation cases of six EU labor law directives and found that, for most member states, "domestic concerns frequently prevail if there is a conflict of interests, and each single act of transposing an EU Directive tends to happen on the basis of a fresh cost-benefit analysis."[28] Christoph Knill examined the implementation of four environmental initiatives passed by the Commission between 1980 and 1993 in Germany, the United Kingdom, and France. He found that implementation of these policies was, at best, inconsistent, and in some cases he found a "dominant pattern of ineffective implementation."[29] One of the gravest examples of this disregard for EU authority is Greece's falsified budget data in its application to join the eurozone. The European Commission's statistical agency failed to alert officials to the suspicious data, which should have prevented Greece's admission to the eurozone.[30] The admission of the eastern European states, which were considerably less developed and more corrupt, led to even more violations.[31]

The net result of proceeding in these ways was a considerable increase in alienation among the electorates of many EU members.

The alienation intensified as the EU policies entered areas of great normative, emotive, and political import. A case in point is the Schengen Agreement, which removed border controls for the movement of people between 25 EU member countries. This led to large numbers of immigrants who entered Europe from the south (where nations were more open to them) moving to northern countries, whose citizens resented them. And it led to large movements of cheap labor from nations such as Poland and the Baltic countries to nations such as France and Ireland, generating still more resentment.

Why is regional community needed?

There are major differences of opinion among scholars about the way in which polities work. Some see them as the coming together of special interest groups, which work out policies that serve their respective constituencies. According to these theorists, the legislature, and more generally the government, serves as a clearinghouse of sorts. There is no need for shared values or consensus building with the public at large. The policies reflect specific interests. Indeed, when these cannot be made to converge, gridlock ensues. If polities could be made to work this way, one could build transnational regional administrative semi-states, based on negotiations among various national and transnational interest groups, with little need for community building.[32]

Members of communities are bonded with one another in affective ways; they share values and not just interests; and they are willing to make sacrifices for one another and the common good of their community—sacrifices they would be unwilling to make for others outside the community. The fact that this holds true for members of nations, but only to a rather limited extent for members of the EU, is highlighted next.

The West Germans gave the equivalent of a trillion U.S. dollars to the East Germans during the decade that followed reunification, with little hesitation. *They are fellow Germans* was about all the explanation that was needed. However, the same Germans have a very hard time granting much smaller amounts to Greece and other EU nations that are in trouble. They are not members of the proverbial tribe. As Alan Bance writes: "Before there can be federalism, it is necessary to create a set of European 'myths' (no doubt as selective as those out of which nineteenth-century nationalism was constructed) to supply 'symbolic justification' for the sacrifice of immediate interests in favour of the collective European enterprise."[33] In short, if Greece had been one of the *neue Länder*, the former East German states, it would have been bailed out without much difficulty.

Americans can readily gain insight into this same phenomenon. Once every few years, some reporter will call attention to the fact that, in the United States, Southern and Midwestern states pay substantially less in taxes but receive a disproportionately larger share of federal outlays than do the northern states. However, such stories have very short legs; *these are fellow Americans, case closed.* In contrast, when Americans are asked to extend to other nations much smaller amounts than the wealthier states (say, Connecticut and New York) give to the poorer states (such as Mississippi and Alabama), it is widely opposed. In other words, if Greece were the fifty-first American state, its troubles would be over.

The clearest demonstration of the powerful communal bonds at the national level is that people are willing to die for their nation; no one is even thinking about dying for the EU, not to mention less advanced transnational unions.

Finally, public policies—in which (since nationalism) the "masses," not just interest groups, are involved—reflect, in part, values, not just interests. This is most obvious in policies that concern so-called cultural issues such as gay marriage, abortion, separation of church and state, attitudes toward minorities and immigrants, and—in the United States—gun control. However, values play a key role in practically all policies, from whether the rich ought to be taxed more than others, to how much we should scale back economic growth in order to protect the environment, to the scope and kind of foreign aid. When there is no normative consensus, forming such policies—and, above all, implementing them—becomes much more arduous.

Indeed, studies show that movement toward building a European community has led to stronger alienation among millions of European citizens.[34] According to an analysis of Eurobarometer surveys from 1973 to 2004, net public support for the EU grew steadily in the 1980s (averaging about 42 percent) and reached an apex of 62 percent in 1991.[35] However, support then declined. By 1997, net support for integration had fallen to 39 percent. Since 2004, it has fluctuated within a 10 percentage point range of roughly 30–40 percent.[36] In 2010, net support was only 31 percent. Moreover, the supporters of the EU are concentrated in countries in which people consider their own government to be particularly inept and corrupt (e.g., Italy), while the critics are in the major European powers, especially Germany and the United Kingdom. The disaffection with the EU further intensified following the financial crisis triggered by Greece.[37]

In response, the EU is actively considering various institutional measures that would increase the power of the EU over the member nations—without any new community-building measures. For instance, Jean-Claude Trichet, president of the European Central Bank from 2003 to 2011, suggested a eurozone-wide Ministry of Finance that would ensure member states' adherence to fiscal and competitiveness policies, control the region's financial sector, and centralize representation of the currency bloc in international financial institutions like the International Monetary Fund.[38] The ministry would also monitor whether countries were pursuing the right policies to be competitive.[39] If the analysis presented here is valid, these measures would increase the tensions and difficulties of the EU, rather than help members to cope with them, because they entail more transnational decision making in matters of great import, without consensus building and the communal foundations on which it must rest.

Legitimacy without consensus?

A political science response to the communitarian block is to point to the movement toward increasing democratization of the EU. Originally, member nations had veto power on practically all matters. However, over time, various changes have been introduced (which are referred to as "deepening") that allow various EU bodies to make decisions based on majority votes of the member states and that do not require unanimity. These changes allow the EU to make more progress in state building without community building, because no single member can block policies (if they are covered under the democracy rule). Furthermore, the changes presumably provide a source of legitimacy, given that democracy is an accepted way to resolve policy differences.[40] (Legitimacy is widely defined as acting in line with established norms.[41])

Democracy, however, presumes community—or at least a measure of community—and a value consensus. As Jean-Marc Ferry puts it, any legal community must overlap with a "moral community" which would be based on "a common political culture and ... a shared historical memory."[42] First of all, those subject to the votes must recognize the legitimacy of the institution, which in turn would reflect their core values. Thus, most Americans would not view policies passed by the UN General Assembly as binding—because the United States has never recognized this body as expressing a community to which the United States belongs and whose basic values it shares. The governments of the EU members agreed to yield a measure of their sovereignty to the EU; however, large segments of their citizens did not. Hence, the fact that a democratic vote takes place often does not build legitimacy, and certainly not consensus. In other words, consensus on basic values and the legitimacy of institutions must be built before or at the least at the same time as democratic power is increased.[43] This largely has yet to take place in the EU.[44]

Of those who agree that the EU needs community building in the sense of the terms used here—not more top-down introduction of institutions, but the formation of a shared ethos—a considerable number hold, in effect, that this observation is irrelevant, because no such ethos can be formed. For instance, Richard Bellamy and Dario Castiglione dispute that a public culture founded on common values can be formed from as diverse (culturally, politically, and not least economically) a body as Europe:

> "Despite the member states sharing a loose set of liberal-democratic values, they often interpret them in different and conflicting ways. For example, they differ over the interpretation of the right to privacy, the ways they tolerate religious differences, their view of human dignity and so on, all of which reflect their very distinct political cultures ... Thus far, what the ECJ [European

Court of Justice] and member states have achieved is not so much a consensus as a series of different sorts of compromise."[45]

EU community building: past and future

The EU has sought to engage in community building through building bonds of affinity among its citizens and promoting shared values, not by introducing more top-down institutions. These efforts have taken place mainly in four areas that are widely considered to be places where community building can happen: education, language, media, and "symbols." It would take an army of social scientists years to review and evaluate all of the attempts made. Here, a few select examples are given to point to the reasons why these measures have not been very effective. One may well contest these assessments individually, but there can be no doubt about the final outcome: there is no EU ethos in the making, and the sense of affinity and shared values among EU citizens is weak and possibly declining.

Education

Currently, education is a national concern and often either excludes European history or examines it from a nation-specific perspective. The movement to Europeanize aspects of national curricula has existed since the 1970s but has met resistance from member states. The Commission strove to reach young audiences with *The Raspberry Ice Cream War*, a comic book released in 1997 that strove to promote the idea of "a peaceful Europe without frontiers" among the children of member nations.[46]

One notes that the suggested changes concern changing some textbooks and the content of some curricula, but not a sweeping Europeanization of the way history, literature, and social sciences are taught. Removing hostile and prejudicial comments is of course of merit, but education continues to be largely national and does not contribute to building a shared ethos. Furthermore, one cannot help but question how much schools can contribute to transmitting a shared ethos and implanting it in future citizens, if no such EU ethos exists in the first place. Any serious attempt to move in this direction faces the fact that integrated education has received the lowest support of all policy initiatives on the Eurobarometer.[47]

Language

Historically, the promotion of a shared language (and in very few cases, more than one) has served as a major ethos-building measure. Nation building often meant that people who spoke different tongues were strongly encouraged to use the newly promoted national language as their primary language, at least in public. Laws were enacted allowing only the use of the national language in court hearings, public documents, street signs, voting ballots, and so on.

For the EU to choose one language as its supranational tongue is neither possible nor desired. The various members have rich cultures that are deeply associated with their particular languages and access to these cultures would be largely lost if all nations chose to speak, say, French from here on out. However, the EU could have chosen for all member nations to lock in on the same second language. (This would be in line with the idea that the supranational community does not seek to replace nations but, rather, to add a layer on top of them.) In effect, English does serve as such in many EU proceedings, mainly for the elites and professionals. However, the Barcelona European Council in 2002 simply established the goal of teaching at least two foreign languages, but which particular languages was left to each individual nation to choose.[48] English is the only serious candidate to become a shared second language, but so far France, Germany, and Italy have strongly opposed this development, thus slowing down the agreement upon a shared European tongue—a major element of community building.

Media

Various attempts to fashion a European newspaper have not truly taken off. The same holds for other media, such as television and radio. One major reason is that the citizens do not share one language. The EU should consider establishing a European Broadcasting Agency, modeled after the BBC, which draws on public funds but has autonomous control of the content of its broadcasts. Its mandate would be to provide news and interpret it from a European perspective.

Europe-wide media, such as the *Financial Times*, are limited to an exclusive group of elites or have expanded to become global publications, as opposed to merely Euro-centric. In the 1980s, an experiment with a European television channel (Eurikon) was conducted by an international consortium of public broadcasters, who rotated responsibility for programming each week. This failed, due to inconsistent programming, cultural barriers, and the lack of a need for, or interest in, transnational advertising (and, therefore, a lack of funds). One observer noted, "While viewers from different countries were united in their dislike for Eurikon's programs, the precise reasons for their dislike tended to diverge along national lines."[49] While the internet has made mass transnational communication much easier, developments have been mainly confined to the private sector. Furthermore, the internet promotes communications with non-EU members just as readily as it does with members, and thus does little for EU community building in particular.

Symbols

In 2008, the European Parliament passed a proposal to display the European flag (a circle of gold stars on a dark blue background) in every meeting room and at official events; to play the European national anthem, based on Beethoven's *Ode to Joy*, at the start of each new Parliament; and to print the European motto—Unity in Diversity—on all Parliament documents. Additionally, Europe Day was formally recognized as a holiday.[50] The EU emblem has been imprinted on license plates, on passports, and in numerous other places.

These and other such measures have done little for EU community building. Some efforts do not capture any particular normative or affective content (e.g., the emblem). Others speak to universal values and neither reflect nor promote EU-specific values (e.g.,

Ode to Joy as the EU anthem). Above all, symbols can express and even help to promote shared values—when they exist—but cannot serve instead of values or be created out of whole cloth.

In short, so far the EU community-building efforts, to the extent that they sought to build a shared ethos, have been particularly ineffectual.

What can be done?

EU megalogues

Societies, even large ones, engage in dialogues about public policies that link many local dialogues into one national give and take—a "megalogue." Typically, just one or two topics top the megalogue's agenda; for instance, whether or not to legalize gay marriage, engage in war, introduce austerity measures during an economic slowdown—or join the eurozone. These dialogues mainly concern values and are not dominated by considerations of facts. They often seem endless and impassionate, but actually frequently lead to new, widely shared public understandings. Such understandings, in turn, often provide a well-grounded normative basis for changes in public policy and institutions; they generate new sources of legitimacy.[51] In the United States, for instance, public dialogues paved the way for new legislation to protect the environment and for the creation of the Environmental Protection Agency, and preceded the abolition of legal segregation and the formation of the Equal Employment Opportunity Commission.

The fact that the majority of EU citizens feel ill-informed about the EU and the actions of its various institutions, and that their views are not considered when policies are changed, suggests the merit of seeking to engender EU-wide megalogues.

Launching EU-wide referendums is one way to launch a megalogue, as long as ample time is allowed before the referendums are taken—that is, a period during which people can consult with one another and their leaders before voting. Megalogues, dialogues, and some referendums do take place in Europe, but they are, as a rule, conducted within each nation. This is in part because people still see themselves primarily as citizens of this or that nation rather than of the EU, and in part because the points of closure—the endpoints or changes in public policy that these dialogues lead to or support—are often on the national level rather than EU-wide. To enhance the formation of a core of shared values associated with the EU, megalogues and referendums had best take place in all member nations at the same time and be tied to decisions to be made on the EU, and not the internal, national level.

The issues to be discussed and voted on at an EU-wide level need to be salient enough to draw people into participating. Suggested changes in immigration policy are an obvious example. Finally, to succeed, participating citizens must be able to trust that the results of these referendums will be binding—that EU officials will be required to heed them, rather than view them as merely advisory.

EU-wide voting

As EU consensus solidifies, the EU should move towards EU-wide voting on EU candidates, rather than the current system in which votes for the EU Parliament are conducted largely for national candidates, on a national basis. Currently, most candidates running for a seat in the European Parliament are put up by national parties and campaign only in their home country. In the European Parliament, most "European parties" are largely comprised of alliances between existing national parties; they function less like political parties and more like international coalitions.

A switch to European parties and candidates raises numerous issues concerning whether different weight should be assigned to the voters of various countries and how to protect minorities.[52] These are concerns that cannot be handled within the confines of this chapter but clearly must be resolved before major progress on this front can be anticipated.

Standing between two steps

The arguments laid out above suggest that if the EU is unable to engage in much stronger community building—if there is no significant transfer of commitment and loyalty from the citizens of the member nations to the evolving supranational community—the EU will be unable to sustain the kind of encompassing state-like, shared governance endeavor that it attempts to advance. The EU needs either to move up to a higher level of community or to retreat to being only a free trade zone enriched by numerous legal and administrative shared arrangements. It will be unable to sustain a shared currency and will be forced to restore national veto power on numerous important policies, in particular those that have a significant normative and emotive content. One the one hand, the EU needs to be able to overcome the nationalism that blocks progress on the communitarian march toward more encompassing social groupings—to parallel the need for more encompassing and effective transnational governance. On the other hand, it seems unable to meet this challenge. Hence, much as one may favor its communitarian advancement, one must acknowledge that the EU is more likely to scale back, as it is already doing with regard to the freedom of movement of people within the EU.[53]

The world is watching, both because of the importance of the EU per se and because several other regional bodies (such as the African Union, the Central American Integration System, and the Association of Southeast Asian Nations) in much earlier stages of development seek ways to engage in community building, with nations as the members of the community.[54]

Part Four
Response to New Technology

ELEVEN

Should AI be regulated?

With Oren Etzioni

Policy makers and academics are raising more and more questions about the ways the legal and moral order can accommodate a large and growing number of machines, robots, and instruments equipped with artificial intelligence (AI)—hereinafter referred to as "smart instruments." Many of these questions spring from the fact that smart instruments, such as driverless cars, have a measure of autonomy; they make many decisions on their own, well beyond the guidelines their programmers provided. Moreover, these smart instruments make decisions in very opaque ways, and they are learning instruments with guidance systems that change as they carry out their missions.

For example, a California policeman issued a warning to the passenger of a Google self-driving car because the car impeded traffic by driving traveling too slowly.[1] But whom should the policeman have cited? The passenger? The owner? The programmer? The car's computer? Similarly, Google faced charges that its search engine discriminated against women by showing ads for well-paying jobs to men more frequently than to women,[2] and that it favored its own shops in search results.[3] The inability of mere mortals to trace how such biases come about illustrates the challenges that smart machines pose to the legal and moral order. The same questions apply to findings that ads for websites providing arrest records were "significantly more likely to show up on searches for distinctively black names or a historically black fraternity."[4] Was there intent? Who or what should be held liable for the resulting harm? How can the government deter repeat offenses by the same instruments? This chapter provides a preliminary response to these and several related questions both in cases of limited harm (e.g., a program that causes a driverless car to crash into another) and with regard to greater potential harm (e.g., the fear that smart instruments may rebel against their makers and harm mankind).[5]

This chapter focuses on the relationship between AI and the legal order; the relationship between AI and the moral order requires a separate analysis.[6] Although both the legal and moral orders reflect the values of one and the same society, the chapter treats them separately because they choose and enforce values in different ways. In the legal realm, long-established institutions such as the legislature and courts sort out which values to enforce, but there are no such authoritative institutions in the social and moral realm. There is no Supreme Court for ethics—nor is one called for. Instead, the moral realm chooses values to enforce through continuous moral dialogues that often lead to new SMUs over time.[7]

We cannot stress enough that by legal order we mean not just law enforcement, but also preventive law, such as routinely auditing businesses, positioning speed cameras, and employing customs officials. We shall see that maintaining the law in the cyber age requires new instruments much more than new laws.

The unique attributes of AI

Reports about the legal challenges posed by smart instruments may at first seem overblown. After all, the law has successfully regulated a wide variety of instruments; regulations govern a great range of things from the level of noise a lawn mower may legally make to the emissions a factory can legally produce.

Some argue that it would be easy to require self-driving (alternately called autonomous or driverless) cars to heed the same laws as old-fashioned cars. However, this would be akin to requiring that Model T cars obey the laws set for horse-drawn carriages. Forcing autonomous cars to abide by prevailing laws would sacrifice many of their capabilities. For example, if granted a lane of their own, driverless cars could travel safely at much greater speeds than old cars. Indeed, history shows that the invention of new technologies—from guns to DNA-typing, from steam engines to unmanned aerial vehicles—has required some new legislation. While bolstering the legal order may require a few new laws, we will see that it is more important to develop new instruments to keep AI legal.

Both new and old laws require the help of AI because of the unique attributes of smart instruments. These devices have *considerable autonomy* in the sense that they make numerous choices "on their own."[8] That is, these instruments use complex algorithms to respond to environmental inputs independently of real-time human input; they "can figure things out for themselves."[9] Smart machines may deviate from or act against the guidelines that the original programmers installed. For instance, self-driving cars decide when to change speed, how much distance to keep from other cars, and may decide to travel faster than the law allows—when they learn that other cars often violate the speed limits. Automatic emergency braking systems,[10] which stop cars in response to perceived dangers without human input, are becoming more common.[11] Consumers complain of false alarms, sudden stops that are dangerous to other cars,[12] and that these brakes force cars to proceed in a straight line even if the driver tries to steer them elsewhere.

AI-equipped autonomous operating systems are becoming *highly opaque* black boxes to human beings. That is, people are unable to follow the steps that these machines are taking to reach whatever conclusions they reach. Viktor Mayer-Schönberger and Kenneth Cukier note: "Today's computer code can be opened and inspected … With big-data analysis, however, this traceability will become much harder. The basis of an algorithm's predictions may often be far too intricate for most people to understand." They add that "the algorithms and datasets behind them, will become black boxes that offer us no accountability, traceability, or confidence."[13]

Moreover, the AI programs that guide smart instruments are *learning systems* that constantly review changing conditions and the performance of the instruments they guide—and then modify the internal guidelines accordingly. Smart instruments do not stop collecting data once they have been launched; instead, further data collection enables smart instruments to keep learning from experience and improve their performance. These AI programs, therefore, may stray considerably from the guidelines their programmers initially gave them. Indeed, smart instruments may counteract their makers' and users' instructions. For instance, the Tesla car that killed its passenger in 2016 was programmed not to violate the rules of the road, but was speeding when the crash occurred. Hence, self-driving cars cannot be tested and certified before hitting the road, and then let loose under the assumption that their guidance systems will not change in response to new information collected as these cars drive about.

AI guardians

Smart instruments' unique attributes pose a legal challenge when these instruments cause harm. Was there intent? Who or what is responsible for the harm? And whom should the law hold liable? The following mental exercise illustrates the issue. Imagine that a bank is sued for denying a disproportionate amount of loan applications made by African Americans, as compared to those made by white Americans. In response, the bank's officials point out that for the past three years the bank has relied on an AI program to grant or deny loans. When selecting a program, the bank stipulated that the software must refrain from using race or any surrogate variable, such as zip code, to determine creditworthiness. Still, the plaintiffs show that the program discriminated, by presenting to the court instances in which the bank denied loans to African American applicants with credit scores as good as or better than white applicants whose loans the bank approved.

A finding of discrimination does not settle the matter. The questions of intent and responsibility for discrimination stand because the law generally punishes deliberate offenses much more harshly than unintended ones—see, for instance, the difference between first-degree murder and involuntary manslaughter.[14] It is hence necessary to answer the questions of intent and responsibility in order to determine whom should be held liable for harm done. To return to our mental exercise—the hypothetical court has established that harm has occurred, but it still needs to determine whether the bank deliberately caused the harm by instructing programmers to use race as a variable—despite its claims. Or did the program "learn" by looking at the data that race can serve as an efficient surrogate variable for other factors such as class, education, and geography?

The court could ask an expert in computer programming to serve as a witness, but she is likely to point out that no human being can "read" an AI program to determine whether the bias it showed reflects the programmers' actions or the program's autonomous actions. Above all, no person can trace the steps that a program went through to reach its autonomous decisions, as the program maintains no records of these steps. (The steps are carried out by the computers involved, on their own, which do not keep a list of the very large number of complex calculations they make.)

This chapter suggests that what the court—and all those who need to determine intent, responsibility, and liability for the acts of smart instruments—needs are *AI programs to examine AI programs.* The law needs smart instruments to deal with smart instruments. Until now, society has treated AI largely as one field that encompasses many programs, ranging from airplane autopilots to surgical robots. From here on, AI should be divided into two categories. The first category would consist of operational AI programs—the computerized "brains" that guide smart instruments. The second category would be composed of oversight AI programs that review the first category's decision making and keep the decisions in line with the law. These oversight programs, which this chapter calls "AI guardians," would include AI programs to interrogate, discover, supervise, audit, and guarantee the compliance of operational AI programs.

Self-driving cars illustrate the role of such AI guardians. Because these cars are programmed to learn and adapt, they need a particular kind of AI guardian program, an AI monitor, to come along for the ride to ensure that the autonomous car's learning and decision making does not lead it to violate the law. Unlike human passengers, these programs would not tire of constantly checking the speed limit and distance from other cars, and they can carry out their oversight duties even in the absence of a passenger.

The AI community has not yet differentiated between operational and oversight AI programs, in large part because many AI scholars shared the original ideals associated with the formation of the internet. Those holding original ideals hoped that the internet would be a "flat" realm, a village in which all people could cooperate.[15] They did not envision a hierarchy in which some supervise and regulate others.[16] However, over the years, the internet has turned from a village into a jungle riddled with hackers, con artists, thieves, bullies, and free riders. It increasingly needs order-enhancing institutions. Hence, the world would benefit from the development of a slew of AI guardians to prevent deviations from the instructions incorporated into AI programs by their human designers.

An interrogator AI would establish whether AI operational programs observe privacy laws by determining whether such programs use personal medical information to target consumers, to make employment decisions, to extend or withdraw credit, and more. Such an AI interrogator could determine not merely whether there was an illegal use of medical information, but also whether the abuse was a deliberate act on the part of the programmers (or those who retained them) or came about as a result of the operation of the AI system. That is, an AI interrogator could find out if the misuse of information was the result of illegally obtaining medical data or of working out medical information from other personal information—the latter being currently legal. For instance, if an AI program at a bank called in a cancer patient's loan, the program's AI interrogator would assess whether the program had acted on information illegally obtained from a hospital or doctor's office or had worked out the person's condition on the basis of consumption decisions (e.g., the person purchased a wig, great amounts of soap, and vitamin supplements).

Other AI guardians could carry out a wide range of oversight roles. Auditor AI programs could determine whether financial planning software directs its users to investments or insurance plans in which those who developed the software have a financial interest. AI auditors could also establish whether search engine results are biased in favor of the corporation that provides the search results or its advertisers. Meanwhile, inspector AI programs could review AI cyber security programs, such as those that restrict access to information, and could report and follow up the response to incidents of unauthorized access. As more instruments incorporate operational AI programs, the need for various AI guardians to carry out oversight tasks will grow. That is, there will be more need for AI programs to keep other AI programs legal.

AI guardians have two major advantages over human "guardians." First, AI guardians are much less likely to violate the intellectual property rights and privacy of those they review, because they have no motives or interests of their own. Second, AI guardians need only a tiny fraction of the resources and time it would take for a human being to carry out the same oversight missions—if humans could carry out such reviews in the first place.

Lock or override?

At first blush, it may seem obvious that there should be an override device to limit smart instruments' autonomous acts. Such a device would provide humans with a sort of veto power over the acts of the smart instruments. For instance, if passengers in an autonomous car witness people trapped in a burning car on the side of the road, they should be able to stop the car in order to get out and help; the self-driving car, without such an override, would otherwise just barrel along. People should be able to slow the car down to enjoy the scenery, or exceed the speed limit to rush to a hospital. So far, all driverless cars have such a mechanism, and several states require that self-driving cars should operate only in the presence of a passenger qualified to drive.[17] New York law even requires that someone should keep one hand on the steering wheel at all times.[18]

By contrast, some have argued that no override should exist because people would abuse it by speeding while intoxicated or driving recklessly out of "road rage" and, in so doing, put themselves and others in danger. As one observer put it, "We often regulate and take control from individuals precisely because we cannot trust them to refrain from acting in their own interest."[19] There is also a communitarian side to this argument: if self-driving cars coordinate their movements, which would greatly enhance safety, individualized overrides would undermine this benefit of autonomous cars.[20]

In response, one notes that the law in free societies rarely prevents people from modifying instruments they own and operate; the exception being those situations in which modifications would cause great harm (e.g., driving without a seat belt). Society deters most "bad" use of tools and instruments by punishing, after the fact, those who abuse their power. The same principle should apply to autonomous instruments.

Moreover, given that AI guardians' oversight programs can accommodate many permutations suggests that the two viewpoints can be reconciled. An AI program could be designed to steer to the side of the road and stop if a person overrides the original program and then engages in dangerous behavior, but otherwise to allow passengers to override the program at will. That is, the program could assess each override and could overrule some. AI programs should also be able to coordinate group behavior even if some members of the group are robots and some are human. None of this may be true of today's AI programs, but it seems reasonable that they will be able to do so in the future.

No fishing

Although it is very rarely phrased in this way, civil societies do not seek full law enforcement. This odd preference stems in part from the likelihood that most, if not all, citizens commit a crime at some point—many commit quite a few. If the authorities fined or arrested everyone who smoked a joint, drove faster than the speed limit after a few drinks, or who did not pay gift tax on large expenditures they made for their children, few citizens, if any, would be spared. Civil societies, hence, tend often to look the other way and rely on sporadic enforcement. This quest for less-than-full law enforcement is one reason why civil libertarians reject "fishing expeditions," that is, cases in which a law enforcement agent abuses a targeted search to try to find evidence of *any* wrongdoing, not covered by the warrant. Such searches are viewed as a violation of one's civil rights.[21] Indeed, this is the reason why warrants include "particularity"—details about what the authorities claim to be looking for, rather than just going fishing.[22] Other reasons for limiting the scope of search warrants include preventing privacy violations, opposition to the surveillance of innocent people, and preventing the authorities from harassing civilians.

Making instruments smarter has a major side-effect: it makes detecting even minor crimes and misdemeanors easy, threatening the ban on fishing and all that it protects. Both the private and the public sectors are developing programs that can track an individual's internet activity;[23] turn cell phones into microphones and tracking devices and computers into cameras;[24] implant tiny radio transmitters into clothes;[25] and much else. The development of these programs is escalating due to the advent of cloud storage and the "internet of things," where objects from refrigerators to thermostats and fitness-tracking bands have sensors that can communicate personal information to third parties and government authorities. [26]

The compilation, analysis, and extrapolation (cybernation)[27] by AI programs of large amounts of personal information, stored or collected by these various smart instruments, further greatly increases the effects of these new technologies, making higher levels of law enforcement much easier. For example, typical CCTVs—private surveillance cameras owned and mounted in one's business, parking lot, or residential lobby—pick up very few facts about one person, at one locality, at one point in time, and keep the information for a short period. The opposite holds true for Microsoft's Domain Awareness System, first tested in New York City in 2012. The program collects information from all over the city from various CCTV cameras, speed cameras, license plate readers, and radiation detectors.[28] While the system does not yet utilize facial recognition, it could be readily expanded to include such data, as well as cell phone location information. The Domain Awareness System stores all this information for five years or more, and authorities can use it at will to draw a full profile of a person's public life. This is but one example of many in which "spot" information about a person is combined with other information about that person, and then those data are subjected to AI analysis that enables authorities to draw conclusions about the person, well beyond what is revealed by direct observation.[29]

To prevent such comprehensive and continuous surveillance of people in public, legislatures should pass new legislation that would require the automatic erasure of information gathered by localized instruments such as toll booths and CCTVs after a short period of time, except in special situations such as following a terrorist attack or an amber alert. Legislation should also prohibit cybernation of all sensitive personal information,[30] for instance information about one's medical condition, and ban the use of insensitive information to divine sensitive information. To enforce these regulations, governments should pass laws mandating the use of AI guardians to audit and monitor operational AI surveillance programs. In short, the law could use AI-assisted oversight to curb AI-enhanced surveillance.

Conclusion

Thoughtful people have asked for centuries: "Who will guard the guardians?"[31] We have no new answer to this question, which has never been answered well. For now, the best we can hope for is that all smart instruments will be outfitted with a readily locatable off-switch—to grant ultimate control to human agents over both operational and oversight AI programs.[32]

TWELVE

A privacy doctrine for the cyber age

Many on the right and on the left feel that technological development is eroding privacy. In addition, the main legal concepts that deal with privacy are obsolete. A privacy doctrine suitable for the cyber age must address a radical change in the type and scale of violations that people face, especially that the greatest current threats to privacy come not at the point that personal information is collected but, rather, from the secondary uses of such information. Often-cited court cases, such as *Katz, Berger, Smith, Karo, Knotts, Kyllo*—and most recently *Jones*—concern whether or not the initial collection of information was in compliance with the U.S. Constitution. They do not address the fact that personal information that was legally obtained may nevertheless be used later to violate privacy—that the ways such information is stored, collated with other pieces of information, analyzed, and distributed or accessed often entail very significant violations of privacy.[1] Moreover, although a considerable number of laws and court cases cover these secondary usages of information, they do not come together to make a coherent doctrine of privacy—and most assuredly not one that addresses the unique challenges of the cyber age.[2]

True, collected personal information was subject to secondary abuses even when it was largely paper bound (e.g., in police blotters or FBI files). Indeed, when Warren and Brandeis published their groundbreaking 1890 article in the *Harvard Law Review*,[3] considered to be the "genesis of the right of privacy,"[4] they were not concerned about gossip per se (a first-order privacy violation) but about the wider distribution of intimate details through the media (a secondary violation).[5] However, the digitization of information, the widespread use of the internet and computers, and the introduction of AI systems to analyze vast amounts of data have increased the extent, volume, scope, and kinds of secondary usages by so many orders of magnitude that it is difficult to find a proper expression to capture the import of this transformation.[6] The main point is not that information can now be processed at a tiny fraction of the cost and at incomparably faster speeds than when it was paper bound, which is certainly the case, but that modes of analysis—which divine new personal information out of personal data previously collected—that are common today were simply inconceivable when most personal information was paper bound.[7] Because these observations are critical to all that follows, and because the term "secondary usages" (which implies usages less important than the first or primary ones) is a rather weak one, from here on I employ the term "cybernation" to refer to information that is digitized, stored, processed, and formatted for mass distribution. Cybernated data can be employed in two distinct ways, and both represent a serious and growing threat to privacy. A discrete piece of personal information, collected at one point in time ("spot" information), may be used for some purpose other than that for which it was originally deemed constitutional, or spot information may be pieced together with other data to generate new information about the person's most inner and intimate life.

The cyber-age privacy doctrine must lay down the foundations on which Congress can develop laws and the courts can accumulate cases that will determine not merely what information the government may legally collect but also what it might do with that data. According to some legal scholars, the District of Columbia Circuit's decision in *Maynard* and the concurring opinion by the Supreme Court's justices in *Jones* provide the building blocks for this new edifice, sometimes referred to as a mosaic theory of the Fourth Amendment, under which "individual actions of law enforcement that are not searches for Fourth Amendment purposes may become searches when taken together en masse."[8] This observation is based on Justice Alito's argument that the GPS tracking of a vehicle on a public highway constituted a search because of the length of time over which the monitoring took place (28 days). This opens the door to taking into account the volume of information collected, and presumes that, while limited amounts of collection may be permissible, large amounts could constitute a violation of privacy. *Jones*, however, still deals only with collection. Hence, most of the work of laying down the foundations for the protection of privacy from cybernation remains to be carried out.

Assumption

Moving beyond Katz

Since 1967, the U.S. legal system has drawn on the twin concepts of personal and societal expectations of privacy to determine whether a Fourth Amendment "search" has taken place. This chapter assumes that relying on both or either expectations of privacy, as articulated by Justice Harlan in his concurring opinion in *Katz*, is indefensible and that it should be allowed to fade from legal practice. Indeed, Justice Harlan himself adopted rather quickly a critical view of his two-pronged test. Four years after *Katz*, in his dissent for *United States v. White*, Harlan wrote, "[w]hile these formulations represent an advance over the unsophisticated trespass analysis of the common law, they too have their limitations and can, ultimately, lead to the substitution of words for analysis. The analysis must, in my view, transcend the search for subjective expectations."[9]

The reasonable expectation of privacy standard has since faced a range of strong criticisms.[10] In his widely cited article on the Fourth Amendment, Anthony G. Amsterdam writes,

> An actual, subjective expectation of privacy obviously has no place in a statement of what Katz held or in a theory of what the fourth amendment protects. It can neither add to, nor can its absence detract from, an individual's claim to fourth amendment protection. If it could, the government could diminish each person's subjective expectations of privacy merely by announcing half-hourly on television that 1984 was being advanced by a decade and that we were all forthwith being placed under comprehensive electronic

surveillance ... Fortunately, neither Katz nor the fourth
amendment asks what we expect of government. They
tell us what we should demand of government.[11]

A leading scholar of the Fourth Amendment and privacy, Orin
Kerr, concedes, "[w]hat counts as a 'reasonable expectation of
privacy' is very much up for grabs,"[12] and much-respected students
of privacy Charles Whitebread and Christopher Slobogin charge
that the Supreme Court has sent "mixed signals" on how to apply
this standard.[13]

The absurdity of *Katz* is revealed by contemplating the
following example: Assume a municipal government announces
that, for public health reasons, anyone who relieves themselves
in a public pool would be charged with a misdemeanor. This
government would then insert a dye (which unfortunately only
exists in Hollywood's fertile imagination) that would form a dark
blue cloud around anyone who violates the ordinance, but would
not announce the introduction of this dye. By *Katz*, surely a person
could argue that their expectation of privacy has been grossly
violated, as they did not expect to be detected when peeing in
the pool. Would it be therefore reasonable to rule this ordinance
unconstitutional and to dismiss the charges against them? And once
the introduction of the dye is made public, how many people would
have to know about it before it is no longer reasonable to expect
privacy in the matter? And who determines what is a reasonable
expectation, and how? Would one announcement about the new
dye suffice, or must it be regularly advertised?

Or, take those who speak in a sizeable political meeting. They
may well have no expectation of privacy. However, surely they
should be protected from government surveillance in such a setting
under most circumstances, to protect their privacy (among other
reasons).[14] And do new technologies change what is expected,
with, say, Facebook lowering the standards of privacy because so
many people post so much private information? The Electronic
Communications Privacy Act (ECPA) protects emails for only 90
days, during which time a warrant is needed for the government
to read them. After that, a subpoena from any prosecutor will do,
without judicial oversight, because in 1986 the thought of keeping
emails around that long was ridiculous because the cost of storing

them was so high. Does anyone expect that their emails are private (to the extent that they are) for 90 days but not for longer?

As to the societal expectation of privacy, a sociologist is keen to know which, if any, communities will be polled to establish what this expectation is.[15] Is it the privacy expected by the community of which the defendant is a member—say Spanish Harlem? Or is it the city of New York, or the United States, or the judge's country club? The fact that judges are free to assume they can rely on their sociological instincts as to what the community expects seems a strange foundation to rely on to determine when a search violates the Constitution.[16]

Finally, the whole notion is circular. Mr. Katz—and all others—either has or does not have an expectation of privacy *depending on what the Supreme Court rules.* Jim Harper put it well when he wrote: "Societal expectations are guided by judicial rulings, which are supposedly guided by societal expectations, which in turn are guided by judicial rulings, and so on."[17]

Four years after the Supreme Court ruled that the police had violated Katz's Fourth Amendment rights by bugging a public pay phone without a warrant, the Court held in *United States v. White* that no warrant was needed to record a conversation in a private home![18] A reasonable person would expect that Mr. White has a higher expectation of privacy in his home than Mr. Katz has in a public phone booth. Nor is there any reason to believe that "society" found the government's surveillance to be more reasonable in White's home than in the public booth.

Particularly relevant to what follows is that various court cases that draw on *Katz* seem not to recognize what might be called a "split condition"—that is, situations in which the government collects information in a way that would be considered constitutional because it was "expected," but then uses and distributes it in "unexpected" ways, which would, thus, be in violation of the Constitution. There are, of course, many such split situations, and these situations should be covered by any comprehensive theory of privacy.

In short, it is difficult for a reasonable person to make sense out of *Katz*. Court rulings on whether a collection of personal information is a "search" by Justice Harlan's formula seem to be highly dependent on what judges think a person or "society" would expect, without determining in any half-objective way what these expectations actually are. And, at the same time, such standards ignore that rulings on privacy recast these expectations. It may take a long time before *Katz* is repealed. Meanwhile, more reasonable criteria for privacy need to be developed and used to, in effect, replace *Katz*.

But not back to "the castle"

To suggest that the time has come to leave behind the reasonable expectation of privacy standard is not to say that the courts should revert to pre-*Katz* Fourth Amendment analysis, which gave considerable weight to the home as the locus of privacy. In *Katz* the majority ruled that "the Fourth Amendment protects people, not places," rejecting the "trespass" doctrine enunciated in *Olmstead*. However, even after this, the home remained largely inviolable in the eyes of the courts. It seems that *Katz* did not detach Fourth Amendment safeguards from the home but, rather, extended the sphere of privacy beyond it to other protected spaces. Information collected about events in one's home is still often considered *a priori* a violation of privacy, while much more license is granted to the state in collecting information about conduct in public and commercial spaces. As Justice Scalia put it, "'[a]t the very core' of the Fourth Amendment 'stands the right of a man to retreat into his own home and there be free from unreasonable governmental intrusion.' With few exceptions, the question whether a warrantless search of a home is reasonable and hence constitutional must be answered no."[19] This is an idea that has deep roots in American and English common law: "Zealous and frequent repetition of the adage that a 'man's house is his castle,' made it abundantly clear that both in England and the Colonies 'the freedom of one's house' was one of the most vital elements of English liberty."[20] In *Dow Chemical Company v. United States*, the Court established that the expectation of privacy was lower in an industrial plant than a home because the latter "is fundamentally a sanctuary, where personal concepts of self and family are forged, where relationships are nurtured and where people normally feel free to express themselves in intimate ways."[21]

Feminist scholars, correctly, roundly criticized the inviolability of the home and the private/public distinction in privacy law. Catharine MacKinnon writes that the problem with granting the home extra protection is that "while the private has been a refuge for some, it has been a hellhole for others, often at the same time."[22] Linda McClain points out that freedom from state interference in the home "renders men unaccountable for what is done in private—rape, battery, and other exploitation."[3]

Moreover, the private/public distinction is rapidly declining in importance in general,[24] and with regard to privacy in particular.[25] We saw considerable evidence to this effect in the discussion of the privatization of force, in particular in the discussion of privacy merchants (see Chapter Two). Marc Jonathon Blitz made the case compelling with regard to the cyber age, and hence is quoted here at some length:

> The 1969 case *Stanley v. Georgia* forbade the government from restricting the books that an individual may read or the films he may watch "in the privacy of his own home." Since that time, the Supreme Court has repeatedly emphasized that *Stanley's* protection applies solely within the physical boundaries of the home: While obscene books or films are protected inside of the home, they are not protected en route to it—whether in a package sent by mail, in a suitcase one is carrying to one's house, or in a stream of data obtained through the Internet.
>
> However adequate this narrow reading of *Stanley* may have been in the four decades since the case was decided, it is ill-suited to the twenty-first century, where the in-home cultural life protected by the Court in *Stanley* inevitably spills over into, or connects with, electronic realms beyond it. Individuals increasingly watch films not, as the defendant in *Stanley* did, by bringing an eight millimeter film or other physical copy of the film into their house, but by streaming it through the Internet. Especially as eReaders, such as the Kindle, and tablets, such as the iPad, proliferate, individuals read books by downloading digital copies of them. They store their

own artistic and written work not in a desk drawer or in a safe, but in the "cloud" of data storage offered to them on far-away servers.[26]

Privacy, it follows, is best viewed as a personal sphere that follows an individual irrespective of location. This is a viewpoint that Christopher Slobogin refers to as the protection-of-personhood theory of privacy, which "views the right to privacy as a means of ensuring individuals are free to define themselves."[27] Privacy plays the same role whether one is in the home or out in public: "Because a substantial part of our personality is developed in public venues, through rituals of our daily lives that occur outside the home and outside the family, cameras that stultify public conduct can stifle personality development."[28] If the government uses a long-distance "shotgun mic" to eavesdrop on the conversations of two persons walking in a public park, such a search is clearly more intrusive than if the government measured the heat setting in their kitchen. This is the case because conversations are much more revealing about the person, including their medical condition, political views, and so on, than their preferred heat setting. In short, privacy is best not home bound but person centered.

A "social policy" model of the Fourth Amendment

The cyber-age privacy doctrine concerns the normative principles that underlie both the evolving interpretations of the Constitution and the laws enacted by Congress, reflecting changes in the moral culture of the society. It hence deals both with the Fourth Amendment and public policy. Such normative comprehensive changes have occurred in other areas. For instance, the civil rights movement has led to changes in the position of the Supreme Court (e.g., from *Plessy v. Ferguson* to *Brown v. Board of Education*) and to acts of Congress (e.g., the Voting Rights Act of 1965). More recently, changes were introduced both by the courts and by various legislatures reflecting changes in the characterization of same-sex marriage in the moral culture. Now such a change is called for with regard to the concept of privacy. This chapter next discusses the normative principles of such a reconstituted concept.

In seeking to base a privacy doctrine neither on expectations of privacy nor on location, this chapter draws on a liberal communitarian philosophy that assumes that individual rights, such as the right to privacy, must be balanced with concerns for the common good, such as those about public health and national security.[29] (By contrast, authoritarian and East Asian communitarians tend to be exclusively concerned with the common good, or pay heed to rights only to the extent that they serve the rulers' aims.[30] At the opposite end of the spectrum, libertarians and several contemporary liberals privilege individual rights and autonomy over societal formulations of the common good.) Although the term "common good" is not one often found in legal literature, its referent is rather close to what is meant by "public interest," which courts frequently recognize, and a similar concept is found in the U.S. Constitution's reference to the quest for a "more perfect union."

The Fourth Amendment reads: "The right of the people to be secure in their persons, houses, papers, and effects, against *unreasonable* searches and seizures, shall not be violated."[31] This is a prime example of a liberal communitarian text because it does not employ the absolute, rights-focused language of many other amendments (e.g., "Congress shall make *no* law"), but recognizes on the face of it that there are reasonable searches, understood as those in which a compelling public interest takes precedence over personal privacy.

This line of analysis assumes that the communitarian balance is meta-stable. That is, for societies to maintain a sound communitarian regime—a careful balance between individual rights and the common good—they must constantly adjust their public policies and laws in response to changing external circumstances (e.g., 9/11) and internal developments (e.g., FBI overreach). Moreover, given that societal steering mechanisms are rather loose, societies tend to over-steer and must correct their corrections with still further adjustments. For example, in the mid-1970s, the Church and Pike Committees investigated abuses by the Central Intelligence Agency, FBI and NSA, uncovering "domestic spying on Americans, harassment and disruption of targeted individuals and groups, assassination plots targeting foreign leaders, infiltration, and manipulation of media and business."[32] As a result, Congress passed the Foreign Intelligence Surveillance Act of 1978 and created the Foreign Intelligence Surveillance Court to limit the surveillance of American citizens by the U.S. government.[33] After 9/11, several reports concluded that the reforms had gone too far by blocking the type of interagency intelligence sharing that could have forestalled the terrorist attacks.[34] As a result, the USA PATRIOT Act was enacted in a great rush and, according to its critics, sacrificed privacy excessively in order to enhance security and "correct" what are considered the excesses of the reforms that the Church and Pike Committees set into motion. Since then, the USA PATRIOT Act itself has been recalibrated.[35]

At each point in time, one must hence ask whether society is tilting too far in one direction or the other. Civil libertarians tend to hold that rights in general and privacy in particular are not adequately protected. The government tends to hold that national security and public safety require additional limitations on privacy. It is the mission of legal scholars, public intellectuals, and concerned citizens to nurture dialogues that help to sort out in which direction corrections must next be made.[36] Note that often some tightening in one area ought to be combined with some easing in others. For instance, currently a case can be made that TSA screening regulations are too tight, while the monitoring of whether visitors and temporary residents committed to leaving the U.S. actually do so is too loose.

Orin Kerr and Peter Swire engage in an important dialogue on whether the issues presented above are best suited for treatment by the courts or by Congress, and whether they are largely viewed through the prism of the Fourth Amendment or congressional acts. The following discussion treats both as if they were an amalgam.

Four criteria help to specify the liberal communitarian approach to privacy.[37] First, a liberal democratic government will limit privacy only if it faces a well-documented and large-scale threat to the common good (such as to public safety or public health), not merely a hypothetical threat or one limited to a few individuals or localities (I avoid the term "clear and present danger," despite the similarity in meaning, because it has a specific legal reference not here intended). The main reason why this threshold must be cleared is because modifying legal precepts—and with them the ethical, social, public philosophies that underlie them—endangers their legitimacy. Changes, therefore, should not be undertaken unless there is strong evidence that either the common good or privacy has been significantly undermined.

Second, if the finding is that the common good needs shoring up, one had best seek to establish whether this goal can be achieved without introducing new limits on privacy. For instance, this is achieved by removing personally identifying information (such as names, addresses, and social security numbers) when medical records are needed by researchers, thus allowing access to data previously not accessible. True, various technical difficulties arise in securing the anonymity of the data. Several ingenious suggestions have been made to cope with this challenge.[38] Conversely, if privacy needs shoring up, one should look for ways to proceed that impose no "losses" to the common good, such as introducing audit trails.

Third, to the extent that privacy-curbing measures must be introduced, they should be as unintrusive as possible. For example, many agree that drug tests should be conducted on those directly responsible for the lives of others, such as school bus drivers. Some employers, however, resort to highly intrusive visual surveillance to ensure that the sample is taken from the person who delivers it. Instead, one can rely on the much less intrusive procedure of measuring the temperature of the sample immediately following delivery.

Fourth, measures that ameliorate the undesirable side-effects of necessary privacy-diminishing measures are to be preferred over those that ignore these effects. Thus, if contact tracing is deemed necessary to curb the spread of infectious diseases so as to protect public health, efforts must be made to protect the anonymity of those involved. A third party may inform those who were in contact with an affected individual about such exposure and the therapeutic and protective measures they ought to next undertake, without disclosing the identity of the diagnosed person.

The combined application of these four balancing criteria helps to determine which correctives to a society's course are both needed and not excessive. This chapter focuses on the third criterion and seeks to address the question: What is least intrusive?

The three dimensions of privacy as a cube

In this section I attempt to show that to maintain privacy in the cyber age, boundaries on information that may be used by the government should be considered along three major dimensions: The level of sensitivity of the information, the volume of information collected, and the extent of cybernation. These considerations guide one to find the lowest level of intrusiveness while holding constant the level of common good. A society ought to tolerate more intrusiveness if there are valid reasons to hold that the threat to the public has significantly increased (e.g., there is an outbreak of a pandemic), and reassert a lower level of intrusiveness when such a threat has subsided.

Sensitivity

The first dimension is the level of sensitivity of the information.[39] For instance, data about a person's medical condition is considered highly sensitive, as is information about one's political beliefs and conduct (e.g., voting), and personal thoughts. Financial information is ranked as less sensitive than medical information, with publicly presented information (e.g., license plates) and routine consumer choices even less so.

These rankings are not based on "expectations of privacy" or on what this or that judge divines as societal expectations.[40] Rather, they reflect shared social values and are the product of politics in the good sense of the term, of liberal democratic processes, and of moral dialogues.[41] Different nations may rank differently what they consider sensitive. For example, France strongly restricts the collection of information by the government about race, ethnicity, and religion (although its rationale is not the protection of privacy but, rather, a strong assimilationist policy and separation of the state and church). For those who analyze the law in terms of the law and economics paradigm, disclosure of sensitive data causes more harm to the person, by objective standards, than does the disclosure of data that is not sensitive. Thus, disclosure of one's medical condition may lead one to lose one's job or not be hired, to be unable obtain a loan, or to incur higher insurance costs, among other harms. By contrast, disclosure of the kinds of bread, cheese, or sheets one buys may affect mainly the kind and amount of spam email one receives.

A re-examination of *Kyllo* helps to highlight this principle. If one goes by *Katz*, the legality of a thermal imaging search from outside the home depends on what one presumes personal and societal expectations to be. At least in middle-class American suburbs, people may consider such a heat reading a violation of their expectations. If one clings to the idea that "my home is my castle," measuring the heat inside the home is indeed a major violation of privacy. However, if one goes by the cyber-age privacy doctrine here outlined, such readings rank very low on sensitivity because they reveal very little or nothing about the resident's medical, financial, or political preferences, let alone their thoughts. And they detect an extremely low bandwidth of information. The information revealed is less consequential than what kind of cereal or which brand of coffee the person purchased. In contrast, taping a person's phone calls is much more revealing. Hence both *Kyllo* and *White* deserve to be reversed.

One may argue that information about the heat inside a home is actually particularly sensitive because it may reveal that a crime is being committed. Preventing crime is obviously a contribution to the common good. And given that in 2011 fewer than half of violent crimes and 22 percent of property crimes in the U.S. were resolved, some may well hold that public authorities are not excessively indulged when dealing with crime.[42] As to harm to the rights of the individuals involved, they would be harmed only if they had a right to commit a crime. As to the presumption of innocence, there is the public safety exception. The arguments against the notion that a crime committed in a home (e.g., spousal abuse) deserves more protection than one committed in public were already presented above. What is new here is that historically, when the Constitution was written, searching a home required a person to enter or peep, which would entail a high level of intrusiveness because the intruder could not but note other potentially sensitive information besides whether or not a crime was being committed. However, technologies that have a very narrow and crime-specific bandwidth (e.g., dogs that sniff for bombs or sensors that measure abnormal levels of heat) and are, hence, very lowly intrusive should be allowed. One may disagree with this line of analysis but still accept the basic point that the less intrusive collection of insensitive information should be tolerated, while the collection of highly sensitive information should be banned under most circumstances.

Many court cases treat the voluntary release of information to others (and by them to still others, discussed below under the third-party doctrine) as if the information disclosed—including phone numbers dialed,[43] copies of written checks,[44] documents given to an accountant,[45] newspaper records,[46] and even papers held by a defendant's attorney[47]—all had the same level of sensitivity.[48] A privacy doctrine that follows the principles here outlined would grant persons more say about the cybernization of sensitive information, while recognizing that the less sensitive information may be used and passed on without the individual's explicit consent.

Over the years, Congress has pieced together privacy law by addressing the protection of one kind of sensitive information at a time, rather than treating all kinds in a comprehensive fashion. Thus, in 1973, the Department of Health, Education and Welfare developed the Code of Fair Information Practices to govern the collection and use of information by the federal government. The principles of the code were incorporated in the Privacy Act of 1974, which "prohibits unauthorized disclosures of the records [the federal government] protects. It also gives individuals the right to review records about themselves, to find out if these records have been disclosed, and to request corrections or amendments of these records, unless the records are legally exempt."[49] The Privacy Act applies only to the federal government and has not been expanded to include records kept by the private sector. In 1986, the ECPA restricted wiretapping, regulated government access to electronic communication stored by third parties, and prohibited the collection of communications content (i.e., what was said, but not who was called) by pen registers. After the Supreme Court ruled in the 1976 case *United States v. Miller* that there was no reasonable expectation of privacy for records at financial institutions, Congress passed the Right to Financial Privacy Act,[50] which extended Fourth Amendment protections to these records. As required by the 1996 HIPAA, in 2002, the Department of Health and Human Services published the final form of "the Privacy Rule," which set the "standards for the electronic exchange, privacy and security of health information."[51] This accumulation of privacy protections includes laws covering specific sectors—or responding to specific events—but did not provide an overarching design. A well-known case in point is Congress' enactment of the Video Privacy Protection Act after the video rental records of Supreme Court nominee Judge Robert Bork were obtained by a Washington, DC newspaper.[52]

Congress could help to establish a privacy doctrine for the cyber age by reviewing what by now has been fairly called an incomplete "patchwork of federal laws and regulations" and providing a comprehensive overall ranking of protections based on the sensitivity of the data.[53] However, many of the building blocks needed for such an edifice are already in place. To develop sensitivity as a criterion for a privacy doctrine does not require a major leap.

Volume

The second dimension on which a cyber-age privacy doctrine should draw is the volume of information collected. Volume refers to the total amount of information collected about the same person, holding constant the level of sensitivity. Volume reflects the extent of time that surveillance is applied (the issue raised in *Jones*), the amount of information collected at each point in time (e.g., only emails sent to a specific person, or all emails stored on a hard drive), and the bandwidth of information collected at any one point in time (e.g., only the addresses of emails sent, or also their content). A single piece of low-sensitivity data deserves the least protection, and a high volume of sensitive information should receive the most protection.

Under such a cyber-age privacy doctrine, different surveillance and search technologies differ in their intrusiveness. Least intrusive are those that collect only discrete pieces of information of the least sensitive kind. These include speed detection cameras, tollbooths, and screening gates, because they all reveal, basically, one piece of information of relatively low sensitivity. Radiation detectors, heat-reading devices and bomb and drug-sniffing dogs belong in this category, not only because of the kind of information (i.e., low or not sensitive) they collect, but also because the bandwidth of the information they collect is very low (i.e., just one facet, indeed a very narrow one, and for a short duration).

Typical closed-circuit televisions (CCTVs)—privately owned, mounted on one's business, parking lot, or residential lobby—belong in the middle range because they pick up several facets (e.g., location, physical appearance, who one associates with), but do so for only a brief period of time and in one locality. The opposite holds for Microsoft's Domain Awareness System, first tested in New York City in 2012.

Phone tapping—especially if not minimized, and if continued for an extended period of time—and computer searches collect considerable volume. (This should not be conflated with considerations that come under the third dimension: Whether these facts are stored, collated, analyzed, and distributed, i.e., the elements of cybernation.) Drones are particularly intrusive because they involve much greater bandwidth and have the potential to engage in very prolonged surveillance at relatively low costs as compared to, say, a stake-out. These volume rankings must be adapted as technologies change. The extent to which combining technologies is intrusive depends on the volume (duration and bandwidth, holding sensitivity constant) of information collected. High-volume searches should be much more circumscribed than low-volume ones.

When the issue of extending privacy protection beyond spot collection arose in *Jones*, several legal scholars, in particular Orin Kerr, pointed to the difficulties of determining when the volume of collection was reasonable and when it became excessively intrusive. Kerr writes:

> In *Jones*, the GPS device was installed for 28 days. Justice Alito stated that this was "surely" long enough to create a mosaic. But he provided no reason why, and he recognized that "other cases may present more difficult questions." They may indeed. If 28 days is too far, how about 21 days, or 14 days, or 3.6 days? Where is the line?[54]

In response, one notes that there are many such cut-off points in law, such as the number of days suspects may be detained before they must be charged or released, the voting and driving ages, the number of jurors necessary for due process, and so on. One may say that they reflect what a "reasonable" person would rule. Actually, they reflect what judges consider a compromise between a restriction that is clearly excessive and one that's clearly inadequate—a line that has been adjusted often. There is no reason why the volume of collection should not be similarly governed.

Cybernation: storing, analysis, and access

The third dimension is the one that is increasing in importance and regarding which law and legal theory have the most catching up to do. To return to the opening deliberations of this chapter, historically, much attention was paid to the question of whether the government can legally collect certain kinds of information under specific conditions. This was reasonable because most violations of privacy occurred through search and surveillance that implicated this first-level collection, that of spot information. True, some significant violations also occurred in the paper age as a result of collating information, storing it, analyzing it, and distributing it. However, to reiterate, as long as records were paper bound, which they practically all were, these secondary violations of privacy were inherently limited when compared to those enabled by the digitization of data and the use of computers (i.e., by cybernation).

To illustrate the scope and effects of cybernation a comparison follows: In one state, a car passes through a tollbooth, a picture of its license plate (but not the driver or others on the front seat) is taken—and then this information is immediately deleted from the computer if the proper payment has been made. In another state, the same information, augmented with a photo of the passengers, is automatically transmitted to a central data bank. There, it is combined with many thousands of other pieces of information about the same person, from locations they have visited (e.g. based on cell tower triangulation) to their magazine subscriptions and recent purchases and so on. The information is regularly analyzed by AI systems to determine if people are engaged in any unusual behavior, what places of worship they frequent (e.g., flagging mosques), which political events they attend (e.g., flagging those who participated in protests), and if they stop at gun shows and so on and on. The findings are widely distributed to local police and the intelligence community and can be gained by the press and divorce lawyers.

Both systems are based on the same spot information, that is, pieces of information pertaining to a very limited, specific event or point in time—as in the case in the first scenario. However, if such information is combined with other information, analyzed, and distributed, as depicted in the second scenario, it provides a very comprehensive and revealing profile of one's personal life. In short, the most serious violations of privacy are often perpetuated not by surveillance or information collection per se, but by combination, manipulation, and data sharing—by cybernation. The more information is cybernated, the more intrusive it becomes.

Limiting intrusion by cybernation

There are in place two major systematic approaches to dealing with privacy violations that result from secondary uses: The third-party doctrine and the EU DPD. The third-party doctrine holds that once a person voluntarily discloses a fact to another party, that party is free (unless explicitly banned) to pass on (or sell) this information to third parties, and those various third parties are free to further process this information, collate it with other data, draw inferences, and so on—in short, to cybernate it.[55]

This approach is challenged by critics who note that in the cyber age much of our private lives are lived in a cyber world operated by third parties like Google and Facebook. Thus, Matthew Lawless writes:

> The third party doctrine gives effect to the criticism often aimed at the "reasonable expectation of privacy" principle, by holding that individuals can only reasonably expect privacy where the Court gives them that privacy. Because the third party doctrine fails to address true societal expectations of privacy (as evident by its failure to protect any information entered into a search engine), it reinforces the privacy norms of a politically and temporally insulated judiciary: once people know their searches are exposed, then—by the

time these cases are contested—there will, in truth, be no expectation of privacy.[56]

However, even without drawing on whatever the societal expectation of privacy is, one notes that considerable harm will come to people and that core societal values will be violated if the third-party doctrine is given free rein. This observation is strengthened by the fact that various exceptions to the third-party doctrine are already in place, such as special rules for medical and financial information. However, according to Greg Nojeim, these rules do not provide the same level of protection as is granted by the Fourth Amendment. He notes that "privacy statutes that protect some categories of sensitive personal information generally do not require warrants for law enforcement access."[57] Furthermore, Matthew Tokson argues that "the conflation of disclosure to automated Internet systems with disclosure to human beings" has led the court to exclude from Fourth Amendment protection a great deal of personal information, including "Internet protocol ('IP') addresses, e-mail to/from information, information about the volume of data transmitted to a user, name, address, and credit card information, and even the contents of a user's e-mails."[58] In short, the third-party doctrine provides very little privacy protection, and the less so the more cybernation is developed and extended.

The EU's DPD in effect takes the opposite view, namely, that any secondary use of personal information released by a person or collected about him requires the explicit *a priori* approval of the original individual "owner" of the information, and that this consent cannot be delegated to an agent or machine.[59] The details of DPD are complex and changing.[60] For instance, it made exceptions from this rule for many areas, such as when the data is needed for the purposes of research, public health, or law enforcement, among others. In January 2012, the European Commission passed draft legislation that would update the existing data protection law. This legislation includes an "opt in" provision: "As a general rule, any processing of personal data will require providing clear and simple information to concerned individuals as well as obtaining specific and explicit consent by such individuals for the processing of their data." Data show that information about a person is used many times each day by a large variety of users. Hence, if such a policy were systematically enforced, each internet user would have to respond to scores if not hundreds of requests per day even for uses of non-sensitive information. It seems that in this area, as in many others, the way DPD rules survive is by very often not enforcing them. Whenever I meet Europeans, and following public lectures in the EU, I ask if anyone has ever been asked to consent to the use of personal information that they had previously released. I have found only one person so far. He said that he got one such request—from Amazon. Other sources indicate that compliance is at best "erratic."[61] The penalties for violating the DPD seem to be miniscule and rarely collected. No wonder a large majority of the EU public—70 percent—fear that their personal data may be misused.[62] In short, neither of these approaches is satisfactory. Taking effect May 25, 2018 the General Data Protection Regulation will replace the DPD and is expected to improve compliance by implementing harsher penalties.

In addition, there are in place a large number of laws, regulations, and guidelines that deal with limited particular usages of personal information beyond the point of collection. However, a very large number of them deal with only one dimension of the cube, and often with only one element of cybernation, limiting either storage, or analysis, or distribution. The laws reflect the helter-skelter way that they were introduced and do not provide a systematic doctrine of cyber privacy. They are best viewed as building blocks, which, if subjected to considerable legal scholarship and legislation, could provide the needed doctrine. They are like a score of characters in search of an author.

One of the key principles for such a doctrine is that the legal system can be more tolerant of the primary-point spot collection of personal information—(a) the more limited the volume (duration and bandwidth) of the collection,[63] (b) the more limited and regulated is the cybernation—holding constant the level of sensitivity of the information. That is, much more latitude can be granted to the collection and cybernation of insensitive information, stricter limitations can be placed on highly sensitive information, and a middle level of protection can be established in between.

In other words, a cyber-age privacy doctrine can be much more tolerant of primary collection conducted within a system of laws and regulations that are effectively enforced to ensure that cybernation is limited, properly supervised, and employed for legitimate purposes—and much less so if the opposite holds. One may refer to this rule as the positive correlation between the level of permissiveness in primary collection and the strictness of controls on secondary usage of personal information.

Another key principle is a ban on using insensitive information to divine the sensitive (e.g., using information about routine consumer purchases to divine a person's medical condition), because it is just as intrusive as collecting and employing sensitive information.[64] This is essential because currently such behavior is rather common.[65] Thus, under the suggested law, Target would be prevented from sending coupons for baby items to a teenage girl after the chain store's analysis of her recent purchases suggests that she might be pregnant.[66] And surely Target would be prevented from selling this information to all comers. To further advance the cyber-age privacy doctrine, much more attention needs to be paid to private actors. Privacy rights, like others, are basically held against the government to protect people from undue intrusion by public authorities. However, increasingly, cybernation is carried out by the private sector. There are corporations that make shadowing internet users—and keeping very detailed dossiers on them—their main line of business. According to Slobogin,

> Companies like Acxiom, Docussearch, ChoicePoint, and Oracle can provide the inquirer with a wide array of data about any of us, including: Basic demographic information, income, net worth, real property holdings, social security number, current and previous addresses, phone numbers and fax numbers, names of neighbors, driver records, license plate and VIN numbers, bankruptcy and debtor filings, employment, business and criminal records, bank account balances and activity, stock purchases, and credit card activity.[67]

And these data are routinely made available to the government, including the FBI. Unless this private cybernation is covered, the cyber-age privacy doctrine will be woefully incomplete.[68]

Given that private actors are very actively engaged in cybernation and often tailor their work so that it might be used by the government (even if no contract is in place and they are, hence, not subject to the limits imposed on the government), extending the privacy doctrine beyond the public/private divide is of pivotal importance for the future of privacy in the cyber age. Admittedly, applying to the private sector similar restrictions and regulations that control the government may well be politically unfeasible in the current environment. However, as one who analyzes the conditions of society from a normative viewpoint, I am duty bound to point out that it makes ever less sense to maintain this distinction.[69] Privacy will be increasingly lost in the cyber age, with little or no gain to the common good, unless private actors—and not just the government—are more reined in. To what extent this may be achieved by self-regulation, changes in norms, increased transparency, or government regulation is a question not addressed here.

For this doctrine to be further developed, laws and court rulings ought to be three-dimensional.[70] These laws and court cases had best specify not only whether a particular collection of personal information is a "search," but also what level of sensitivity can be tolerated and to what extent the information may be stored, analyzed, and distributed. This may seem—and is—a tall, if not impossible, order. However, as is illustrated next, a considerable number of measures are already in place that are, in effect, at least two-dimensional. These, though, suffer from the fact that they have been introduced each on its own and do not reflect an overarching doctrine of privacy; hence, they reveal great inconsistencies that need to be remedied. I cannot stress enough that the following are but selective examples of such measures.

One should note that a very early attempt to deal with the issue—basically, by banning a form of cybernation—utterly failed. In 2003, Congress shut down the Pentagon's Total Information Awareness (TIA) program, which was created to detect potential terrorists by using data-mining technologies to analyze unprecedented amounts of personal transaction data. However, a report by the *Wall Street Journal* in 2008 revealed that the most important components of TIA were simply "shifted to the NSA" and "put in the so-called black budget, where it would receive less scrutiny and bolster other data-sifting efforts."[71]

Minimization is one way of addressing the volume issue, as Swire pointed out in his groundbreaking article on *Jones* and the mosaic theory.[72] Accordingly, when the FBI taps a phone, even for an extended period of time, the intrusion can be reduced significantly if the FBI either stops listening when it hears that the conversation is not relevant to the investigation (e.g., a child is calling the suspect under surveillance) or locks away those segments of the taped correspondence that turn out to be irrelevant.[73] For this rule to be integrated into the doctrine, it may be waived for insensitive information. That is, there would be no need to minimize if the child asked, say, to watch TV, but minimization would be activated if she asked, say, about medical news concerning a family member.

Another example of a safeguard against excessive privacy intrusions is the requirement that certain content be deleted after a specific time period. Most private companies that utilize CCTV erase video footage after a set number of days, such as after a week. Admittedly, their reasons for doing so may be simply economic; however, the effect is still to limit the volume of collection and potential for subsequent abuse. Note that there are no legal requirements to erase these tapes. However, such laws ought to be considered (Europeans are increasingly recognizing a "right to be forgotten"). It would be in the public interest to require that footage be kept for a fixed period of time (as it has proven useful in fighting crime and terrorism), but also to ban under most circumstances the integration of the video feed into encompassing and cybernated systems of the kind Microsoft has developed.

The treatment of private local CCTVs should be examined in the context of the ways other such spot-collection information is treated. Because the bandwidth of information collected by toll booths, speed cameras, and radiation detectors is very narrow, one might be permitted to store it for longer and feed it into cybernated systems. By contrast, cell phone tracking can be utilized to collect a great volume and bandwidth of information about a person's location and activities. People carry their phones to many places they cannot take their cars, where no video cameras or radiation detectors will be found, including sensitive places such as political meetings, houses of worship, and residences. These rules must be constantly updated as what various technologies can observe and retain constantly changes.

Regulations to keep information paper bound have been introduced for reasons other than protecting privacy, but these requirements still have the effect of limiting intrusiveness. For example, Congress prevents the Bureau of Alcohol, Tobacco, Firearms and Explosives from computerizing gun records when such information is collected during background checks.[74] In 2013, an amendment to the anti-insider trading STOCK Act exempted 28,000 executive branch staff from having to post their financial disclosure forms "online in a searchable, sortable and downloadable format."[75] These bans remind one that not all the privacy measures that are in place are legitimate and that some are best scaled back rather than enhanced.[76]

A related issue is raised by the cybernation of arrest records. Arrest records should be, but are not, considered highly sensitive information. When these records, especially those concerning people who were subsequently released without any charges, were paper bound, the damage they inflicted on most people's reputations was limited. However, as a result of cybernation, they have become much more problematic. Under the suggested doctrine, arrest records of people not charged after a given period of time would be available only to law enforcement officers. The opposite might be said about data banks that alert the public to physicians that have been denied privileges for cause—a very high threshold that indicates serious ethical shortcomings.

Many computer systems ("clouds" included) encrypt their data and a few have introduced audit trails. The cyber-age privacy doctrine might require that all data banks that contain sensitive information be encrypted and include at least some rudimentary form of audit trail.

Technologies can be recalibrated to collect the "need to know" information, while shielding extraneous but highly sensitive information from observation. For example, when law enforcement collects DNA samples from convicted criminals or arrested individuals, FBI analysts create DNA profiles using so-called "junk DNA" "because it is not 'associated with any known physical or medical characteristics,' and thus theoretically poses only a minimal invasion of privacy."[77] Storing these "genetic fingerprints" in national databases is much less intrusive than retaining data produced by blood samples, which "reveal sensitive medical or biological information."[78] In 2013, the TSA stopped its use of body scanners that revealed almost-nude images, using instead scanners that produce "cartoon-like" images on which they mark the places where hidden objects are found.[79] This did not affect the volume of collection, but lessened the sensitivity of the content.

Other measures must address the fact that often data can be "re-identified" or "de-anonymized." In 2006, AOL released the search records—stripped of "personal identifiers"—of over 600,000 people. An investigation by the *New York Times*, however, demonstrated that intimate information—including names and faces—could be gleaned from such purportedly anonymous data. This risk is mitigated by the development of statistical methods that prevent such undertakings, such as "differential privacy," which allows curators of large databases to release the results of socially beneficial data analysis without compromising the privacy of the respondents who make up the sample.[80]

Many more examples could be provided. However, the above list may suffice to show that, while there are numerous measures in place that deal with various elements of the privacy cube, these have not been introduced with systematic attention to the guiding principles needed for the cyber age.

Notes

Introduction

[1] See, for example, Gallup, "Satisfaction With the United States," http://www.gallup.com/poll/1669/general-mood-country.aspx.

[2] Gallup, "Americans' Confidence in Institutions Stays Low," June 13, 2016, http://www.gallup.com/poll/192581/americans-confidence-institutions-stays-low.aspx.

[3] As Lynn Mather puts it, "*Law is in society*, and most now agree with the argument Laura Nader made initially that the field should have been named 'Law *in* Society' rather than law *and* society." Lynn Mather, "Law and Society." Oxford Handbooks Online. May 24, 2017. http://www.oxfordhandbooks.com/view/10.1093/oxfordhb/9780199208425.001.0001/oxfordhb-9780199208425-e-39.

[4] Lawrence Friedman, "The Law and Society Movement," *Stanford Law Review* 38 (1986): 763.

[5] Lynn Mather, "Law and Society."

[6] Friedman, "The Law and Society Movement," 763.

[7] Mather, "Law and Society."

[8] Robert Ellickson, *Order Without Law, How Neighbors Settle Disputes* (Cambridge, MA: Harvard University Press, 1995) quoted in Austin Sarat and Patricia Ewick eds. *The Handbook of Law and Society* (Chichester, UK: Wiley Blackwell, 2015), xiv.

[9] Austin Sarat and Patricia Ewick eds. *The Handbook of Law and Society* (Chichester, UK: Wiley Blackwell, 2015).

[10] Ibid.

Chapter One

[1] Cas Mudde, "The Populist Zeitgeist," *Government and Opposition* 39, no. 4 (2004).

[2] Jan-Werner Müller, *What is Populism* (Philadelphia: University of Pennsylvania Press, 2016).

[3] See Amy Chozick, "Hillary Clinton Calls Many Trump Backers 'Deplorables,' and G.O.P. Pounces," *New York Times*, September 10, 2016,

https://www.nytimes.com/2016/09/11/us/politics/hillary-clinton-basket-of-deplorables.html?_r=0.

4 Michael Lind, "This is What the Future of American Politics Looks Like," *Politico*, May 22, 2016, http://www.politico.com/magazine/story/2016/05/2016-election-realignment-partisan-political-party-policy-democrats-republicans-politics-213909; Jonathan Haidt, "When and Why Nationalism Beats Globalism," *The American Interest*, July 10, 2016, http://www.the-american-interest.com/2016/07/10/when-and-why-nationalism-beats-globalism/.

5 George Monbiot, "The New Chauvinism," *Guardian*, August 8, 2005, https://www.theguardian.com/politics/2005/aug/09/july7.britishidentity.

6 Pankaj Mishra, "How Rousseau Predicted Trump," *New Yorker*, August 1, 2016, http://www.newyorker.com/magazine/2016/08/01/how-rousseau-predicted-trump.

7 Ferdinand Tönnies, *Community and Society*, trans. and ed. Charles P. Loomis (East Lansing: Michigan State University Press, 1957).

8 A reviewer of a previous draft noted here that the transition Tönnies points to is not from social relations to atomization but merely a change in the kind of relations people have, from communal to associational. This is indeed the case, but the point is that these relations are not thick enough.

9 David Redles, "The Nazi Old Guard: Identity Formation During Apocalyptic Times," *Nova Religio: The Journal of Alternative and Emergent Religions* 14, no. 1 (2010): 31.

10 Yuval Levin notes that both conservative and liberals are nostalgic for a bygone era: liberals miss the 1960s and the Great Society, conservatives miss the 1980s and both are nostalgic for the 1950s, but for different reasons. See Yuval Levin, *The Fractured Republic: Renewing America's Social Contract in the Age of Individualism* (New York: Basic Books, 2016).

11 Program for Public Consultation (University of Maryland), "Support for Trump Fed by Near-Universal Frustration that Government Ignores the People," November 18, 2016, http://www.publicconsultation.org/redblue/support-for-trump-fed-by-near-universal-frustration-that-government-ignores-the-people/.

12 Roberto Stefan Foa and Yascha Mounk, "The Democratic Disconnect," *Journal of Democracy* 27, no 3 (2016): 13.

13 Ibid., 12.

14 Ibid.

15 Peter Singer, "Famine, Affluence, and Morality," *Philosophy & Public Affairs* 1, no. 3 (1972): 229.

16 Martha Craven Nussbaum and Joshua Cohen. *For Love of Country?* (Boston: Beacon Press, 1996).

17 *See, e.g.*, John F. Helliwell, "Well-Being, Social Capital and Public Policy: What's New?" *Economic Modelling*, 20 (2003) and L. Fratiglioni et al. "'Influence of Social Networks on Occurrence of Dementia," *The Lancet* (2000).

18 Isaiah Berlin, "Joseph de Maistre and the Origins of Fascism," in *The Crooked Timber of Humanity: Chapters in the History of Ideas*, ed. Henry Hardy (New York: Alfred A. Knopf, 1991), 100 (emphasis in original).
19 Michael Sandel, *Liberalism and the Limits of Justice*, 2nd ed. (New York: Cambridge University Press, 1998), 179.
20 Arlie Russell Hochschild, *Strangers in Their Own Land* (New York: The New Press, 2017); Amy Goldstein, *Janesville: An American Story* (New York: Simon &Schuster, 2017).
21 David B. Wong, "On Flourishing and Finding One's Identity in Community," in *Midwest Studies in Philosophy*, Vol. XIII, Ethical Theory: Character and Virtue, ed. Peter A. French, Theodore E. Uehling, Jr., and Howard K. Wettstein (Notre Dame, IN: University of Notre Dame Press, 1988), 333.
22 Dennis Wrong, *The Problem of Order* (New York: Simon & Schuster, 1994).
23 See Michael Walzer, *Thick And Thin: Moral Argument at Home and Abroad* (Notre Dame, IN: University of Notre Dame Press, 1994).
24 Levin, *The Fractured Republic*.
25 M. Daly, introduction to *Communitarianism: A New Public Ethics*, ed. M. Daly (Belmont, CA: Wadsworth Publishing Company, 1994), xix. Cf. S. Mulhall and A. Swift, *Liberals and Communitarians* (Cambridge: Blackwell, 1992), vii; N. Lacey and E. Frazer, "Blind Alleys: Communitarianism," *Politics* 14, no. 2 (1994): 75; A. Vincent, "Liberal Nationalism and Communitarianism: An Ambiguous Association," *Australian Journal of Politics & History* 43 (1997).
26 David Brooks, "The View from Trump Tower," *New York Times*, November 11, 2016, https://www.nytimes.com/2016/11/12/opinion/the-view-from-trump-tower.html.
27 Ibid.
28 Heather Long, "U.S. Has Lost 5 Million Manufacturing Jobs Since 2000," *CNN*, March 29, 2016, http://money.cnn.com/2016/03/29/news/economy/us-manufacturing-jobs/.
29 For a fuller treatment of reactionary thinking, see Mark Lilla, *The Shipwrecked Mind: On Political Reaction* (New York: New York Review of Books, 2016).
30 Jonathan Haidt, "When and Why Nationalism Beats Globalism," *The American Interest*, July 10, 2016, http://www.the-american-interest.com/2016/07/10/when-and-why-nationalism-beats-globalism/.
31 Jacob Hornberger, "There Is Only One Libertarian Position on Immigration," *Future of Freedom Foundation*, August 25, 2016, http://www.fff.org/2015/08/25/one-libertarian-position-immigration/.
32 William Galston, "Immigration Reaches Critical Mass," *Wall Street Journal*, November 22, 2016. http://www.wsj.com/articles/immigration-reaches-critical-mass-1479857623.
33 Ibid.
34 Frédéric Mayet, "Laïcité à Montpellier: Des Jupes Longues Font Débat au Collège des Garrigues," *Midi Libre*, March 31, 2015, http://www.midilibre.fr/2015/03/31/le-college-des-garrigues-est-soucieux-de-sa-laicite,1144142.php.

[35] Alain Auffray and Laure Equy, "Le Burkini Interdit dans une Quinzaine de Communes," *Liberation*, August 19, 2016, http://www.liberation.fr/france/2016/08/19/le-burkini-interdit-dans-une-quinzaine-de-communes_1473469.

[36] Angelique Chrisafis, "Pork or Nothing: How School Dinners Are Dividing France," *Guardian*, October 13, 2015, http://www.theguardian.com/world/2015/oct/13/pork-school-dinners-france-secularism-children-religious-intolerance.

[37] The Community Associations Institute estimates that 68 million Americans common-interest communities, including homeowners' associations, condominium communities and cooperatives. See https://www.caionline.org/AboutCommunityAssociations/Pages/StatisticalInformation.aspx.

[38] *See, e.g.*, Evan McKenzie, *Privatopia: Homeowner Associations and the Rise of Residential Private Government* (New Haven, CT:Yale University Press, 1994).

[39] L. Joe Morgan, "Gated Communities: Institutionalizing Social Stratification," *The Geographical Bulletin* 54, no. 1 (2013), 28.

[40] Robert D. Putnam, *Bowling Alone: The Collapse and Revival of American Community* (New York: Simon & Schuster, 2000).

[41] "Chelsea Clinton Campaigns in Michigan," October 29, 2016, https://hillaryspeeches.com/tag/equality/.

[42] Matt Apuzzo and Alan Blinder, "North Carolina Law May Risk Federal Aid," *New York Times*, April 1, 2016, http://www.nytimes.com/2016/04/02/us/politics/north-carolina-anti-discrimination-law-obama-federal-funds.html.

[43] Amitai Etzioni, *The Spirit of Community* (New York: Simon & Schuster, 1993), 5–6.

[44] Robert Reinhold, "In Land of Liberals, Restroom Rights are Rolled Back," *New York Times*, November 15, 1991, A14.

[45] Daniel Seligman, "Keeping Up," *Fortune*, February 10, 1992, 145.

[46] "Mother Scolded for Suit over Son's Honors," *New York Times*, November 23, 1991, 28.

[47] American Bankers Association ad, *Washington Post*, November 17, 1991, A13.

[48] Frank Bruni, "Tempest in a Toilet," *New York Times*, April 23, 2016, https://www.nytimes.com/2016/04/24/opinion/sunday/tempest-in-a-toilet.html.

[49] Ibid.

[50] David Benkoff, "Both Sides in the Transgender 'Bathroom Battle' Are Wrong," *Daily Caller*, November 10, 2015, http://dailycaller.com/2015/11/10/both-sides-in-the-transgender-bathroom-battle-are-wrong/#ixzz4a6CBgYP3.

[51] Duaa Eldeib and Robert McCoppin, "Feds Reject School District's Plan for Transgender Student Locker Room," *Chicago Tribune*, October 13, 2015, http://www.chicagotribune.com/news/local/breaking/ct-transgender-student-locker-room-palatine-met-20151012-story.html.

[52] Ibid.

53 American Civil Liberties Union, Complaint to United States Department of Justice against Gloucester County Public Schools on behalf of Gavin Grimm, December 18, 2014, https://acluva.org/wp-content/uploads/2014/12/141218-dojcomplaintltrGRIMM.pdf.

54 Steven Petrow, "Civilities: Is It Time to Include 'Mx.' in the Mix with 'Ms.' and 'Mr.'?" *Washington Post*, August 3, 2016, https://www.washingtonpost.com/lifestyle/style/civilities-is-it-time-to-include-mx-in-the-mix-with-ms-and-mr/2015/07/31/b0b91868-37b5-11e5-9739-170df8af8eb9_story.html?utm_term=.95724011abc9.

55 Ibid.

56 Jessica Kenwood, "Vancouver School Board Adopts Progressive Transgender Policy," *Vice News*, June 19, 2014, https://news.vice.com/article/vancouver-school-board-adopts-progressive-transgender-policy.

57 Al Donato, "He And She, Ze And Xe: The Case For Gender-Neutral Pronouns," November 25, 2014, *Plaid Zebra*, http://www.theplaidzebra.com/ze-xe-case-gender-neutral-pronouns/.

58 Arlie Russell Hochschild, *Strangers in Their Own Land: Anger and Mourning on the American Right* (New York: The New Press, 2016).

59 Ibid., 218–219.

60 Justin McCarthy, "Same-Sex Marriage Support Reaches New High at 55%," Gallup, 21 May, 2014.

61 See Dan Rather, interview by Ana Marie Cox, *New York Times Magazine*, April 12, 2017, https://www.nytimes.com/2017/04/12/magazine/dan-rather-thinks-we-need-patriotism-not-nationalism.html?_r=0.

62 E.J. Dionne, Jr., "Why We Don't Call It Nationalists' Day," *Washington Post*, April 17, 2017, https://www.washingtonpost.com/opinions/why-we-dont-call-it-nationalists-day/2017/04/16/2baa4a72-2145-11e7-a0a7-8b2a45e3dc84_story.html?utm_term=.3cbdebeeda07.

63 Ibid. Dionne adds that "Mona Charen of the Ethics and Public Policy Center had it exactly right when she argued: 'Patriotism is enough—it needs no improving or expanding.' She called nationalism 'a demagogue's patriotism' more likely to be converted 'into something aggressive.'" Furthermore, "columnist Jonah Goldberg caught something important when he wrote that 'nationalism is ultimately the fire of tribalism, having too much of it tends to melt away important distinctions, from the rule of law to the right to dissent to the sovereignty of the individual." Ibid.

64 Lawrence Summers, "How to Embrace Nationalism Responsibly," *Washington Post*, July 10, 2016, https://www.washingtonpost.com/opinions/global-opinions/how-to-embrace-nationalism-responsibly/2016/07/10/faf7a100-4507-11e6-8856-f26de2537a9d_story.html?utm_term=.8a8be33df9c4.

Chapter Two

1 Moreover, private agents can be limited through civil suits.

2 True, an oft-cited article by Samuel Warren and Louis Brandeis conceived of privacy as a right to be let alone, mainly from the press; however, this

was a law review article, not the law of the land. *See* Samuel D. Warren & Louis D. Brandeis, *The Right to Privacy, Harvard Law Review* 4 (1890).

3 *See Griswold v. Connecticut*, 381 U.S. 479 (1965).

4 Privacy Act of 1974, 5 U.S.C. § 552 (1974).

5 U.S. Const. amend. IV.

6 *See, e.g., Maryland v. King*, 133 S. Ct. 1958 (2013) (on intrusiveness); *Brigham City v. Stuart*, 547 U.S. 398 (2006) (on exigent circumstances); *California v. Greenwood*, 486 U.S. 35 (1988) (on expectations of privacy); *New Jersey v. T.L.O.*, 469 U.S. 325 (1985) (on special needs); *Schneckloth v. Bustamonte*, 412 U.S. 218 (1972) (on consent); *Katz v. United States*, 389 U.S. 347 (1967) (on expectations of privacy and attendant safeguards).

7 Sabrina Siddiqui, "Congress Passes NSA Surveillance Reform in Vindication for Snowden," *Guardian*, June 3, 2015, https://www.theguardian.com/us-news/2015/jun/02/congress-surveillance-reform-edward-snowden.

8 *See, e.g.*, Gil Press, "6 Predictions for the $125 Billion Big Data Analytics Market in 2015," *Forbes*, December 11, 2014, http://www.forbes.com/sites/gilpress/2014/12/11/6-predictions-for-the-125-billion-big-data-analytics-market-in-2015/#1aafe71a2b20.

9 Amitai Etzioni, "The Privacy Merchants: What Is To Be Done?" *Journal of Constitutional Law* 14, no. 4 (2012).

10 Federal Trade Commission, "Protecting Consumer Privacy in an Era of Rapid Change," FTC Report 1 (2012), https://www.ftc.gov/sites/default/files/documents/reports/federal-trade-commission-report-protecting-consumer-privacy-era-rapid-change-recommendations/120326privacyreport.pdf, 68.

11 Natasha Singer, "Mapping, and Sharing, the Consumer Genome," *New York Times*, June 6, 2012, BU1.

12 Government Accountability Office, "Information Resellers: Consumer Privacy Framework Needs to Reflect Changes in Technology and the Marketplace " (2013): 5, http://www.gao.gov/assets/660/658151.pdf.

13 Press Release, "Markey, Rockefeller Introduce Data Broker Bill to Ensure Accuracy, Accountability for Consumers," February 12, 2014, http://www.markey.senate.gov/news/press-releases/markey-rockefeller-introduce-data-broker-bill-to-ensure-accuracy-accountability-for-consumers.

14 Federation of American Scientists, "Intelligence Budget Data," http://fas.org/irp/budget/ (last visited September 28, 2016).

15 Senate Committee on Commerce, Science, and Transportation, "A Review of the Data Broker Industry: Collection, Use, and Sale of Consumer Data for Marketing Purposes," December 18, 2013, https://www.commerce.senate.gov/public/_cache/files/0d2b3642-6221-4888-a631-08f2f255b577/AE5D72CBE7F44F5BFC846BECE22C875B.12.18.13-senate-commerce-committee-report-on-data-broker-industry.pdf, ii.

16 Ibid.

17 Frank Pasquale, "The Dark Market for Personal Data," *New York Times*, October 16, 2014, http://www.nytimes.com/2014/10/17/opinion/the-dark-market-for-personal-data.html.

18 *See, e.g.*, Chris Jay Hoofnagle, "Big Brother's Little Helpers: How ChoicePoint and Other Commercial Data Brokers Collect and Package Your Data for Law Enforcement," *North Carolina Journal of International Law and Commercial Regulation* 29 (2004).

19 ChoicePoint has since been rebranded "LexisNexis Risk Solutions" after its acquisition by Reed Elsevier.

20 Daniel J. Solove & Chris Jay Hoofnagle, "A Model Regime of Privacy Protection," *University of Illinois Law Review* (2006): 362.

21 Ibid., 363.

22 Nicole Duarte, "Commercial Data Uses by Law Enforcement Raises Questions about Accuracy, Oversight," *News21*, August 16, 2006, http://news21.com/story/2006/08/16/commercial_data_use_by_law.

23 Melanie Hicken, "What Information is the Government Buying aboutYou?" *CNN Money*, October 30, 2013, http://money.cnn.com/2013/10/30/pf/government-data-broker/.

24 Christopher Slobogin, "Government Data Mining and the Fourth Amendment," *University of Chicago Law Review*, 75 (2008): 320.

25 Hoofnagle, "Big Brother's Little Helpers," 637.

26 Scott Shane, "Shifting Mood May End Blank Check for U.S. Security Effort," *New York Times*, October 24, 2012, A1.

27 "LexisNexis Accurint for Law Enforcement," *Lexis Nexis*, 2011, http://www.lexisnexis.com/government/solutions/literature/accurintle_ss.pdf.

28 Robert Gellman & Pam Dixon, "Data Brokers and the Federal Government: A New Front in the Battle for Privacy Opens," 2013, http://www.worldprivacyforum.org/wp-content/uploads/2013/10/WPF_DataBrokersPart3_fs.pdf, 11.

29 Fair Credit Reporting Act, 15 U.S.C. § 1681 (1968).

30 Ibid.

31 "Data Brokers and 'People Search' Sites," *Privacy Rights Clearinghouse*, https://www.privacyrights.org/consumer-guides/data-brokers-and-people-search-sites (last visited September 28, 2016).

32 Erin McCann, "FTC Calls Out Health Data Brokers," *Healthcare IT News*, May 28, 2014, http://www.healthcareitnews.com/news/ftc-calls-out-dealth-data-brokers.

33 Gramm-Leach-Bliley Act, 15 U.S.C. §§ 6801–6809 (1999).

343 Federal Trade Commission, "In Brief: The Financial Privacy Requirements of the Gramm-Leach-Bliley Act," 2002, https://www.ftc.gov/tips-advice/business-center/guidance/brief-financial-privacy-requirements-gramm-leach-bliley-act.

35 "Financial Privacy," *Privacy Rights Clearinghouse*, October 5, 2016, https://www.privacyrights.org/consumer-guides/financial-privacy#3.

36 "Data Brokers and 'People Search' Sites," *Privacy Rights Clearinghouse*, https://www.privacyrights.org/consumer-guides/data-brokers-and-people-search-sites (last visited September 28, 2016).

37 Gellman and Dixon, "Data Brokers and the Federal Government," 10.

[38] Christopher Slobogin, "Transaction Surveillance by the Government," *Mississippi Law Journal*, 75 (2005): 141.

[39] One exception is the Electronic Communications Privacy Act's treatment of communications records stored for fewer than 180 days. Slobogin, "Transaction Surveillance by the Government."

[40] Slobogin, "Transaction Surveillance by the Government," 153.

[41] Gellman and Dixon, "Data Brokers and the Federal Government," 5.

[42] Slobogin, "Transaction Surveillance by the Government," 161.

[43] Directive 95/46/EC of the European Parliament and of the Council of October 24, 1995 on the Protection of Individuals with Regard to the Processing of Personal Data and on the Free Movement of Such Data, 1995, *Official Journal* (L 281): 31.

[44] To Directive 95/46/EC of the European Parliament and of the Council, October 24, 1995, http://eur-lex.europa.eu/legal-content/en/TXT/?uri=CELEX%3A31995L0046.

[45] European Commission, "Exceptions to Data Protection Rules," http://ec.europa.eu/justice/data-protection/individuals/exceptions/index_en.htm (last visited September 28, 2016).

[46] European Commission, "Comparative Study on Different Approaches to New Privacy Challenges, in Particular in the Light of Technological Developments" (2010), http://ec.europa.eu/justice/policies/privacy/docs/studies/new_privacy_challenges/final_report_en.pdf, 15.

[47] Amitai Etzioni, *Privacy in a Cyber Age: Policy and Practice* (New York: Palgrave Macmillan, 2015).

[48] For more discussion of this approach, see Chapter Twelve.

[49] Federal Trade Commission, "A Summary of Your Rights under the Fair Credit Reporting Act," https://www.consumer.ftc.gov/articles/pdf-0096-fair-credit-reporting-act.pdf (last visited September 29, 2016).

[50] Electronic Communications Privacy Act of 1986, Pub. L. No. 99-508, 100 Stat. 1848 (1986) (codified as amended in various sections of the United States Code, such as 18 U.S.C. § 2510 (1986)).

[51] For additional discussion of private policing *see* Jeannine Bell, "The Police and Policing," in *Blackwell Companion to Law and Society*, ed. Austin Sarat (Malden, MA: Blackwell, 2004), 131–145.

[52] Elizabeth E. Joh, "Conceptualizing the Private Police," 2005 *Utah Law Review*, 573, 577 (2005) at 586; *see also* James F. Pastor, *The Privatization of Police in America: An Analysis and Case Study* (Jefferson, NC: Mcfarland, 2003) (chronicling the growth of the private police force in the U.S.).

[53] David A. Sklansky, "The Private Police," 46 *UCLA Law Review* 1165, 1174 (1999); Shoshana Walter & Ryan Gabrielson, "America's Gun-Toting Guards Armed with Poor Training, Little Oversight," *Reveal*, December 14, 2014, https://www.revealnews.org/article/americas-gun-toting-security-guards-may-not-be-fit-for-duty/.

[54] "Law Enforcement Facts," accessed March 16, 2018, http://www.nleomf.org/facts/enforcement/.

[55] John S. Dempsey, *Introduction to Private Security* (Belmont, CA: Thompson, 2010), 66–67.

[56] *See, e.g.*, Jon Swaine, Oliver Laughland, & Jamiles Lartey, "Black Americans Killed by Police Twice as Likely to be Unarmed as White People," *Guardian*, June 1, 2015, https://www.theguardian.com/us-news/2015/jun/01/black-americans-killed-by-police-analysis.

[57] Walter & Gabrielson, "America's Gun-Toting Guards"; *see also* Lauren Kirchner, "The Surprisingly Lax Oversight of the Security Guard Industry," *Pacific Standard*, July 1, 2014, https://psmag.com/the-surprisingly-lax-oversight-of-the-security-guard-industry-1b3e5f9a7d83#.mcfufvpom.

[58] Walter & Gabrielson, "America's Gun-Toting Guards."

[59] Ibid.

[60] David A. Sklansky, "The Private Police," *UCLA Law Review* 46 (1998): 1183.

[61] *Miranda v. Arizona* 384 U.S. 436 (1966).

[62] Ibid., 1167.

[63] Malcolm K. Sparrow, "Managing the Boundary Between Public and Private Policing", *New Perspectives In Policing* 8 (2014), https://www.hks.harvard.edu/content/download/67532/1242938/version/1/file/ManagingBoundariesPolicing.pdf, 9.

[64] Ibid.

[65] 42 U.S.C. § 1983 (1996).

[66] Jack M. Beermann, "Why Do Plaintiffs Sue Private Parties under Section 1983?" *Cardozo Law Review* 26 (2005): 21.

[67] Sklansky, "The Private Police," 1229.

[68] Elizabeth E. Joh, "The Paradox of Private Policing," 95 *Journal of Criminal Law & Criminology* 49, 62–63 (2004).

[69] Heidi Boghosian, Applying Restraints to Private Police, 70 *Missouri Law Review* 177, 185 (2005).

[70] Karena Rahall, "The Siren Is Calling: Economic and Ideological Trends Toward Privatization of Public Police Forces," 68 *University of Miami Law Review* 633, 647 (2014).

[71] Joh, "The Paradox of Private Policing," 116.

[72] Richard Ericson, *Crime in an Insecure World* (Cambridge, UK: Polity Press, 2007), 179.

[73] David Alan Sklansky, "Private Police and Democracy," *American Journal of Criminal Law* 45 (2006): 105.

[74] Ibid., 104–105.

[75] M. Rhead Enion, "Constitutional Limits on Private Policing and the State's Allocation of Force," *Duke Law Journal*, 59 (2009): 553.

[76] Ibid., 552–553; *see also* John M. Burkoff, "Not So Private Searches and the Constitution," *Cornell Law Review* 66 (1981): 628 ("State involvement with nominally private law enforcers is often pervasive even when it appears to fall short of an actual agency relationship. This is particularly true when the unlawful private search and seizure activity results in criminal prosecution in state or federal criminal courts.").

77 Sklansky, "The Private Police," 1235–1236.

78 Max Weber, "Politics as a Vocation," Speech at Munich University (January 28, 1919) (transcript http://anthropos-lab.net/wp/wp-content/uploads/2011/12/Weber-Politics-as-a-Vocation.pdf).

79 "Overview of Awards by Fiscal Year," *USA Spending*, https://www.usaspending.gov/transparency/Pages/OverviewOfAwards.aspx (last visited September 28, 2016).

80 Robert O'Harrow, Jr., Dana Priest, & Marjorie Censer, "NSA Leaks Put Focus on Intelligence Apparatus's Reliance on Outside Contractors," *Washington Post*, June 10, 2013, http://www.washingtonpost.com/business/nsa-leaks-put-focus-on-intelligence-apparatuss-reliance-on-outside-contractors/2013/06/10/e940c4ba-d20e-11e2-9f1a-1a7cdee20287_story.html.

81 Associated Press, "Case Against Contractors Resurfaces," *New York Times*, October 17, 2013, A17.

82 Jeremy Scahill, "Blackwater's Black Ops," *Nation*, September 15, 2010, http://www.thenation.com/article/154739/blackwaters-black-ops.

83 Commission on Wartime Contracting in Iraq and Afghanistan, "At What Risk? Correcting Over-Reliance on Contractors in Contingency Operations," February 24, 2011, http://cybercemetery.unt.edu/archive/cwc/20110929221313/http://www.wartimecontracting.gov/docs/CWC_InterimReport2-lowres.pdf ("Congress established the Commission on Wartime Contracting to reduce the extensive amount of waste, fraud, and abuse in Iraq and Afghanistan and in future contingency operations … Criminal behavior and blatant corruption sap dollars from what could otherwise be successful project outcomes and, more disturbingly, contribute to a climate in which huge amounts of waste are accepted as the norm.").

84 Ibid., 4.

85 Ibid., 1.

86 *See, e.g.*, "Recent Criminal Cases," *Special Inspector General for Afghanistan Reconstruction*, https://www.sigar.mil/investigations/criminalcases/index.aspx?SSR=3&SubSSR=20&WP=Criminal%20Cases; Carlo Munoz, "2 Soldiers Convicted in Fuel-selling Scam in Afghanistan," *Stars and Stripes*, February 18, 2015, http://www.stripes.com/news/middle-east/afghanistan/2-soldiers-convicted-in-fuel-selling-scam-in-afghanistan-1.330236; U.S. Department of Justice, "Two Department of Defense Contractors Charged in Bribery Conspiracy Related to DOD Contracts in Afghanistan," press release, April 9, 2009, http://www.justice.gov/atr/public/press_releases/2009/244643.htm.

87 *See, e.g.*, Human Rights Council, "Report of the Working Group on the Use of Mercenaries as a Means of Violating Human Rights and Impeding the Exercise of the Right of Peoples to Self-determination," U.N. Doc A/HRC/15/25/Add.3 (2010).

88 *See, e.g.*, Jeremy Scahill, *Blackwater: The Rise of the World's Most Powerful Mercenary Army* (New York: Nation Books, 2007); David Isenberg, *Shadow Force: Private Security Contractors in Iraq* (Westport, CT: Praeger Security

International, 2008); Robert Young Pelton, *Licensed to Kill: Hired Guns in the War on Terror* (New York: Crown Publishers, 2006).

89 *See, e.g.*, "Iraq: A Decade of Abuses," *Amnesty International*, March 11, 2013, https://www.amnesty.org/en/documents/MDE14/001/2013/en/.

90 Ibid.; "Iraq Prison Abuse Scandal Fast Facts," *CNN*, March 12, 2016, http://www.cnn.com/2013/10/30/world/meast/iraq-prison-abuse-scandal-fast-facts/.

91 "Abu Ghraib, 10 Years Later," *New York Times*, April 23, 2015, A22.

92 "Will Anyone Pay for Abu Ghraib?" *New York Times*, February 5, 2015, A25.

93 Noah Bierman, "Few Have Faced Consequences for Abuses at Abu Ghraib Prison in Iraq," *Los Angeles Times*, March 17, 2005, http://www.latimes.com/nation/la-na-abu-ghraib-lawsuit-20150317-story.html.

94 Another PMC involved in the scandal, L-3 Services, a subsidiary of Engility Holdings, settled with the detainees. "Iraqis Awarded $5m Over Abu Ghraib Abuse," *Al-Jazeera*, January 9, 2013, http://www.aljazeera.com/news/middleeast/2013/01/2013193300675421.html; "Iraq Prison Abuse Scandal Fast Facts," *CNN*, March 12, 2016, http://www.cnn.com/2013/10/30/world/meast/iraq-prison-abuse-scandal-fast-facts/.

95 Mark W. Bina, "Private Military Contractor Liability and Accountability after Abu Ghraib," *John Marshall Law Review*, 38, no. 4 (2005): 1242.

96 Ibid.

97 Marc Lindemann, "Civilian Contractors Under Military Law," *Parameters* 37 (2007): 89

98 "Contractors' Support of U.S. Operations in Iraq," *Congressional Budget Office*, 2008, https://www.cbo.gov/sites/default/files/110th-congress-2007-2008/reports/08-12-iraqcontractors.pdf, 20.

99 Deborah Avant & Lee Sigelman, "What Does Private Security in Iraq Mean for US Democracy at Home?" January 24, 2008 (presented at the Burkle Center, UCLA), https://bc.sas.upenn.edu/system/files/Avant_08.pdf.

100 Letter from Ronald Weich, Assistant Attorney General, U.S. Department of Justice, to Hon. Patrick J. Leahy & Hon. Dianne Feinstein, Chairmen, U.S. Senate, Committee on the Judiciary, October 7, 2011, http://www.justice.gov/sites/default/files/ola/legacy/2011/11/08/100711-ltr-res1145-civilian-extraterritorial-jurisdiction-act.pdf.

101 Charles Doyle, *Civilian Extraterritorial Jurisdiction Act: Federal Contractor Criminal Liability Overseas* (CRS Report No. R42358) (Washington, DC: Congressional Research Service, 2012), http://www.fas.org/sgp/crs/misc/R42358.pdf; Overview of S. 1145 (112th): Ceja, *GovTrack*, https://www.govtrack.us/congress/bills/112/s1145 (last visited November 14, 2016).

102 Peter Singer, *Corporate Warriors: The Rise of the Privatized Military Industry* (Ithaca, NY: Cornell University Press, 2003), 238.

103 Katherine Fallah, "Corporate Actors: The Legal Status of Mercenaries in Armed Conflict," *International Review of the Red Cross* 88, no. 863 (2006).

104 Ibid.

105 *See, e.g.*, "S. 674 (110th): Transparency and Accountability in Military and Security Contracting Act of 2007," *GovTrack*, https://www.govtrack.us/congress/bills/110/s674 (last visited October 23, 2016).

106 "H.R. 2740 (110th): MEJA Expansion and Enforcement Act of 2007," *GovTrack*, https://www.govtrack.us/congress/bills/110/hr2740 (last visited October 23, 2016).

107 Lindsay Wise, "Sen. Claire McCaskill Leaps Hurdles to Overhauling Wartime Contracting," *McClatchy DC*, January 19, 2013, http://www.mcclatchydc.com/news/politics-government/congress/article24743218.html; Press Release, "Sen. Claire McCaskill, Fight Against ISIS Gets Independent Watchdog as McCaskill's Wartime Contracting Reforms Kick-in," December 23, 2014, https://www.mccaskill.senate.gov/media-center/news-releases/fight-against-isis-gets-independent-watchdog-as-mccaskills-wartime-contracting-reforms-kick-in.

108 "Constellis Holdings, Inc. Acquires Constellis Group, Inc.," *Academi*, June 6, 2015, https://www.academi.com/news_room/press_releases/95.

109 "Defense," *Center for Responsive Politics*, https://www.opensecrets.org/industries/indus.php?Ind=D (last visited October 23, 2016).

110 Laura T. Dickinson, "Public Law Values in a Privatized World," 31 *Yale Journal of International Law*, 383 (2006).

111 Laura Dickinson, *Outsourcing War and Peace: Preserving Public Values in a World of Privatized Foreign Affairs* (New Haven, CT: Yale University Press, 2011), 71–73.

112 Ibid., 143–145.

113 Ibid., 194.

114 Paul Verkuil, *Outsourcing Sovereignty: Why Privatization of Government Functions Threatens Democracy and What We Can Do About It* (New York: Cambridge University Press, 2007).

115 Commission on Wartime Contracting in Iraq and Afghanistan, "Transforming Wartime Contracting: Controlling Costs, Reducing Risks," 2011, http://www.wartimecontracting.gov/docs/CWC_FinalReport-lowres.pdf, 34.

116 Singer, *Corporate Warriors*, 235.

117 Commission on Wartime Contracting in Iraq and Afghanistan, "Transforming Wartime Contracting," 58–61.

118 Alan McLean & Archie Tse, "American Forces in Afghanistan and Iraq," *New York Times*, http://www.nytimes.com/interactive/2011/06/22/world/asia/american-forces-in-afghanistan-and-iraq.html (last visited October 23, 2016).

119 Mark Thompson, "Obama's Afghanistan Speech: What to Watch For," *Time*, December 1, 2009, http://content.time.com/time/nation/article/0,8599,1943707,00.html.

120 McLean & Tse, "American Forces."

121 August Cole, "Afghanistan Contractors Outnumber Troops," *Wall Street Journal*, August 22, 2009, http://www.wsj.com/articles/SB125089638739950599.

[122] Moshe Schwartz & Jennifer Church, *Department of Defense's Use of Contractors to Support Military Operations: Background, Analysis and Issues for Congress* (CRS Report No. R43074) (Washington, DC: Congressional Research Service, 2013), http://www.fas.org/sgp/crs/natsec/R43074.pdf.

[123] Micah Zenko, "The New Unknown Soldiers of Iraq and Afghanistan," *Foreign Policy* (May 29, 2015), http://foreignpolicy.com/2015/05/29/the-new-unknown-soldiers-of-afghanistan-and-iraq/.

[124] *Berwick v. Uber Techs., Inc.*, No. 11-46739 EK, slip op. at 9 (California Labor Commissioner, June 3, 2015).

[125] Noam Scheiber & Stephanie Strom, "Labor Board Ruling Eases Way for Fast-Food Unions' Efforts," *New York Times*, August 27, 2015, http://www.nytimes.com/2015/08/28/business/labor-board-says-franchise-workers-can-bargain-with-parent-company.html.

[126] James Surowiecki, "Gigs with Benefits," *New Yorker*, July 6, 2015, http://www.newyorker.com/magazine/2015/07/06/gigs-with-benefits.

[127] "Independent Contractor (Self-Employed) or Employee?" *Internal Revenue Service*, https://www.irs.gov/businesses/small-businesses-self-employed/independent-contractor-self-employed-or-employee (last visited October 23, 2016).

[128] For more discussion on this point, see Amitai Etzioni, "The Bankruptcy of Liberalism and Conservatism," *Political Science Quarterly* 128, no. 1 (2013).

[129] Ibid.

Chapter Three

[1] George J. Stigler, "The Theory of Economic Regulation," *Bell Journal of Economics and Management Science* 2, no. 1 (1971).

[2] George J. Stigler & Claire Friedland, "What Can Regulators Regulate? The Case of Electricity," *Journal of Law and Economics* 5 (1962).

[3] Eric Lipton & Ben Protess, "Banks' Lobbyists Help in Drafting Financial Bills," *New York Times*, May 23, 2013, https://dealbook.nytimes.com/2013/05/23/banks-lobbyists-help-in-drafting-financial-bills/?ref=politics.

[4] "Setting the Rules," *The Economist*, January 9, 2003, http://www.economist.com/node/1558898.

[5] Jerry Markham, *A Financial History of the United States from Enron-Era Scandals to the Subprime Crisis (2004–2009)* (2011; repr., London: Routledge, 2015), 77.

[6] Nadja Popovich & Tatiana Schlossberg, "23 Environmental Rules Rolled Back in Trump's First 100 Days," *New York Times*, May 2, 2017, https://www.nytimes.com/interactive/2017/05/02/climate/environmental-rules-reversed-trump-100-days.html?mcubz=1.

[7] *See* Craig Timberg, "FTC under fire for passing on Google's search practices," *Washington Post*, December 18, 2012, https://www.washingtonpost.com/business/economy/ftc-under-fire-for-passing-on-googles-search-practices-critics-say/2012/12/18/aec0d708-487f-11e2-b6f0-e851e741d196_story.html?utm_term=.59f0b6e76688; Brody Mullins, Rolfe Winkler, & Brent Kendall, "Inside the U.S. Antitrust Probe of Google," *Wall Street Journal*,

March 19, 2015, https://www.wsj.com/articles/inside-the-u-s-antitrust-probe-of-google-1426793274.

8 Mullins et al., "Inside the U.S. Antitrust Probe of Google."

9 Binyamin Appelbaum & Ellen Nakashima, "Banking Regulator Played Advocate Over Enforcer," *Washington Post*, November 23, 2008, http://www.washingtonpost.com/wp-dyn/content/article/2008/11/22/AR2008112202213.html.

10 Ibid.

11 Judith Lewis, "How We Almost Blew Up Ohio," *Mother Jones*, April 24, 2008, http://www.motherjones.com/environment/2008/04/how-we-almost-blew-ohio/.

12 Ibid.

13 Gerald P. O'Driscoll, Jr., "The Gulf Spill, the Financial Crisis and Government Failure," *Wall Street Journal*, June 12, 2010, http://online.wsj.com/article/SB10001424052748704575304575296873167457684.html.

14 John C. Coates IV, "The Goals and Promise of the Sarbane-Oxley Act," *Journal of Economic Perspectives* 21, no. 2 (2007).

15 Cass Sunsetin & Richard Thaler, "Libertarian Paternalism is not an Oxymoron," *The University of Chicago Law Review* 70, no. 4 (2003).

16 Richard Thaler & Cass Sunstein, *Nudge: Improving Decisions About Health, Wealth, and Happiness* (New Haven, CT: Yale University Press, 2008).

17 Jill Ornitz & Ryan Struyk, "Donald Trump's Surprisingly Honest Lessons About Big Money in Politics," *ABC News*, August 11, 2015, http://abcnews.go.com/Politics/donald-trumps-surprisingly-honest-lessons-big-money-politics/story?id=32993736.

18 Anahad O'Connor, "Herbal Supplements Are Often Not What They Seem," *New York Times*, November 3, 2013, http://www.nytimes.com/2013/11/05/science/herbal-supplements-are-often-not-what-they-seem.html.

19 Evan Osnos, "Embrace the Irony," *New Yorker*, October 13, 2014, http://www.newyorker.com/magazine/2014/10/13/embrace-irony.

20 *Citizens United v. Federal Election Commission*, 558 U. S. 310, 360 (2010).

21 Paul Blumenthal, "Fossil Fuel Company Super PAC Gifts Came before Congress Ended the Oil Export Ban," *Huffington Post*, February 3, 2015, http://www.huffingtonpost.com/entry/fossil-fuel-super-pac-donors_us_56b25c5ae4b04f9b57d82d06.

22 "Congress Passes U.S. Spending Bill to End Oil Export Ban," *Bloomberg News*, http://www.bloomberg.com/politics/articles/2015-12-18/house-passes-u-s-spending-bill-that-ends-crude-oil-export-ban.

23 Clifford Krauss & Diane Cardwell, "Expected Repeal of Oil Export Ban Unlikely to Have Immediate Impact," *New York Times*, December 16, 2015, http://www.nytimes.com/2015/12/17/business/energy-environment/expected-repeal-of-oil-export-ban-unlikely-to-have-immediate-impact.html.

24 Emily Atkin, "Senate Passes Bill to Approve Construction of Keystone XL Pipeline," *ThinkProgress*, January 29, 2015, https://thinkprogress.

org/senate-passes-bill-to-approve-construction-of-keystone-xl-pipeline-13451fc504a0#.k8ctzrh3h.

[25] Anne Baker, "The More Outside Money Politicians Take, the Less Well They Represent Their Constituents," *Washington Post*, August 17, 2016, https://www.washingtonpost.com/news/monkey-cage/wp/2016/08/17/members-of-congress-follow-the-money-not-the-voters-heres-the-evidence/#comments.

[26] Complaint at 10–11, *McCutcheon v. Federal Elections Commission*, 893 F. Supp. 2d 133 (D.D.C. 2012) (No. l:12-cv-01034-JEB).

[27] Ibid., 11–12.

[28] Richard Briffault, "Of Constituents and Contributors," *University of Chicago Legal Forum* (2016): 31.

[29] Ibid., 34.

[30] "The term *independent expenditure* means an expenditure by a person for a communication expressly advocating the election or defeat of a clearly identified candidate that is not made in cooperation, consultation, or concert with, or at the request or suggestion of, a candidate, a candidate's authorized committee, or their agents, or a political party committee or its agents." 11 CFR §100.16(a).

[31] *Buckley v. Valeo*, 424 U.S. 1, 47 (1976).

[32] *Citizens United v. Federal Election Commission*, 558 U.S. 310 (2010).

[33] Matea Gold, "It's Bold, but Legal: How Campaigns and Their Super PAC Backers Work Together," *Washington Post*, July 6, 2015, https://www.washingtonpost.com/politics/here-are-the-secret-ways-super-pacs-and-campaigns-can-work-together/2015/07/06/bda78210-1539-11e5-89f3-61410da94eb1_story.html.

[34] Matea Gold, "Election 2014: A New Level of Collaboration Between Candidates and Big-Money Allies," *Washington Post*, November 3, 2014, https://www.washingtonpost.com/politics/election-2014-a-new-level-of-collaboration-between-candidates-and-big-money-allies/2014/11/03/ec2bda9a-636f-11e4-836c-83bc4f26eb67_story.html.

[35] Matea Gold, "Now It's Even Easier for Candidates and Their Aides to Help Super PACs," *Washington Post*, December 24, 2015, https://www.washingtonpost.com/politics/now-its-even-easier-for-candidates-and-their-aides-to-help-super-pacs/2015/12/24/d8d1ff4a-a989-11e5-9b92-dea7cd4b1a4d_story.html.

[36] "Strengthen Rules Preventing Candidate Coordination with Super PACs," *Brennan Center for Justice*, February 4, 2016, https://www.brennancenter.org/analysis/strengthen-rules-preventing-candidate-coordination-super-pacs#_ftn3.

[37] Gold, "It's Bold, but Legal."

[38] Gold, "Election 2014: A New Level of Collaboration."

[39] Eric Schmitt, "Senate Rejects Campaign Finance Amendment," *New York Times*, March 19, 1997, http://www.nytimes.com/1997/03/19/us/senate-rejects-campaign-finance-amendment.html; Associated Press, "Campaign

Spending Curb Defeated," September 11, 2014, http://www.nytimes. com/2014/09/12/us/campaign-spending-curb-defeated.html?_r=0.

[40] Derek Willis, "Every Election Is the Most Expensive Election. Or Not," *New York Times*, December 16, 2014, http://www.nytimes.com/2014/12/17/ upshot/every-election-is-the-most-expensive-election-or-not.html.

[41] "Cost of Election," *Center for Responsive Politics*, https://www.opensecrets. org/overview/cost.php?display=T&infl=N.

[42] "Nine Things You Need to Know about Super PACs," *Sunlight Foundation*, January 31, 2012, https://sunlightfoundation.com/blog/2012/01/31/nine- things-you-need-know-about-super-pacs/.

[43] *McCutcheon v. Federal Election Commission*, Slip. Op. No. 12-536 at 35 (2014).

[44] "Political Nonprofits (Dark Money)," *Center for Responsive Politics*, https:// www.opensecrets.org/outsidespending/nonprof_summ.php.

[45] Fredreka Schouten, "Super PACs Hide Their Intentions Behind Fuzzy Names," *USA Today*, February 11, 2014, http://www.usatoday.com/story/ news/politics/2014/02/11/super-pac-names/5375699/.

[46] *Buckley v. Valeo*, 424 U.S. 1 (1976).

Chapter Four

[1] Belief in the legitimacy of the laws, not fear of punishment, is what drives people to comply with laws. Tom Tyler, *Why People Obey the Law* (New Haven, CT: Yale University Press, 1990). Thus it is imperative that laws are perceived to have a legitimate base.

[2] Andrew Perrin, *Citizen Speak: The Democratic Imagination in American Life* (Chicago: University of Chicago Press, 2006).

[3] Ibid.

[4] Jon D. Miller, 2010. "Attentive Public," in *Encyclopedia of Science and Technology Communication*, ed. Susanna H. Priest (ed.), (Thousand Oaks, CA: SAGE Publications, Inc.), 73–75.

[5] Encyclopædia Britannica Online. s.v. "ideal type" (2016), http://www. britannica.com/topic/ideal-type.

[6] Paul A. Offit, *Pandora's Lab: Seven Stories of Science Gone Wrong* (Washington, DC: National Geographic Partners, 2017), 173.

[7] Denis H. Wu & Renita Coleman, "Advancing Agenda-Setting Theory: The Comparative Strength and New Contingent Conditions of the Two Levels of Agenda-Setting," *Journalism and Mass Communication Quarterly* 86, no. 4 (Winter 2009): 776.

[8] James M. Jasper, "The Emotions of Protest: Affective and Reactive Emotions in and around Social Movements," *Sociological Forum* 13, no. 3 (1998): 409.

[9] Amitai Etzioni, "COIN: A Study of Strategic Illusion," *Small Wars & Insurgencies* 26, no. 3 (2015): 345–376.

[10] Kristin Luker, *Abortion and the Politics of Motherhood* (Berkeley: University of California Press, 1985), 226.

[11] Aldon D. Morris, "A Retrospective on the Civil Rights Movement: Political and Intellectual Landmarks," *Annual Review of Sociology* 25 (1999).

[12] Data source: Google Trends, www.google.com/trends.

[13] The Montreux Declaration, August 23, 1947, http://www.cvce.eu/content/publication/1999/1/1/adf279f7-80a4-4855-9215-48a5184328aa/publishable_en.pdf.

[14] Data source: Google Trends, www.google.com/trends.

[15] George Stigler and Gary Becker, "De Gustibus Non Est Disputandum," *The American Economic Review* 67, no. 2 (1977).

[16] *See* Amartya Sen, "Rational Fools: A Critique of the Behavioral Foundations of Economic Theory," *Philosophy & Public Affairs* 6, no. 4 (1977); Richard Thaler, *Misbehaving: The Making of Behavioral Economics* (New York: W.W. Norton & Company, 2015); Herbert Simon, *Administrative Behavior: A Study of Decision-Making Processes in Administrative Organizations*, 4th ed. (1947; New York: The Free Press, 1997).

[17] James H. Kuklinski, Ellen Riggle, & Victor Ottati, "The Cognitive and Affective Bases of Political Tolerance Judgments," *American Journal of Political Science* 35 (1991): 1–27; John S. Dryzek, "Democratization as Deliberative Capacity Building," *Comparative Political Studies* 42 (2008): 11.

[18] James Q. Wilson, "Interests and Deliberation in the American Republic, or Why James Madison Would Have Never Received the James Madison Award," *PS: Political Science and Politics* 23, no. 4 (1990): 559.

[19] Ernest R. House, "Unfinished Business: Causes and Values," *American Journal of Evaluation* 22, no. 3 (2005): 313 cited in: Robert A. Harris, "A Summary Critique of The Fact/Value Dichotomy," *virtualsalt.com* (2005): 2.

[20] Cheryl Hall, "Recognizing the Passion in Deliberation: Toward a More Democratic Theory of Deliberative Democracy," *Hypatia* (2007): 81.

[21] Ibid., 82.

[22] Jonathan Haidt, *The Righteous Mind: Why Good People Are Divided by Politics and Religion* (New York: Pantheon Books, 2012).

[23] Bernard Cohen, *The Press and Foreign Policy* (Princeton, NJ: Princeton University Press, 1963).

[24] Robert E. Goodin, *No Smoking: The Ethical Issues* (Chicago: The University of Chicago Press, 1989).

[25] Michael Lerner and Cornel West, *Jews and Blacks: Let the Healing Begin* (New York: G.P. Putnam's Sons, 1995).

[26] For additional examples, see Michael LaBossiere, *Moral Methods* (self-published, 2012).

[27] OED Online, "culture, n.," Oxford University Press (2016), http://www.oed.com/view/Entry/45746?redirectedFrom=culture+war.

[28] Stephen Prothero, *Why the Liberals Win the Culture Wars (Even When They Lose Elections)* (New York: Harper Collins, 2016).

[29] On the emotional role of *Brown v. Board of Education* (1954), see Jeff Goodwin, James M. Jasper, & Francesa Polletta (eds.), *Passionate Politics: Emotions and Social Movements* (Chicago: The University of Chicago Press, 2001), 7–8.

[30] Monica Anderson, "For Earth Day, Here's How Americans View Environmental Issues," *Pew Research Center*, April 22, 2016, http://www.

pewresearch.org/fact-tank/2016/04/22/for-earth-day-heres-how-americans-view-environmental-issues/.

31 Zac Auter, "In U.S., 73% Now Prioritize Alternative Energy Over Oil, Gas," *Gallup*, March 24, 2016, http://www.gallup.com/poll/190268/prioritize-alternative-energy-oil-gas.aspx.

32 Richard H. Thaler & Cass R. Sunstein, *Nudge: Improving Decisions About Health, Wealth, and Happiness* (New Haven, CT: Yale University Press, 2008).

33 Amitai Etzioni, *A Comparative Analysis of Complex Organizations* (New York: Free Press of Glencoe, 1961).

34 Amitai Etzioni, *A Comparative Analysis of Complex Organizations, Revised and Enlarged Edition* (New York: The Free Press, 1975).

35 *See, e.g.*, James Warren, "Should We Pay Kids to Read?" *The Atlantic*, October 16, 2012, http://www.theatlantic.com/national/archive/2012/10/should-we-pay-kids-to-read/263677/.

36 *See, e.g.*, Dion Haynes & Michael Birnbaum, "DC Tries Cash as a Motivator in Schools," *Washington Post*, August 22, 2008, http://www.washingtonpost.com/wp-dyn/content/article/2008/08/21/AR2008082103874.html.

37 Dennis Hume Wrong, *The Problem of Order: What Unites and Divides Society* (New York: The Free Press, 1994).

38 Alan Lewis, *The Psychology of Taxation* (New York: St. Martin's, 1982): 5–6.

39 Amitai Etzioni, *The New Golden Rule: Community and Morality in a Democratic Society* (New York: Basic Books, 1996), 146.

40 Ibid., 143.

41 "Bowers v. Hardwick," Oyez. Chicago-Kent College of Law at Illinois Tech, n.d., accessed June 9, 2016, https://www.oyez.org/cases/1985/85-140.

42 H.R. 3396 (104th) (1996a). Defense of Marriage Act. https://www.govtrack.us/congress/votes/104-1996/h316.

43 H.R. 3396 (104th) (1996b). Defense of Marriage Act. https://www.govtrack.us/congress/votes/104-1996/s280.

44 David Cole, *Engines of Liberty: The Power of Citizen Activists to Make Constitutional Law* (New York: Basic Books, 2016), 28.

45 William J. Clinton, *Public Papers of the Presidents of the United States, Book 2. July 1 to December 31, 1996* (Washington: United States Government Printing Office, 1996), 1635.

46 Gallup, "Marriage" (2016), http://www.gallup.com/poll/117328/marriage.aspx.

47 Pew Research Center, "Gay Marriage" (2015), http://www.pewresearch.org/data-trend/domestic-issues/attitudes-on-gay-marriage/.

48 Jeffrey Schmalz, "In Hawaii, Step Toward Legalized Gay Marriage," *New York Times*, May 7, 1993, http://www.nytimes.com/1993/05/07/us/in-hawaii-step-toward-legalized-gay-marriage.html.

49 Cole, *Engines of Liberty*.

50 Pam Belluck, "Massachusetts Arrives at Moment for Same-sex Marriage," *New York Times*, May 17, 2004, http://www.nytimes.com/2004/05/17/us/massachusetts-arrives-at-moment-for-same-sex-marriage.html?_r=0.

51 Cole, *Engines of Liberty*, 82.

52 Ibid., 49.

53 Ibid., 51.

54 Ibid., 48–49.

55 Ibid.

56 Ibid., 70.

57 Ibid., 69.

58 Ibid., 68–70.

59 Ibid., 74.

60 Associated Press, "Number of Gay and Lesbian TV Characters Growing, Says GLAAD," October 1, 2014, http://www.cbsnews.com/news/number-of-gay-and-lesbian-tv-characters-growing-says-glaad/.

61 Eliana Dockterman, "These Shows Helped Shape America's Attitudes About Gay Relationships," *Time*, June 26, 2015, http://time.com/3937496/gay-marriage-supreme-court-ruling-tv-shows-changed-america/.

62 Paul Hitlin & Sovini Tan, "In Social Media, Support for Same-Sex Marriage," *Pew Research Center*, May 17, 2012, http://www.journalism.org/2012/05/17/social-media-support-samesex-marriage/.

63 Ibid.

64 Ibid.

65 Alexis Kleinman, "How the Red Equal Sign Took Over Facebook, According to Facebook's Own Data," *Huffington Post*, March 29, 2013, http://www.huffingtonpost.com/2013/03/29/red-equal-sign-facebook_n_2980489.html.

66 Maureen McCarty, "One Year Out, The Little Red Logo that Transformed the Marriage Equality Narrative," *Human Rights Campaign*, March 25, 2014, http://www.hrc.org/blog/one-year-out-the-little-red-logo-that-transformed-the-marriage-equality-nar.

67 Paul Hitlin, Mark Jurkowitz, & Amy Mitchell, "News Coverage Conveys Strong Momentum for Same-Sex Marriage," *Pew Research Center*, June 17, 2013, http://www.journalism.org/2013/06/17/news-coverage-conveys-strong-momentum/.

68 Ibid.

69 Associated Press, "In California, Protests Over Gay Marriage Vote," November 9, 2008, http://www.nytimes.com/2008/11/10/us/10protest.html.

70 Ibid.

71 "United States v. Windsor," Oyez. Chicago-Kent College of Law at Illinois Tech, n.d., accessed June 9, 2016, https://www.oyez.org/cases/2012/12-307.

72 "Obergefell v. Hodges," Oyez. Chicago-Kent College of Law at Illinois Tech, n.d. June 9, 2016, accessed June 9, 2016, https://www.oyez.org/cases/2014/14-556.

73 Gallup, "Marriage" (2016), http://www.gallup.com/poll/117328/marriage.aspx.

74 Cole, *Engines of Liberty*, 92.

[75] Jimmy Carter, "Airline Deregulation Act of 1978 Remarks on Signing S. 2493 into Law," October 24, 1978, *The American Presidency Project*, http://www.presidency.ucsb.edu/ws/?pid=30038.

[76] Jon Kamp & Valerie Bauerlein, "PayPal Cancels Plan for Facility in North Carolina, Citing Transgender Law," April 5, 2016, https://www.wsj.com/articles/paypal-cancels-plans-for-operations-center-400-jobs-over-north-carolinas-transgender-law-1459872277.

[77] Ryan Bort, "A Comprehensive Timeline of Public Figures Boycotting North Carolina over The HB2 'Bathroom Bill,'" *Newsweek*, September 14, 2016, http://www.newsweek.com/north-carolina-hb2-bathroom-bill-timeline-498052.

[78] Stephen Peters, "More Than 100 Major CEOs & Business Leaders Urge North Carolina To Repeal Anti-LGBT Law," *Human Rights Campaign*, March 31, 2016, http://www.hrc.org/blog/more-than-100-major-ceos-business-leaders-demanding-north-carolina-repeal-r#prclt-8yvIPm11.

[79] Cass Sunstein, "On the Expressive Function of Law," *The University of Pennsylvania Law Review* 144, no. 5 (1996): 2022.

[80] Ibid., 2051.

[81] Alexandra Natapoff , "Misdemeanor Decriminalization," *Vanderbilt Law Review* 68, no. 4 (2015): 1074.

[82] Janice Nadler, "Expressive Law, Social Norms, and Social Groups," *Law & Social Inquiry*, 42, no. 1 (2017): 68; *See also* Richard H. McAdams, "An Attitudinal Theory of Expressive Law," *Oregon Law Review* 78 (2000).

[83] John L. Newby II, "The Fight for the Right to Fight and the Forgotten Negro Protest Movement: The History of Executive Order 9981 and Its Effect upon Brown v. Board Of Education and Beyond," *Texas Journal on Civil Liberties & Civil Rights* 10, no. 1 (2004): 84.

[84] Richard McAdams, "An Attitudinal Theory of Expressive Law," *Oregon Law Review* 79 (2000): 389.

[85] Etzioni, *The New Golden Rule*.

[86] Ferdinand Tönnies, *Community and Society*, trans. and ed. Charles P. Loomis (East Lansing: Michigan State University Press, 1957).

[87] Edward Blakely, "In Gated Communities, Such As Where Trayvon Martin Died, A Dangerous Mind-Set," *Washington Post*, April 6, 2012, https://www.washingtonpost.com/opinions/in-gated-communities-such-as-where-trayvon-martin-died-a-dangerous-mind-set/2012/04/06/gIQAwWG8zS_story.html?utm_term=.d8cc39afee59.

[88] Amy Gutmann, "Communitarian Critics of Liberalism," *Philosophy and Public Affairs* 14, no. 3 (Summer 1985): 319.

[89] L.B. Parekh, *The Future of Multi-Ethnic Britain: Report of the Commission on the Future of Multi-Ethnic Britain* (London: Profile Books, 2000).

[90] Amitai Etzioni, *Security First* (New Haven, CT: Yale University Press, 2007), 186–192.

Chapter Five

[1] Plato, *Republic*, 505e.

2 Plato, *Republic*, 464b.

3 Aristotle, *Politics*, 1280a31–32.

4 Cicero, *On the Commonwealth* , trans. George Holland Sabine and Stanley Barney Smith (New York: Macmillan, 1929), 129.

5 Aquinas, *Summa Theologiae*, Ia, IIae, q. 19, art. 10.

6 Andrew M. Yuengert, "The Common Good for Economists," *Faith and Economics* 38 (2001), https://www.gordon.edu/ace/pdf/Yuengert=F&E38. pdf.

7 Adam Smith, *An Inquiry into the Nature and Causes of the Wealth of Nations* (1776; repr., Chicago: Chicago University Press, 1977), 477.

8 Friedrich von Hayek, *The Road to Serfdom* (Chicago: University of Chicago Press, 1944).

9 Kenneth Joseph Arrow, "Economic Welfare and the Allocation of Resources for Invention" in *The Rate and Direction of Inventive Activity: Economic and Social Factors*, ed. Universities-National Bureau Committee for Economic Research, Committee on Economic Growth of the Social Science Research Council (Princeton: Princeton University Press, 1962), 619, http://www. nber.org/chapters/c2144.pdf.

10 Frank Sorauf, *Party and Representation: Legislative Politics in Pennsylvania* (New York: Atherton Press, 1963).

11 Ayn Rand, "The Monument Builders," in *The Virtue of Selfishness* (New York: Signet, 1964), 88.

12 *Abrams v. United States*, 250 U.S. 616 (1919).

13 Private conversation with Scott L. Cummings.

14 *See* Amitai Etzioni, *Security First* (New Haven, CT: Yale University Press, 2007), 5–7.

15 Dennis C. Mueller, *Public Choice III* (Cambridge, UK: Cambridge University Press, 2003), 304.

16 André Blais, *To Vote or not to Vote? The Merits and Limits of Rational Choice Theory* (Pittsburgh, PA: University of Pittsburgh Press, 2000).

Chapter Six

1 David R. Jones, *Party Polarization and Legislative Gridlock, Political Research Quarterly* 54 (2001): 125–141.

2 *See, e.g.,*Ashley Fantz & Paul Courson,"Prosecutors: Bradley Manning'Craved' Notoriety," *CNN,* June 3, 2013, http://www.cnn.com/2013/06/03/US/ manning-court-martial.

3 Ibid.

4 Ibid.

5 Ibid.

6 Ibid.

7 David E. Pozen, "The Leaky Leviathan: Why the Government Condemns and Condones Unlawful Disclosures of Information," *Harvard Law Review* 127 (2013): 512, 542–543 (citations omitted).

8 *See* Lydia Saad, "'Pro-Choice'Americans at Record-Low 41%," *Gallup,* May 23, 2012, http://www.gallup.com/poll/154838/pro-choice-americans-

record-low.aspx (highlighting the close divide between pro-choice and pro-life Americans).

[9] *See* "Gun Control: Key Data Points," *Pew Research Center*, July 27, 2013, http://www.pewresearch.org/key-data-points/gun-control-key-data-points-from-pew-research (reporting that the division among Americans on the gun rights debate is virtually even).

[10] *See* "Market Troubles," *Economist*, April 6, 2011, http://www.economist.com/blogs/dailychart/2011/04/public_opinion_capitalism (noting a split in Americans' opinion of the free market).

[11] For more discussion on the fragmentations of the media, see Rebecca Chalif, "Political Media Fragmentation: Echo Chambers in Cable News," *Electronic Media & Policy* 1 (2011): 46, http://www.emandp.com/site_content_uploads/main_content/Political Media Fragmentation - Echo Chambers in Cable News (1).pdf. For more evidence of political polarization, *see* David R. Jones, "Party Polarization and Legislative Gridlock," *Political Research Quarterly* 54 (2001): 125; Amitai Etzioni, "Gridlock?" *The Forum* 10, no. 3 (2012), http://icps.gwu.edu/files/2013/01/Gridlock.pdf.

[12] I choose the word "seeks" deliberately because the media endeavors, but does not necessarily achieve, this goal.

[13] Ann E. Marimow, "A Rare Peek into a Justice Department Leak Probe," *Washington Post*, May 19, 2013, http://www.washingtonpost.com/local/a-rare-peek-into-a-justice-department-leak-probe/2013/05/19/0bc473de-be5e-11e2-97d4-a479289a31f9_story.html.

[14] Mark Hosenball & Tabassum Zakaria, "AP Records Seizure Just Latest Step in Sweeping U.S. Leak Probe," *Reuters*, May 15, 2013, http://www.reuters.com/article/2013/05/16/us-usa-justice-ap-investigation-idUSBRE94F01F20130516.

[15] Charlie Savage & Leslie Kaufman, "Phone Records of Journalists Seized by U.S.," *New York Times*, May 14, 2013, A1.

[16] *See, e.g.*, Nick Gillespie, "Obama's War on Journalism: 'An Unconstitutional Act'," *Daily Beast*, May 22, 2013, http://www.thedailybeast.com/articles/2013/05/22/obama-s-war-on-journalism-an-unconstitutional-act.html.

[17] Dana Milbank, "In AP, Rosen Investigations, Government Makes Criminals of Reporters," *Washington Post*, May 21, 2013, http://articles.washingtonpost.com/2013-05-21/opinions/39419370_1_obama-administration-watergate-benghazi.

[18] Ibid.

[19] "Another Chilling Leak Investigation," *New York Times*, May 21, 2013, A26.

[20] Gillespie, "Obama's War on Journalism."

[21] "Justice Department Run Amok on Journalists' Sources," *The San Francisco Chronicle*, May 22, 2013, http://www.sfchronicle.com/opinion/editorials/article/Justice-Department-run-amok-on-journalists-4540632.php.

[22] Ron Fournier, "You Know What Really Risks National Security? Leak Investigations," *National Journal*, May 30, 2013, http://www.nationaljournal.

com/politics/you-know-what-really-risks-national-security-leak-investigations-20130517.

[23] Alex Weprin, "Tom Brokaw: 'The Press Always Has to Be Careful About Having a Glass Jaw,'" *TVNewser*, May 29, 2013, http://www.mediabistro.com/tvnewser/tom-brokaw-on-the-brokaw-files-the-state-of-media-and-the-presidents-press-policy_b181138.

[24] Walter Pincus, "A Knee-Jerk Circling of the Media Wagons," *Washington Post*, May 28, 2013, A9.

[25] "Correspondents' Association Statement on Monitoring of Journalists," *Fox News*, May 21, 2013, http://www.foxnews.com/politics/2013/05/21/correspondents-association-statement-on-monitoring-journalists/.

[26] Pincus, "A Knee-Jerk Circling of the Media Wagons."

[27] Tom Curry, "Holder Addresses AP Leaks Investigation, Announces IRS Probe," *NBC News*, May 14, 2013, http://nbcpolitics.nbcnews.com/_news/2013/05/14/18253923-holder-addresses-ap-leaks-investigation-announces-irs-probe?lite.

[28] Daniel Klaidman, "Holder's Regrets and Repairs," *Daily Beast*, May 28, 2013, http://www.thedailybeast.com/articles/2013/05/28/holder-s-regrets-and-repairs.html.

[29] Barack Obama, "Remarks at the National Defense University," May 23, 2013, http://www.whitehouse.gov/the-press-office/2013/05/23/remarks-president-national-defense-university.

[30] Ibid.

[31] Ibid.

[32] Pozen, "The Leaky Leviathan," 577.

[33] Ibid., 514.

[34] See Jeffrey M. Jones, "Americans' Trust in Government Generally Down this Year," *Gallup*, September 26, 2013, http://www.gallup.com/poll/164663/americans-trust-government-generally-down-year.aspx (reporting that trust in the executive branch fell to 51 percent in 2013).

[35] Pozen, "The Leaky Leviathan," 573.

[36] Matthew Cooper, "Why a Media Shield Law Isn't Enough to Save Journalists," *National Journal*, May 29, 2013, http://www.nationaljournal.com/politics/why-a-media-shield-law-isn-t-enough-to-save-journalists_20130529.

[37] *See* Amitai Etzioni, *The Common Good* (Cambridge: Polity Press, 2004), 3–4.

[38] *See, e.g.*, Kostas Vlassopoulos, "Free Spaces: Identity, Experience and Democracy in Classical Athens," *Classical Quarterly* 57 (2007): 33.

[39] *See* "Q&A: What is a Loya Jirga?" *BBC News*, July 1, 2002, http://news.bbc.co.UK/2/hi/south_asia/1782079.stm.

[40] *See* Dylan Matthews, "It's Official: The 112th Congress was the Most Polarized Ever," *Washington Post*, January 17, 2013, http://www.washingtonpost.com/blogs/wonkblog/wp/2013/01/17/its-official-the-112th-congress-was-the-most-polarized-ever/.

[41] *See generally*, Amitai Etzioni, "Communitarianism," *Encyclopedia Britannica Online*, http://www.britannica.com/EBchecked/topic/1366457/communitarianism (accessed January 13, 2014).

[42] Etzioni, *The Common Good*. In contrast, authoritarian and East Asian communitarians tend be concerned with the common good and pay heed to rights mainly insofar as they serve the rulers' aims. *See* Etzioni, "Communitarianism." At the opposite end of the spectrum, contemporary liberals emphasize individual rights and autonomy over societal formulations of the common good. Ibid.

[43] Ibid.

[44] U.S. Const. amend. IV.

[45] *See generally*, "National Terrorism Advisory System," *Department of Homeland Security*, http://www.dhs.gov/national-terrorism-advisory-system (accessed January 15, 2014) (stating that "Americans ... should always be aware of the heightened risk of terrorist attack in the United States").

[46] *See* "The Comprehensive National Cybersecurity Initiative," *White House*, http://www.whitehouse.gov/issues/foreignpolicy/cybersecurity/nationa-initiative (accessed January 14, 2014) (identifying "cybersecurity as one of the most serious economic and national security challenges we face as a nation, but one that we as a government or as a country are not adequately prepared to counter").

[47] Ibid.

[48] *See, e.g.*, Marc Ambinder, "WikiLeaks: One Analyst, So Many Documents," *National Journal*, November 29, 2010, http://www.nationaljournal.com/whitehouse/wikileaks-one-analyst-so-many-documents-20101129. Mark Feldstein writes that Wikileaks'"instantaneous global reach poses a challenge not only to state secrets everywhere, but even perhaps to the very idea of government itself." Mark Feldstein, "The Implications of Wikileaks," *American Journalism Review*, December 14, 2010, http://www.ajrarchive.org/Article.asp?id=4999.

[49] *See* Etzioni, "Communitarianism."

Chapter Seven

[1] *See generally*, Amitai Etzioni, *The New Golden Rule: Community and Morality in a Democratic Society* (New York: Basic Books, 1996).

[2] *See generally*, Amitai Etzioni, *The Limits of Privacy* (New York: Basic Books, 1999) (discussing this balance in the context of privacy and public health, public safety, sex offenders, and freedom of the press, among other rights); *see also* Amitai Etzioni, "The Privacy Merchants: What Is To Be Done?" *Journal of Constitutional Law* 14, no. 4 (2012); Amitai Etzioni, *How Patriotic is the Patriot Act? Freedom Versus Security in the Age of Terrorism* (New York: Routledge, 2004).

[3] Gerald Gaus & Shane D. Courtland, "Liberalism," in *Stanford Encyclopedia of Philosophy*, ed. Edward N. Zalta, 2011, http://plato.stanford.edu/entries/liberalism. *See also* John Rawls, *A Theory of Justice* (Cambridge, MA: Belknap Press, 1999).

[4] Gregory Ferenstein, "Obama's Shift Towards Communitarianism," *Daily Beast*, June 30, 2013, http://www.thedailybeast.com/articles/2013/06/30/obama-s-shift-toward- communitarianism.html.

5 *See generally*, Russell A. Fox, "Confucian and Communitarian Responses to Liberal Democracy," *Review of Politics* 59, no. 3 (1997) (discussing more broadly this strand of communitarianism).

6 *See* The Institute for Communitarian Policy Studies, *Responsive Community Platform*, http://www.gwu.edu/~ccps/rcplatform.html.

7 U.S. Const. amend. IV.

8 For a more detailed discussion of the advocacy model, see Chapter Six.

9 Nate Silver, "Poll Finds a Shift Towards More Libertarian Views," *NEW YORK TIMES*, June 20, 2011, http://fivethirtyeight.blogs.nytimes.com/2011/06/20/poll-finds-a-shift-toward-more-libertarian-views/.

10 Hendrik Hertzberg, "Snoop Scoops," *New Yorker*, June 24, 2013, http://www.newyorker.com/talk/comment/2013/06/24/130624taco_talk_hertzberg.

11 Ibid. (quoting Tim Shorrock, "A Modern-Day Stasi State," *NATION*, June 11, 2013, http://www.thenation.com/article/174746/modern-day-stasi-state#axzz2WlXb09AW).

12 Al Gore via Twitter, June 5, 2013, https://twitter.com/algore/status/342455655057211393 (last visited June 20, 2013).

13 Conor Friedersdorf, "All the Infrastructure a Tyrant Would Need, Courtesy of Bush and Obama," *Atlantic*, June 7, 2013, http://www.theatlantic.com/politics/archive/2013/06/all-the-infrastructure-a-tyrant-would-need-courtesy-of-bush-and-obama/276635/.

14 Andrew C. McCarthy, "What Is Private, What Is Not," *National Review Online*, June 8, 2013, http://www.nationalreview.com/article/350546/what-private-what-not-andrew-c-mccarthy.

15 Ibid.

16 Andrew C. McCarthy, "Andrew C. McCarthy on the NSA and PRISM Controversies," interview with Hugh Hewitt, June 8, 2013, http://www.hughhewitt.com/andrew-c-mccarthy-on-the-nsa-and-prism-controversies/.

17 "Big Brother and Big Data," *Wall Street Journal*, June 9, 2013, http://online.wsj.com/article/SB10001424127887323495604578535552983978828.html.

18 Donna Cassata and Matt Apuzzo, "Sen. Dianne Feinstein Defends NSA Phone Record Program," *NBC Bay Area*, June 6, 2013, http://www.nbcbayarea.com/news/local/Sen-Dianne-Feinstein-Defends-NSA-Phone-Record-Program-210477781.html.

19 "Spying on citizens: 'It's called protecting America,'" *Washington Post*, June 6, 2013, http://www.washingtonpost.com/video/thefold/spying-on-citizens-its-called-protecting-america/2013/06/06/736102e0-ced6-11e2-8845-d970ccb04497_video.html (author anonymous).

20 Barack Obama, as reported by the New York Times: "Obama's Remarks on Health Care and Surveillance," *New York Times*, June 7, 2013, http://www.nytimes.com/2013/06/08/us/obamas-remarks-on-health-care-and-surveillance.html?pagewanted=all.

21 Private communication with the author.

[22] Stewart Baker, *Skating on Stilts: Why We Aren't Stopping Tomorrow's Terrorism* (Stanford, CA: Hoover Institution Press, 2010), 27.

[23] *See* Amitai Etzioni, *The Limits of Privacy* (Basic Books, 1999).

[24] Sara Carter, "Al Qaeda gaining strength in Mali, North Africa," *Washington Times*, March 26, 2013, http://www.washingtontimes.com/news/2013/mar/26/key-mali-lawmaker-challenges-obama-on-al-qaida-thr/?page=all. *See also* Sudarsan Raghavan, "Nigerian Islamist Militants Return from Mali with Weapons, Skills," *Washington Post*, May 31, 2013, http://articles.washingtonpost.com/2013-05-31/world/39642133_1_northern-mali-boko-haram-nigerian-islamist; Adam Entous, Drew Hinshaw, & David Gauthier-Villars, "Militants, Chased from Mali, Pose New Threats," *Wall Street Journal*, May 24, 2013, http://online.wsj.com/article/SB10001424127887323336104578503464066163002.html.

[25] Cory Bennett, "How Al-Qaida in Yemen Became the Biggest Terrorist Threat to the U.S.," *National Journal*, May 30, 2013, http://www.nationaljournal.com/political-landscape-podcast/how-al-qaida-in-yemen-became-the-biggest-terrorist-threat-to-the-u-s-20121214. *See also* Lt. Col. Douglas A. Pryer, "The Rise of the Machines," *Military Review* (2013): 17.

[26] Bruce Riedel, "Al Qaeda Comeback," *Daily Beast*, April 12, 2013, http://www.thedailybeast.com/articles/2013/04/12/al-qaeda-comeback.html.

[27] *See* Paul K. Kerr and Mary Beth Nikitin, *Pakistan's Nuclear Weapons: Proliferation and Security Issues* (CRS Report No. RL34248) (Washington, DC: Congressional Research Service, 2013), http://www.fas.org/sgp/crs/nuke/RL34248.pdf (for a detailed discussion of this point); Amy F. Woolf, *Nonstrategic Nuclear Weapons* (CRS Report No. RL 32572) (Washington, DC: Congressional Research Service, 2012), http://www.fas.org/sgp/crs/nuke/RL32572.pdf.

[28] Shaun Gregory, "The Terrorist Threat to Pakistan's Nuclear Weapons," *CTC Sentinel*, July 15, 2009, 2, 7, http://www.ctc.usma.edu/wp-content/uploads/2010/06/Vol2Iss7-Art1.pdf.

[29] "House Select Intelligence Committee Holds Hearing on Disclosure of National Security Agency Surveillance Programs," June 18, 2013, https://www.fas.org/irp/congress/2013_hr/disclosure.pdf, 10–11.

[30] Ibid.

[31] Ibid.

[32] Ibid.; *see also* Erin McClam, "Surveillance Helped Stop Plots against NYSE and New York Subway, Official Says," *NBC News*, June 18, 2013, http://usnews.nbcnews.com/_news/2013/06/18/19022364-surveillance-helped-stop-plots-against-nyse-and-new-york-subway-official-says?lite.

[33] "House Select Intelligence Committee Holds Hearing on Disclosure of National Security Agency Surveillance Programs," 11–13.

[34] *See* Marc Ambinder, "How the NSA Uses Your Telephone Records," *Week*, June 6, 2013, http://theweek.com/article/index/245285/how-the-nsa-uses-your-telephone-records (this is a bit of a simplification, but largely captures the NSA's operating procedures).

[35] Jack Nicas, "TSA to Halt Revealing Body Scans at Airports," *Wall Street Journal*, January 18, 2013.

[36] Courtney Kube, "NSA Chief Says Surveillance Programs Helped Foil 54 Plots," *NBC News*, June 27, 2013, http://usnews.nbcnews.com/_ news/2013/06/27/19175466-nsa-chief-says-surveillance-programs-helped-foil-54-plots?lite.

[37] Hendrik Hertzberg, "Snoop Scoops."

[38] Jameel Jaffer, "Privacy Is Worth Protecting," *New York Times*, June 9, 2013, http://www.nytimes.com/roomfordebate/2013/06/09/is-the-nsa-surveillance-threat-real-or-imagined.

[39] "Morning Edition, Snowden's Leaks Puts National Security Agency in a Bind," *NPR*, July 9, 2013, http://www.npr.org/player/v2/mediaPlayer.ht ml?action=1&t=1&islist=false&id=200285742&m=200286159.

[40] Legal Information Institute, "Fourth Amendment," *Cornell University Law School*, http://www.law.cornell.edu/wex/fourth_amendment (accessed 12 July 2013).

[41] *See Electronic Privacy Information Center v. United States Department of Homeland Security*, 653 F.3d 1, 10–11 (D.C. Cir. 2011); *see also National Treasury Employees Union v. Von Raab*, 489 U.S. 656, 674–675 I&N 3 (1989).

[42] *See Michigan Department of State Police v. Sitz*, 110 S. Ct. 2481 (1990).

[43] *See Skinner v. Railway Labor Executives Association*, 489 U.S. 602 (1989); *see also National Treasury Employees Union v. Von Raab*, 489 U.S. 656 (1989).

[44] Ibid., 613.

[45] Scott Shane & David E. Sanger, "Job Title Key to Inner Access Held by Snowden," *New York Times*, June 30, 2013, http://www.nytimes.com/2013/07/01/us/job-title-key-to-inner-access-held-by-snowden.html?pagewanted=all.

[46] Paul Rosenzweig, "The NSA's Phone Collection Order—It May be Legal, But Is It Wise?" *Heritage Foundation*, June 7, 2013, http://www.heritage.org/research/commentary/2013/6/the-nsas-phone-collection-order-it-may-be-legal-but-i.s-it-wise.

[47] Bob Cesca, "CNET Reporter Posts Wildly Inaccurate Yet Totally Viral 'Bombshell' about NSA Eavesdropping," *Daily Banter*, June 16, 2013, http://thedailybanter.com/2013/06/ cnet-reporter-posts-wildly-inaccurate-yet-totally-viral-bombshell-about-nsa-eavesdropping/.

[48] *See* Allie Bohm, "How Long Is Your Cell Phone Company Hanging On To Your Data?" *American Civil Liberties Union*, September 28, 2011, http://www.aclu.org/blog/technology-and-liberty/how-long-your-cell- phone-company-hanging-your-data (discussing the data retention policies of the U.S. telecommunication giants, which vary from company to company, depending on the type of information. In 2011, the ACLU of North Carolina obtained, through a FOIA request, a chart created by the Department of Justice that details how long six major cellular service providers kept their data. Cell tower information was kept on a rolling one-year basis by Verizon; for 18–24 months by Sprint; and indefinitely since 2008 by AT&T. In contrast, the content of text messages was not

retained at all by four of the companies, and kept for 3–5 days by Verizon and 90 days by Virgin Mobile (but accessible to law enforcement only with a warrant)).

49 "This Week: Sen. Dianne Feinstein and Rep. Mike Rogers," *ABC This Week*, June 9, 2013, http://abcnews.go.com/Politics/week-transcript-sen-dianne-feinstein-rep-mike-rogers/story?id=19343314&page=4#. Udsm2jtilJl.

50 National Security Agency/Central Security Service, "SIGINT Frequently Asked Questions," January 15, 2009, http://www.nsa.gov/sigint/faqs.shtml#sigint4.

51 *See* Amitai Etzioni, "A Cyber Age Privacy Doctrine: A Liberal Communitarian Approach," *I/S: A Journal of Law and Policy for the Information Society* 10, no. 2 (2014).

52 "Big Brother and Big Data," Wall Street Journal, June 9, 2013, http://online.wsj.com/article/SB100014241278873234956045785355529839788828.html.

53 In 2008, ChoicePoint was acquired by Reed Elsevier (of which LexisNexis is a subsidiary), and was merged with the LexisNexis Risk Information and Analytics Group.

54 For more on this point, *see* Etzioni, "The Privacy Merchants".

55 Daniel Solove, *The Digital Person: Technology and Privacy in the information Age* (New York: NYU Press, 2004), 169.

56 *See* Etzioni, "The Privacy Merchants," 935–936.

57 Jeffrey Rosen, "The Naked Crowd: Balancing Privacy and Security in an Age of Terror," *ARIZONA LAW REVIEW* 46 (2004): 611.

58 Beth Givens, "Public Records on the Internet: The Privacy Dilemma," *Privacy Rights Clearinghouse*, http://www.cfp2002.org/proceedings/proceedings/givens.pdf.

59 *See* Amitai Etzioni & Radhika Bhat, "Second Chances, Social Forgiveness, and the Internet," *American Scholar* (Spring 2009), http://theamericanscholar.org/second-chances-social-forgiveness-and-the-internet/#.Udx70DtilJk.

60 Federal Bureau of Investigation, "Clearances," *Crime in the United States (2011)*, http://www.fbi.gov/about-us/cjis/ucr/crime-in-the-u.s/2011/crime-in-the-u.s.-2011/clearances (discussing the most recent numbers from 2011 as indicated by this report).

61 Matthew C. Waxman, in an interview with Jonathan Masters, entitled: "Has the FISA Court Gone Too Far?" *Council on Foreign Relations*, July 12, 2013, http://www.cfr.org/intelligence/has-fisa-court-gone-too-far/p31095. *See also* Shaun Waterman, "Officials say Americans protected by Prism surveillance program," *Washington Times*, June 10, 2013, http://www.washingtontimes.com/news/2013/jun/10/officials-say-americans-protected-by-prism-surveil/?page=all.

62 *See, e.g.*, U.S. Government Accountability Office, "Agencies Have Taken Key Steps to Protect Privacy in Selected Efforts, But Significant Compliance Issues Remain" (GAO-05-866, August 2005); U.S. Government Accountability Office, "Alternatives Exist for Enhancing Protection of

Personally Identifiable Information" (GAO-08-536, May 2008); U.S. Government Accountability Office, "Federal Law Should Be Updated to Address Changing Technology Landscape" (GAO-12-961T, July 2012); U.S. Government Accountability Office, "Measuring Progress and Addressing Potential Privacy Concerns Would Facilitate Integration into the National Airspace System" (OfficeGAO-12-98,1September 2012).

63 David Jackson, "Obama: NSA Surveillance Programs Are 'Transparent,'" *USA Today*, June 18, 2013, http://www.usatoday.com/story/theoval/2013/06/18/obama-charlie-rose-program-nsa-surveillance/2433549.

64 Peter Baker, "After Leaks, Obama Leads Damage Control Effort," *New York Times*, June 28, 2013, http://www.nytimes.com/2013/06/29/us/politics/after-leaks-obama-leads-damage-control-effort.html?pagewanted=all.

65 Trevor Timm, "The NSA Leaks Are Forcing More Transparency on Both Companies and the Government," *Freedom of the Press Foundation*, June 15, 2013, https://pressfreedomfoundation.org/blog/2013/06/nsa-leaks-are-forcing-more-transparency-both-companies-and-government.

66 Ellen Nakashima, "Bipartisan Group of Senators Urges Transparency on Phone Record Surveillance," *Washington Post*, June 28, 2013, http://articles.washingtonpost.com/2013-06-28/world/40251889_1_phone-records-bulk-collection-senators.

67 Scott Shane & David E. Sanger, "Job Title Key to Inner Access Held by Snowden," *New York Times*, June 30, 2013, http://www.nytimes.com/2013/07/01/us/job-title-key-to-inner-access-held-by-snowden.html?pagewanted=al.

68 Vindu Goel & Claire Cain Miller, "More Data on Privacy, but Picture Is No Clearer," *New York Times*, June 17, 2013, http://www.nytimes.com/2013/06/18/technology/more-data-on-privacy-but-picture-is-no-clearer.html.

69 Spencer Ackerman, "Senators Press NSA Director for Answers on Secret Surveillance Program," *Guardian*, June 12, 2013, http://www.guardian.co.uk/world/2013/jun/12/senate-nsa-director-keith-alexander.

70 In 2001, six men from Buffalo, New York took a trip to Pakistan for a spiritual retreat sponsored by Tablighi Jamaat—a group that, while associated with radicalism, was not designated as a terrorist organization. While there, however, the six men were accused of attending a terrorist training camp called Al Farooq and supposedly listened to a speech delivered by Osama bin Laden. No evidence was presented of a forthcoming plot on their part. There were no weapons found, no history of violence uncovered, nor was there any "clear and convincing evidence" that the six men were planning any sort of terrorist act. Yet they were still charged under the Antiterrorism and Effective Death Penalty Act with a possible 15 years in prison and $250,000 fine for their activities. JoAnn Wypijewski, "Living in an Age of Fire," *Mother Jones*, March/April 2003, http://www.motherjones.com/politics/2003/03/living-age-fire.

[71] Kim Dotcom, "Prism: Concerns over Government Tyranny Are Legitimate," *Guardian*, June 13, 2013, http://www.guardian.co.uk/commentisfree/2013/jun/13/prism-utah-data-center-surveillance.

Chapter Eight

[1] Senator Patrick Leahy, speaking on ABC News, This Week (Burwell's Information Services, November 18, 2001).

[2] American Civil Liberties Union, "Insatiable Appetite: The Government's Demand for New and Unnecessary Powers after September 11," (Washington, DC: American Civil Liberties Union, Washington National Office, April 2002), https://www.aclu.org/other/insatiable-appetite-governments-demand-new-and-unnecessary-powers-after-september-11.

[3] Wendy Kaminer, "Ashcroft's Lies," *American Prospect*, July 15, 2002, 9.

[4] Rich Connell and Richard A. Serrano, "L.A. Is Warned of New Unrest," *Los Angeles Times*, October 22, 1992, A1.

[5] "Beating Case: Tempers Flare at Rally," *USA Today*, April 16, 1996, 3A.

Chapter Nine

[1] G. John Ikenberry, "The Future of the Liberal World Order," *Foreign Affairs* 90, no. 3 (2011).

[2] The historical question whether this conception of sovereignty arose out of the Treaty of Westphalia is the subject of significant debate within the literature. For a concurring view, see Daniel Philpott, *Revolutions in Sovereignty: How Ideas Shaped Modern International Relations* (Princeton, NJ: Princeton University Press, 2001), 76. For dissenting views, see Daniel Nexon, "Zeitgeist? Neo-idealism and International Political Change," *Review of International Political Economy* 12, no. 4 (2005): 700–719; and Stephen Krasner, *Sovereignty: Organized Hypocrisy* (Princeton, NJ: Princeton University Press, 1999), 20–25.

[3] For a recent example, see Romit Guha and Brian Spegele, "China–India Border Tensions Rise," *Wall Street Journal*, April 26, 2013, online.wsj.com/article/SB10001424127887323789704578446970130137416.html.

[4] Some scholars (e.g., John Ikenberry) hold that the international order centered on Westphalian sovereignty is a decidedly liberal order, while others (e.g., Anne Marie Slaughter) associate the Westphalian model of sovereignty with realism as distinct from a liberal notion of sovereignty under which states have responsibilities, especially to protect their citizens, as well as rights. For Ikenberry's view, see G. John Ikenberry, *Liberal Leviathan* (Princeton, NJ: Princeton University Press, 2011). For Slaughter's, see Anne Marie Slaughter, "Sovereignty and Power in a Networked World Order," *Stanford Law Review* 40 (2004): 283–329, and Anne Marie Slaughter, "Intervention, Libya, and the Future of Sovereignty," *Atlantic*, September 4, 2011, www.theatlantic.com/international/archive/2011/09/intervention-libya-and-the-future-of-sovereignty/244537/.

5   Daniel Philpott, "Sovereignty," in *Stanford Encyclopedia of Philosophy*, ed. Edward N. Zalta (Summer 2010 Edition), plato.stanford.edu/cgi-bin/encyclopedia/archinfo.cgi?entry=sovereignty. *See also* Jack Goldsmith and Daryl Levinson, "Law for States: International Law, Constitutional Law, Public Law," *Harvard Law Review* 122, no. 7 (2009): 1844.

6   Rome Statute of the International Criminal Court, July 17, 1998.

7   Charter of the United Nations, June 26, 1945.

8   One might observe a certain similarity between this view and and the view outlined by Immanuel Kant in his essay "Perpetual Peace" (1795).

9   General Assembly Draft Resolution, "2005 World Summit Outcome," U.N. Doc. A/60/L.1 (2005), available at www.who.int/hiv/universalaccess2010/worldsummit.pdf.

10 Francis Deng, Sadikiel Kimaro, Terrence Lyons, Donald Rothchild, & I. William Zartman, *Sovereignty as Responsibility* (Washington, DC: Brookings Institution, 1996).

11 Ibid., xvii.

12 Gareth Evans, Mohamed Sahnoun et al., *The Responsibility to Protect: Report of the International Commission on Intervention and State Sovereignty* (Ottawa: International Development Research Centre, 2001), 13.

13 *A More Secure World: Our Shared Responsibility* (New York: United Nations Department of Public Information, 2004), 17.

14 Ibid.

15 U.N. Security Council Resolution 1674, U.N. Doc. S/RES/1674 (2006).

16 Luke Glanville, "The Responsibility to Protect Beyond Borders," *Human Rights Law Review* 12, no. 1 (2012): 1.

17 Bruce Ackerman, "Obama's Unconstitutional War," *Foreign Policy*, March 24, 2011; Richard Norton-Taylor, "Libya Campaign 'Has Made UN Missions to Protect Civilians Less Likely,'" *Guardian*, March 19, 2012, www.guardian.co.uk/world/2012/mar/19/libya-un-missions-civilians.

18 Amitai Etzioni, "The Democratisation Mirage," *Survival: Global Politics and Strategy* 57, no. 4 (2015).

19 Ikenberry, *Liberal Leviathan*, 250.

20 For example, both China and Russia have endorsed the "Responsibility to Protect," and the two nations (reluctantly) permitted the intervention in Libya by declining to veto the United Nations Security Council's authorization of the use of force in the country. See Dan Bilefsky and Mark Landler, "As U.N. Backs Military Action in Libya, U.S. Role Is Unclear," *New York Times*, March 17, 2011, www.nytimes.com/2011/03/18/world/africa/18nations.html?pagewanted=all.

21 Ramesh Thakur, "Law, Legitimacy and United Nations," *Melbourne Journal of International Law* 11, no. 1 (2010).

Chapter Ten

1   Theodore J. Lowi, "Globalization, War, and the Withering Away of the State," *Brown Journal of World Affairs* 17, no. 2 (2011): 243.

2   Daniel H. Deudney, *Bounding Power* (Princeton, NJ: Princeton University Press, 2007), 1.

3   Ibid., 3.

4   Daniel H. Deudney, personal communication with the author.

5   Kent V. Flannery, "The Cultural Evolution of Civilizations," *Annual Review of Ecology and Systematics* 3 (1972).

6   Jürgen Klüver, "The Socio-Cultural Evolution of Human Societies and Civilizations," *EMBO Reports* 9 (2008): S55–S58.

7   Benedict Anderson, *Imagined Communities: Reflections on the Origin and Spread of Nationalism* (New York: Verso, 1983).

8   The state function, of keeping order, was carried out by members of the community who were so designated by the leaders of the community—or by ad hoc forces put together when the occasion arose.

9   Daniel Lerner, *The Passing of Traditional Society: Modernizing the Middle East* (New York: Macmillan, 1958).

10 Michael E. Howard, *The Franco-Prussian War: The German Invasion of France, 1870–1871* (New York: Routledge, 2001), 11.

11 Ibid., 235.

12 Allison R. Hayward, "Revisiting the Fable of Reform," *Harvard Journal on Legislation* 45 (2008): 429.

13 For further analysis of this phenomenon, see Sean Carey, "Undivided Loyalties: Is National Identity an Obstacle to European Integration?" *European Union Politics* 3, no. 4 (2002) and Adam Luedke, "European Integration, Public Opinion and Immigration Policy: Testing the Impact of National Identity," *European Union Politics* 6, no. 1 (2005).

14 Ruud Koopmans and Paul Statham, "Challenging the Liberal Nation-State? Postnationalism, Multiculturalism, and the Collective Claims Making of Migrants and Ethnic Minorities in Britain and Germany," *American Journal of Sociology* 105, no. 3 (1999).

15 Jürgen Habermas, *The Postnational Constellation: Political Essays* (Cambridge, MA: MIT Press, 2001): 49.

16 Mark Juergensmeyer, "Religious Nationalism and Transnationalism in a Global World," http://juergensmeyer.org/religious-nationalism-and-transnationalism-in-a-global-world/.

17 Habermas, *Postnational Constellation*, 68.

18 Ibid., 81.

19 Pablo Jiménez Lobeira, "Exploring Cosmopolitan Communitarianist: EU Citizenship—An Analogical Reading," *Open Insight: Revista de Filosofía* 2, no. 2 (2011): 145.

20 Ibid.

21 For more, see Amitai Etzioni, *From Empire to Community* (New York: Palgrave Macmillan, 2004).

22 Ibid.

23 For the various approaches to EU governance, see James Caporaso, "The European Union and Forms of State: Westphalian, Regulatory or Post-

Modern? A Logical and Empirical Assessment," *Journal of Common Market Studies* 34, no. 1 (1996).

24 For extensive analysis of the evolution of the EU community experiment, see Willem Maas, *Creating European Citizens* (Lanham, MD: Rowman & Littlefield, 2007).

25 Council Resolution, "On a New Approach to Technical Harmonization and Standards," May 7, 1985, http://eur-lex.europa.eu/LexUriServ/LexUriServ.do?uri=CELEX:31985Y0604(01):EN:HTML

26 "European Standards: List of References of Harmonised Standards," *European Commission*, February 1, 2011, http://ec.europa.eu/enterprise/policies/european-standards/documents/harmonised-standards-legislation/list-references/index_en.htm.

27 Business Green Staff, "Green Groups Take EU to Court over Biofuels—Again," *Guardian*, May 2011, http://www.guardian.co.uk/environment/2011/may/26/biofuels-energy.

28 Gerda Falkner & Oliver Treib, "Three Worlds of Compliance or Four? The EU-15 Compared to New Member States," *Journal of Common Market Studies* 46, no. 2 (2008): 297.

29 Christoph Knill, "European Politics: Impact of National Administrative Traditions," *Journal of Public Policy* 18, no. 1 (1998), 11.

30 Manuela Saragosa, "Greece Warned on False Euro Data," *BBC News*, December 1, 2004, http://news.bbc.co.uk/2/hi/business/4058327.stm.

31 Falkner & Treib, "Three Worlds of Compliance or Four?" 293–313, 303.

32 For an example of this argument, see Andrew Moravcsik, "In Defense of the 'Democratic Deficit': Reassessing Legitimacy in the EU," *Journal of Common Market Studies* 40, no. 4 (2002).

33 Alan Bance, "The Idea of Europe: from Erasmus to ERASMUS," *Journal of European Studies* 22, no. 1 (1992).

34 For additional studies of patterns in public support for the EU not discussed here, see Matthew Gabel, "Public Support for European Integration: An Empirical Test of Five Theories," *The Journal of Politics* 60, no. 2 (1998): 333–354; and Liesbet Hooghe & Gary Marks, "A Postfunctionalist Theory of European Integration: From Permissive Consensus to Constraining Dissensus," *British Journal of Political Science* 39 (2009).

35 The Eurobarometer is a bi-yearly survey of public opinion by the European Commission, http://ec.europa.eu/public_opinion/index_en.htm. Net public support refers to the percentage of those who say their country's membership in the EU is a good thing minus those who say it is a bad thing. Richard C. Eichenberg and Russell J. Dalton, "Post-Maastricht Blues: The Transformation of Citizen Support for European Integration, 1973–2004," *Acta Politica* 42 (2007): Figure 1.

36 Eurobarometer surveys, 2004–2010, *European Commission: Public Opinion*, http://ec.europa.eu/public_opinion/index_en.htm.

37 For a study of the financial crisis' impact on public opinion, see Felix Roth, Felicitas Nowak-Lehmann D. & Thomas Otter, "Has the Financial Crisis Shattered Citizens' Trust in National and European Governmental

Institutions?: Evidence from the EU Member States, 1999–2010" *Center for European Policy Studies* no. 343 (June 2011).

[38] Jean-Claude Trichet ,"Building Europe, Building Institutions" (speech, Aachen, Germany, June 2, 2011) http://www.ecb.int/press/key/date/2011/html/sp110602.en.html.

[39] Jack Ewing & Niki Kitsantonis, "Trichet Urges Creation of Euro Oversight Panel," *New York Times*, June 2, 2011, http://www.nytimes.com/2011/06/03/business/global/03euro.html?_r=1. For additional discussion of efforts to centralize fiscal policy in the Eurozone, see Emiliano Grossman & Patrick LeBlond, "European Financial Integration: Finally the Great Leap Forward?" *Journal of Common Market Studies* 49, no. 2 (2011).

[40] For further arguments that the democratic process creates legitimacy, see Renaud DeHousse, "Constitutional Reform in the European Community: Are there Alternatives to the Majoritarian Avenue?" in *The Crisis of Representation in Europe*, ed. Jack Hayward (London: Frank Cass, 1995) and Jurgen Habermas, "Why Europe Needs a Constitution," *New Left Review* 11 (September–October 2001).

[41] Seymour Martin Lipset, *Political Man: The Social Basis of Politics* (New York: Doubleday, 1960), 77.

[42] Jean-Marc Ferry, "Ten Normative Theses on the European Union," *Ethical Perspectives* 15 no. 4 (2008).

[43] For different approaches to the problem of consensus-building, see Justine Lacroix, "For a European Constitutional Patriotism," *Political Studies* 50 (2002); and Joschka Fischer, "From Confederacy to Federation: Thoughts on the Finality of European Integration" (speech, Humboldt University, Berlin, Germany, May 12, 2000).

[44] Claus Offe, "Is There, or Can There Be, a 'European Society?'" in *Civil Society: Berlin Perspectives*, ed. John Keane (New York: Berghahn Books, 2007), 169–188.

[45] Richard Bellamy & Dario Castiglione, "Lacroix's European Constitutional Patriotism: A Response," *Political Studies,* 52 (2004), 190.

[46] "General Publications: Young People," *European Commission* website, http://ec.europa.eu/publications/archives/young/01/index_en.htm (accessed 30 September 2011).

[47] Lars-Erik Cederman, "Nationalism and Bounded Integration: What It Would Take to Construct a European Demos," *European Journal of International Relations* 7 (2001).

[48] "Presidency Conclusions," *Barcelona European Council*, March 15 and 16, 2002, http://ec.europa.eu/research/era/docs/en/council-eu-30.pdf; Commissioners Leonard Orban and Jan Figel, "Key Data on Teaching Languages at School in Europe," *Eurydice Network* (2008 edition).

[49] Tobias Theiler, "Viewers into Europeans? How the European Union Tried to Europeanize the Audiovisual Sector, and Why It Failed," *Canadian Journal of Communication* 24, no. 4 (1999), http://www.cjc-online.ca/index.php/journal/article/view/1126/1035.

50 "Symbols of the Union to be Adopted by Parliament," press release, *European Parliament*, September 11, 2008, http://www.europarl.europa. eu/sides/getDoc.do?language=en&type=IM-PRESS&reference=20080 909IPR36656 .

51 For proposals on how to create a climate of discourse, see Claudia Schrag, "The Quest for EU Legitimacy: How to Study a Never-Ending Crisis," *Perspectives on Europe* 40, no. 2 (Autumn 2010), 27–34.

52 For more detailed discussion of these issues, see J.H.H. Weiler, "A Constitution for Europe? Some Hard Choices," *Journal for Common Market Studies* 40, no. 4 (2002).

53 Dean Carroll, "Strengthened Schengen to 'Europeanise' borders," *Public Service Europe*, September 16, 2011, http://www.publicserviceeurope.com/ article/864/strengthened-schengen-to-europeanise-borders; Martin Banks, "Mixed Response to EU Plans for Shake-Up of Schengen Area," *Parliament*, September 19, 2011, http://www.theparliament.com/latest-news/article/ newsarticle/mixed-response-to-eu-plans-for-shake-up-of-schengen-area.

54 The author advanced this thesis long before the current difficulties faced by the EU. See Amitai Etzioni, *Political Unification: On Building Supranational Communities* (New York: Holt, Rinehart and Winston, 1965) and Amitai Etzioni, *Political Unification Revisited: On Building Supranational Communities* (Lanham, MD: Lexington Books, 2001).

Chapter Eleven

1 Don Melvin, "Cop Pulls Over Google Self-Driving Car, Finds No Driver To Ticket," *CNN*, November 13, 2015, http://www.cnn. com/2015/11/13/us/google-self-driving-car-pulled-over/.

2 Julia Carpenter, "Google's Algorithm Shows Prestigious Job Ads To Men, But Not To Women. Here's Why That Should Worry You," *Washington Post*, July 6, 2015, https://www.washingtonpost.com/news/the-intersect/ wp/2015/07/06/googles-algorithm-shows-prestigious-job-ads-to-men-but-not-to-women-heres-why-that-should-worry-you/; Kristen V. Brown, "Google Showed Women Ads for Lower-Paying Jobs," *Fusion*, July 8, 2015, http://fusion.net/story/162685/google-ad-algorithms-gender-discrimination/; Claire Cain Miller, "When Algorithms Discriminate," *New York Times*, July 9, 2015, http://www.nytimes.com/2015/07/10/ upshot/when-algorithms-discriminate.html.

3 Brian Souter has voiced concerns regarding the fairness of Google's PageRank and search results after their websites disappeared from Google's first-page results. In the case of MyTriggers.com, the Ohio-based shopping comparison search site accused Google of favoring its own services in search results (although the judge eventually ruled that the site failed to show harm to other similar businesses). "Disappearing Tycoon Souter Blames Google," *BBC News*, September 12, 2011.

4 Claire Cain Miller, "When Algorithms Discriminate."

[5] Nick Bostrom, "When Machines Outsmart Humans," *CNN*, September 8, 2014, http://www.cnn.com/2014/09/09/opinion/bostrom-machine-superintelligence/index.html.

[6] For a consideration of the relationship between AI and the moral order, see Amitai Etzioni & Oren Etzioni, "AI Assisted Ethics," *Ethics and Information Technology* 18, no. 2 (2016).

[7] Amitai Etzioni, *Moral Dialogues in Public Debates*, 11 *Public Perspective* 2 (2000).

[8] Viktor Mayer-Schönberger & Kenneth Cukier, *Big Data: A Revolution that Will Transform How We Live, Work, and Think* (New York: Houghton Mifflin Harcourt, 2014), 16–17.

[9] "New Algorithm Lets Autonomous Robots Divvy Up Assembly Tasks on the Fly," *Science Daily*, May 27, 2015, http://www.sciencedaily.com/releases/2015/05/150527142100.htm.

[10] Chris Kapnan, "Auto-Braking: A Quantum Leap for Road Safety," *Telegraph*, August 14, 2012, http://www.telegraph.co.uk/motoring/road-safety/9429746/Auto-braking-a-quantum-leap-for-road-safety.html.

[11] Mark Phelan, "Automatic Braking Coming, But Not All Systems Are Equal," *Detroit Free Press*, January 1, 2016, http://www.freep.com/story/money/cars/mark-phelan/2016/01/01/automatic-braking-safety-pedestrian-detection-nhtsa-iihs/78029322/.

[12] Eric Limer, "Automatic Brakes Are Stopping for No Good Reason," *Popular Mechanics*, June 19, 2015, www.popularmechanics.com/cars/a16103/automatic-brakes-are-triggering-for-no-good-reason/.

[13] Mayer-Schönberger and Cukier, *Big Data*, 178.

[14] *Griggs v. Duke Power*, 401 U.S. 424 (1971) (further highlights the import of establishing whether the harm was deliberately inflicted).

[15] Shane Greenstein, "How the Internet Became Commercial: Innovation, Privatization, and the Birth of a New Network" (Princeton, NJ: Princeton University Press, 2015).

[16] John Perry Barlow, "A Declaration of the Independence of Cyberspace," February 8, 1996, https://projects.eff.org/~barlow/Declaration-Final.html.

[17] Bryant Walker Smith, "Automated Vehicles Are Probably Legal in the United States," *Texas A&M Law Review* (2014).

[18] New York Vehicle and Traffic Law Tit. 7 Art. 33 § 1226.

[19] Joshua Gans, "Who Should Control Your Car's Software," *Digitopoly*, December 28, 2015, https://medium.com/@joshgans/who-should-control-your-cars-software-c5ecd8c1e129#.5qkj39p8k.

[20] Ibid.

[21] See Katherine M. Shelfer & Hiaohua Hu, "Making Better Sense of the Demographic Data Value in the Data Mining Procedure," in *Foundations and Novel Approaches in Data Mining*, ed. Tsau Young Lin, Setsuo Ohsuga, Churn-Jung Liau, & Xiaohua Hu, 331–361 (Berlin: Springer Science & Business Media, 2005); Brent Skorup, "Cops Scan Social Media to Help Assess Your 'Threat Rating,'" *Reuters*, December 12, 2014, http://

blogs.reuters.com/great-debate/2014/12/12/police-data-mining-looks-through-social-media-assigns-you-a-threat-level/.

[22] *See, e.g., The State of Ohio, Appellee, v. Retherford, Appellant*, 93 Ohio App.3d 586 (1994).

[23] *See, e.g.*, Peter Eckersley, "How Online Tracking Companies Know Most of What You Do Online (and What Social Networks Are Doing to Help Them," *Electronic Frontier Foundation*, 2009, https://www.eff.org/deeplinks/2009/09/online-trackers-and-social-networks.

[24] *See, e.g.*, Mike Masnick, "Smartphone Apps Quietly Using Phone Microphones and Cameras To Gather Data," *Tech Dirt*, April 17, 2011, https://www.techdirt.com/blog/wireless/articles/20110417/21485513927/smartphone-apps-quietly-using-phone-microphones-cameras-to-gather-data.shtml.

[25] Jenny Strasburg & Matthew Yi, "Clothing Will Have Transmitters / Benetton to Keep Track of Clothing with Tiny Transmitters," *SF Gate*, March 12, 2003, http://www.sfgate.com/business/article/Clothing-will-have-transmitters-Benetton-to-2628532.php.

[26] Andrew Hilts, Christopher Parsons, & Jeffrey Knockel, "Every Step You Fake: A Comparative Analysis of Fitness Tracker Privacy and Security," *Open Effect Report* (2016), https: //openeffect.ca/reports/Every_Step_You_Fake.pdf.

[27] Amitai Etzioni, *Privacy in a Cyber Age: Policy and Practice* (New York: Palgrave Macmillan, 2015).

[28] Joe Coscarelli, "The NYPD's Domain Awareness System Is Watching You," *New York Magazine*, August 9, 2012, http://nymag.com/daily/intelligencer/2012/08/nypd-domain-awareness-system-microsoft-is-watching-you.html.

[29] *United States v. Jones*, 132 S. Ct. 945, 565 U.S. (2012).

[30] Etzioni, *Privacy in a Cyber Age*.

[31] The question "Quis custodiet ipsos custodies" was first posed by the Roman author Juvenal. *See* Lindsay Watson and Patricia Watson, eds. *Juvenal: Satire 6.* (Cambridge, UK: Cambridge University Press, 2014).

[32] This last line may seem to contradict an earlier statement that oversight programs should be protected from human override. This previous statement refers to the use of smart instruments, but not to avoiding their use. Thus, as long as one drives a car, one will be subject to its monitoring program. But both its operational and oversight program can be avoided, if one idles the car, if one stops using it. The same should hold for all instruments.

Chapter Twelve

[1] Amitai Etzioni, "The Privacy Merchants: What Is To Be Done?" *Journal of Constitutional Law* 14, no. 4 (2012).

[2] Peter P. Swire, "Katz is Dead. Long Live Katz," *Michigan Law Review* 102, no. 5 (2002): 912 ("[t]he increasing storage of telephone calls is part of the much broader expansion since 1967 of stored records in the hands

of third parties. Although there are no Supreme Court cases on most of these categories of stored records, the *Miller* and *Smith* line of cases make it quite possible that the government can take all of these records without navigating Fourth Amendment protections."). Some scholars have suggested that Fourth Amendment restrictions should apply to subsequent use, although the analysis is not sufficiently developed in the courts to constitute a meaningful privacy doctrine. Harold J. Krent, "Of Diaries and Data Banks: Use Restrictions Under the Fourth Amendment," *Texas Law Review* 74 (1995): 51 ("[i]f the state can obtain the information only through means constituting a search or seizure, then use restrictions should apply, confining the governmental authorities to uses consistent with the [Fourth] Amendment's reasonableness requirement.").

3   Samuel D. Warren & Louis D. Brandeis, "The Right to Privacy," *Harvard Law Review* 4 (1890).

4   N.T.O. "The Virginia 'Right of Privacy' Statute," *Virginia Law Review*, 38, no. 1 (1952): 117.

5   Warren & Brandeis, "The Right to Privacy."

6   For an excellent overview of how advances in information and communication technologies have rendered obsolete the privacy laws (and the doctrines on which these laws are based) of the 1980s and 1990s, see Omer Tene, "Privacy: The New Generations," *International Data Privacy Law* 1, no. 1 (2011). For a discussion of how these changes have particularly affected the privacy expectations of the 'Facebook generation,' see Mary Graw Leary, "Reasonable Expectations of Privacy for Youth in a Digital Age," *Mississippi Law Journal* 80 (2011).

7   This is of course not a terribly new position—legal scholars have been discussing the implications for privacy and the Fourth Amendment of the Internet since its introduction as publically available technology. *See* Lawrence Lessig, *Code and Other Laws of Cyberspace* (New York: Basic Books, 1999), 222–223; and Laurence H. Tribe, "The Constitution in Cyberspace" (speech, First Conference on Computers, Freedom, & Privacy, March 26, 1991), http://groups.csail.mit.edu/mac/classes/6.805/articles/tribe-constitution.txt.

8   Erin Smith Dennis, "A Mosaic Shield: Maynard, the Fourth Amendment, and Privacy Rights in the Digital Age," *Cardozo Law Review* 33 (2012): 738. *See also* Orin Kerr, "The Mosaic Theory of the Fourth Amendment," *Michigan Law Review* 111, no. 3 (2012): 320 ("[u]nder mosaic theory, searches can be defined collectively as a sequence of discrete steps rather than as individualized steps. Identifying Fourth Amendment search requires analyzing police actions over time as a collective 'mosaic' of surveillance."); Madelaine Virginia Ford, "Mosaic Theory and the Fourth Amendment: How Jones Can Save Privacy in the Face of Evolving Technology," *American University Journal of Gender Social Policy and Law* 19 (2011): 1353; Bethany L. Dickman, "Untying Knotts: The Application of Mosaic Theory to GPS Surveillance in United States v. Maryland," *American University Law Review* 60 (2011).

[9]   *U.S. v. White*, 401 U.S. 745, 786 (1971).

[10] Shaun B. Spencer, "Reasonable Expectations and the Erosion of Privacy," *San Diego Law Review* 39 (2002); Jim Harper, "Reforming the Fourth Amendment Privacy Doctrine," *American University Law Review* 57 (2008); Haley Plourde-Cole, "Back to Katz: Reasonable Expectation of Privacy in the Facebook Age," *Fordham Urban Law Journal* 38, no. 2 (2010); Christopher Slobogin & Joseph E. Schumacher, "Reasonable Expectations of Privacy and Autonomy in Fourth Amendment Cases: An Empirical Look at Understandings Recognized and Permitted by Society," *Duke Law Journal* 42 (1993); Richard G. Wilkins, "Defining the 'Reasonable Expectation of Privacy': An Emerging Tripartite Analysis," *Vanderbilt Law Review* 40 (1987): 1108; Sherry F. Colb, "What Is A Search? Two Conceptual Flaws in Fourth Amendment Doctrine and Some Hints of a Remedy," *Stanford Law Review* 55 (2002): 122; Silas Wasserstom & Louis Michael Seidman, "The Fourth Amendment as Constitutional Theory," *Georgetown Law Journal* 77 (1988).

[11] Anthony G. Amsterdam, "Perspectives on the Fourth Amendment," *Minnesota Law Review* 58 (1974): 383.

[12] Orin S. Kerr, "The Fourth Amendment and New Technologies: Constitutional Myths and the Case for Caution," *Michigan Law Review* 102 (2004): 808.

[13] Charles H. Whitebread and Christopher Slobogin, *Criminal Procedure: An Analysis of Cases and Concepts*, 3rd ed. (Westbury, NY: Foundation Press, 1993), 116.

[14] Further, what is considered a reasonable expectation is in constant flux due to technological changes. Thus, as the use of the Internet for personal communications grew, the Electronic Communications Privacy Act of 1986 failed to protect stored private emails because it was passed in a time when most emails were related to business records, which are expected to be afforded a lesser degree of privacy. *See* Deirdre L. Mulligan, "Reasonable Expectations in Electronic Communications: A Critical Perspective on the Electronic Communications Privacy Act," *George Washington Law Review* 72 (2004).

[15] Slobogin & Schumacher, "Reasonable Expectations of Privacy and Autonomy," 732 ("a sense of how [innocent] U.S. citizens gauge the impact of police investigative techniques on their privacy and autonomy is highly relevant to current Fourth Amendment jurisprudence. This Article describes an effort to obtain some preliminary data in this regard.").

[16] Robert M. Bloom, *Searches, Seizures, and Warrants* (Westport, CT: Praeger, 2003), 46 ("[b]ecause there is no straightforward answer to this question, 'reasonable' has largely come to mean what a majority of the Supreme Court Justices say is reasonable").

[17] Jim Harper, "Reforming Fourth Amendment Privacy Doctrines," *American University Law Review* 57 (2008): 1392. *See also* Jeffrey Rosen, *The Unwanted Gaze: The Destruction of Privacy in America* (New York: Vintage Books, 2001), 60 ("Harlan's test was applauded as a victory for privacy, but it

soon became clear that it was entirely circular"); Michael Abramowicz, "Constitutional Circularity," *UCLA Law Review* 49 (2001): 60–61 ("Fourth Amendment doctrine, moreover, is circular, for someone can have a reasonable expectation of privacy in an area if and only if the Court has held that a search in that area would be unreasonable").

18 A. Morgan Cloud, "Rube Goldberg Meets the Constitution: The Supreme Court, Technology and the Fourth Amendment," *Mississippi Law Journal* 72 (2002).

19 *Kyllo v. United States*, 533 U.S. 27, 31 (2001) (quoting *Silverman v. United States*, 365 U.S. 505, 511 (1961)).

20 *Payton v. New York*, 445 U.S. 573, 591–598 (1980).

21 *Dow Chemical Company v. United States*, 749 F.2d 307, 314 (6th Cir. 1984), *aff'd*, 476 U.S. 227 (1986).

22 Catharine A. MacKinnon, "Reflections on Sex Equality Under Law," *Yale Law Journal* 100 (1991): 1311.

23 Linda C. McClain, "Inviolability and Privacy: The Castle, the Sanctuary, and the Body," *Yale Journal of Law & the Humanities* 7, no. 1 (1995): 209.

24 Amitai Etzioni, "The Bankruptcy of Liberalism and Conservatism," *Political Science Quarterly* 128, no. 1 (2013).

25 Christopher Slobogin, "Public Privacy: Camera Surveillance of Public Places and the Right to Anonymity," *Mississippi Law Journal* 72 (2002). Scott E. Sundby, "Everyman's Fourth Amendment: Privacy or Mutual Trust between Government and Citizen?" *Columbia Law Review* 94 (1994): 1758–1759; Bethany L. Dickman, "Untying Knotts: The Application of Mosaic Theory to GPS Surveillance in United States v. Maryland," *American University Law Review* 60 (2011).

26 Marc Jonathan Blitz, "Stanley in Cyberspace: Why the Privacy Protection of the First Amendment Should Be More Like That of the Fourth," *Hastings Law Journal* 62 (2010).

27 Slobogin, "Public Privacy," 254.

28 Ibid., 255.

29 Amitai Etzioni, "Community," in *Encyclopedia of Political Thought*, ed. Michael Gibbons (Chichester, UK: John Wiley & Sons, Ltd., 2015).

30 Ibid.

31 U.S. Const. amend. IV (emphasis added).

32 Mary Ferrell Foundation, "Post-Watergate Intelligence Investigations," http://www.maryferrell.org/wiki/index.php/Post-Watergate_Intelligence_Investigations (last visited March 13, 2014).

33 Ibid.

34 Thomas B. Hunter, "The Challenges of Intelligence Sharing," *Operational Studies* 3 (2004).

35 For a critical analysis of the "Information Sharing Paradigm" that has arisen in law enforcement and intelligence community since 9/11, see Peter P. Swire, "Privacy and Information Sharing in the War on Terrorism," *Villanova Law Review* 51 (2006).

36 Alexander Aleinikoff, writing in 1987, argued that the courts had entered the "age of balancing." "Balancing has been a vehicle primarily for weakening earlier categorical doctrines restricting governmental power to search and seize." T. Alexander Aleinikoff, "Constitutional Law in the Age of Balancing," *Yale Law Journal* 96 (1987): 965. Many civil libertarians have argued that post-9/11, Fourth Amendment rights are being systematically eroded in the name of national security. *See* Jay Stanley, "Reviving the Fourth Amendment and American Privacy," *ACLU*, May 28, 2010, http://www.aclu.org/blog/national-security-technology-and-liberty/reviving-fourth-amendment-and-american-privacy. *See also* Orin S. Kerr, "An Equilibrium-Adjustment Theory of the Fourth Amendment," *Harvard Law Review* 125 (2011): 478 ("[t]he theory of equilibrium-adjustment posits that the Supreme Court adjusts the scope of Fourth Amendment protection in response to new facts in order to restore the status quo level of protection. When changing technology or social practice expands government power, the Supreme Court tightens Fourth Amendment protection; when it threatens government power, the Supreme Court loosens constitutional protection").

37 *See* Amitai Etzioni, *The Limits of Privacy* (New York: Basic Books, 1999), 5.

38 *See* Anna C. Henning, *Compulsory DNA Collection: A Fourth Amendment Analysis* (CRS Report Number R40077) (Washington, DC: Congressional Research Service, 2010), 2, https://fas.org/sgp/crs/misc/R40077.pdf (quoting *United States v. Kincade*, 379 F.3d 813, 818 (9th Cir. 2004) (en banc)).

39 American Bar Association, "ABA Standards for Criminal Justice, 3rd Edition: Law Enforcement Access to Third Party Records Standards," 2013, http://www.americanbar.org/content/dam/aba/publications/criminal_justice_standards/third_party_access.authcheckdam.pdf.

40 Shaun Spencer raises concerns around legislating privacy protections. *See* Spencer, "Reasonable Expectations and the Erosion of Privacy," 860 ("[g]iven the powerful influence of various lobbies opposed to strong privacy protection, that role may best be described as a sine qua non. That is, unless the public has a strong desire for privacy in a particular area, attempts to pass legislation establishing that area as a private sphere are doomed to fail … To the extent that legislatures base privacy legislation on social values and norms, they necessarily rely on the same changing expectations as the judicial conception of privacy").

41 Amitai Etzioni, *From Empire to Community: A New Approach to International Relations* (New York: Palgrave Macmillan, 2004), 67–71.

42 Federal Bureau of Investigation, "Uniform Crime Report: Crime in the United States 2011," October 2012.

43 *Smith v. Maryland*, 442 U.S. 735, 745 (1979).

44 *United States v. Miller*, 425 U.S. 435 (1976).

45 *Couch v. United States*, 409 U.S. 322 (1973).

46 *Zurcher v. Stanford Daily*, 436 U.S. 547 (1978).

47 *Fisher v. United States*, 425 U.S. 391 (1976).

48 The preceding examples are laid out in Swire, "Katz is Dead. Long Live Katz," 908–909.

49 "Privacy and Internet," *DIPLO*, http://textus.diplomacy.edu/portals/ PrivacyAndInternet/oview.asp?FilterTopic=/46434/46464&ShowBlog= false (accessed April 7, 2013).

50 The Right to Financial Privacy Act of 1978, 12 U.S.C. §§ 3401–3402 (West 2011).

51 "Summary of the HIPAA Privacy Rule," *Department of Health and Human Services*, http://www.hhs.gov/ocr/privacy/hipaa/understanding/summary (last visited March 4, 2014).

52 The Video Privacy Protection Act of 1988, 18 U.S.C. § 2710 (West 2013).

53 Gina Stevens, *Privacy Protections for Personal Information Online* (CRS Report No. R41756) (Washington, DC: Congressional Research Service, 2011), https://fas.org/sgp/crs/misc/R41756.pdf.

54 Kerr, "The Mosaic Theory of the Fourth Amendment," 333.

55 Information voluntarily handed over to another party does not receive Fourth Amendment protection "even if the information is revealed on the assumption that it will be used only for a limited purpose and the confidence placed in the third party will not be betrayed," *United States v. Miller*, 425 U.S. 435, 443 (1976); *see also* Orin Kerr, "The Case for the Third Party Doctrine," *Michigan Law Review* 107 (2009): 569–570. Earlier cases that built up this doctrine include *Couch v. United States*, 409 U.S. 322 (1973); *Lee v. United States*, 343 U.S. 747 (1952).

56 Matthew D. Lawless, "The Third Party Doctrine Redux: Internet Search Records and the Case for a 'Crazy Quilt' of Fourth Amendment Protection," *UCLA Journal of Law & Technology* 2 (2007).

57 Orin Kerr and Greg Nojeim, "The Data Question: Should the Third-Party Records Doctrine Be Revisited?," *ABA Journal*, August 1, 2012, http:// www.abajournal.com/magazine/article/the_data_question_should_the_ third-party_records_doctrine_be_revisited.

58 Matthew Tokson, "Automation and the Fourth Amendment," *Iowa Law Review* 96 (2011): 586.

59 Daniel Cooper, *Consent in EU Data Protection Law*, European Privacy Association, http://www.europeanprivacyassociation.eu/public/ download/EPA%20Editorial_%20Consent%20in%20EU%20Data%20 Protection%20Law.pdf (last visited March 13, 2014).

60 "Why Do We Need an EU Data Protection Reform?," *European Commission*, http://ec.europa.eu/justice/data-protection/document/ review2012/factsheets/1_en.pdf .(last visited March 13, 2014).

61 Erica Newland, "CDT Comments on EU Data Protection Directive," *Center for Democracy and Technology*, January 20, 2011, https://www.cdt. org/blogs/erica-newland/cdt-comments-eu-data-protection-directive.

62 "Data Protection Reform: Frequently Asked Questions," *European Commission*, January 25, 2012, http://europa.eu/rapid/press-release_ MEMO-12-41_en.htm?locale=fr.

[63] In the wake of *Jones*, Professor Susan Freiwald identified four factors that the courts use to extend Fourth Amendment protection to new surveillance technologies that "make sense." These include whether the target is unaware of the surveillance; it covers items that the people consider private; it is continuous; and it is indiscriminate (covers more information than is necessary for establishing guilt). Susan Freiwald, "The Four Factor Test," *The Selected Works of Susan Freiwald* (2013), available at http://works.bepress. com/susan_freiwald/11.

[64] People often trust assurances that their sensitive information (names and social security number) can be deleted when their data is collected in large databases. In fact, scientists have shown that individuals can be easily "deanonymized." Paul Ohm writes that this misunderstanding has given the public a false sense of security and has led to inadequate privacy protections, laws, and regulations. *See* Paul Ohm, "Broken Promises of Privacy: Responding to the Surprising Failure of Anonymization," *UCLA Law Review* 57 (2010). *See also* Marcia Stepanek, "Weblining," *Businessweek*, April 3, 2000, http://www.businessweek.com/2000/00_14/b3675027. htm; Jennifer Golbeck, Christina Robles & Karen Turner, "Predicting Personality with Social Media" (paper, ACM conference on Human Factors in Computing Systems, Vancouver, Canada, May 7–12, 2011).

[65] Marcy Peek, "Passing Beyond Identity on the Internet: Espionage and Counterespionage in the Internet Age," *Vermont Law Review* 28 (2003): 94 (evaluating ways to resist discriminatory marketing in cyberspace); Stepanek, "Weblining" ([a] data broker company Acxiom matches names against housing, education, and incomes in order to identify the unpublicized ethnicity of an individual or group); Nicholas Carr, "Tracking Is an Assault on Liberty, With Real Dangers," *Wall Street Journal*, August 6, 2010, http:// online.wsj.com/news/articles/SB10001424052748703748904575441168 2714389888 ("[i]t used to be ... you had to get a warrant to monitor a person or a group of people. Today, it is increasingly easy to monitor ideas"); Etzioni, "The Privacy Merchants," 948–950.

[66] "How Target Figured Out a Teen Girl Was Pregnant Before Her Father Did," *Forbes*, February 16, 2012, http://www.forbes.com/sites/ kashmirhill/2012/02/16/how-target-figured-out-a-teen-girl-was-pregnant-before-her-father-did.

[67] Christopher Slobogin, "Government Data Mining and the Fourth Amendment," *University of Chicago Law Review* 75 (2008): 320.

[68] For further discussion on these matters, see Etzioni, "The Privacy Merchants"; Etzioni, "The Bankruptcy of Liberalism and Conservatism" (discussing the collapse of the public–private divide).

[69] For more discussion, see Etzioni, "The Bankruptcy of Liberalism and Conservatism."

[70] Kerr sees a greater role here for Congress, while Swire sees a greater role for the courts. *See* Swire, "Katz is Dead. Long Live Katz," 912; Kerr, "The Fourth Amendment and New Technologies." This chapter is unable to add

to these deliberations other than to recognize that both are needed and neither seems able to keep up with changing technologies.

71 Siobhan Gorman, "NSA's Domestic Spying Grows as Agency Sweeps Up Data," *Wall Street Journal*, March 10, 2008, http://online.wsj.com/news/articles/SB120511973377523845.

72 Peter P. Swire, "A Reasonableness Approach to Searches After the Jones GPS Tracking Case," *Stanford Law Review Online* 64 (2012).

73 Gary T. Marx, "Ethics for the New Surveillance," *The Information Society* 14, no. 3 (1998): 178.

74 Erica Goode and Sheryl Gay Stolberg, "Legal Curbs Said to Hamper A.T.F. in Gun Inquiries," *New York Times*, December 25, 2012, http://www.nytimes.com/2012/12/26/us/legislative-handcuffs-limit-atfs-ability-to-fight-gun-crime.html?pagewanted=all&_r=0.

75 Tamara Keith, "How Congress Quietly Overhauled Its Insider-Trading Law," *NPR*, April 16, 2013, http://m.npr.org/news/Politics/177496734.

76 See Etzioni, *The Limits of Privacy*.

77 Henning, *Compulsory DNA Collection*.

78 Ibid., 13.

79 Jack Nicas, "TSA to Halt Revealing Body Scans at Airports," *Wall Street Journal*, January 18, 2013, http://online.wsj.com/news/articles/SB10001424127887323783704578250152613273568.

80 Cynthia Dwork, "Differential Privacy: A Survey of Results," in *Theory and Applications of Models of Computation: 5th International Conference, TAMC 2008*, ed. Manindra Agrawal et al. (Berlin: Springer, 2008), 1–19 ("[r]oughly speaking, differential privacy ensures that the removal or addition of a single database item does not [substantially] affect the outcome of any analysis. It follows that no risk is incurred by joining the database, providing a mathematically rigorous means of coping with the fact that distributional information may be disclosive").

Index

CPSIA information can be obtained
at www.ICGtesting.com
Printed in the USA
JSHW021153200323
39186JS00008B/453

9 781529 200263